Thanks — especially if you read it!

Melvyn

CINEMA, LITERATURE AND SOCIETY

CROOM HELM STUDIES ON FILM, TELEVISION
AND THE MEDIA
General Editor: Dr Anthony Aldgate,
The Open University

CINEMA, LITERATURE & SOCIETY

Elite and Mass Culture in Interwar Britain

Peter Miles and Malcolm Smith

CROOM HELM
London • New York • Sydney

© 1987 P. Miles and M. Smith
Croom Helm Ltd, Provident House, Burrell Row,
Beckenham, Kent, BR3 1AT
Croom Helm Australia, 44-50 Waterloo Road,
North Ryde, 2113, New South Wales

Published in the USA by
Croom Helm
in association with Methuen, Inc.
29 West 35th Street
New York, NY 10001

British Library Cataloguing in Publication Data

Miles, Peter
    Cinema, literature and society: elite
    and mass culture in interwar Britain.
    1. Arts and society — Great Britain
    2. Arts — Political aspects — Great
    Britain
    I. Title II. Smith, Malcolm
    306'.47'0941   NX180.S6

    ISBN 0-7099-3363-0

Library of Congress Cataloging in Publication Data

Miles, Peter
    Cinema, literature, and society.

    (Croom Helm studies on film, television, and the media)
    Bibliography: p.
    Includes index.
    1. Great Britain — Intellectual life — 20th century.
2. Great Britain — Popular culture — History — 20th century.
3. English literature — 20th century — History and criticism.
4. Literature and society — Great Britain — History — 20th
century. 5. Moving-pictures — Great Britain — History.
I. Smith, Malcolm. 1947– II. Title. III. Series.
DA566.4.F565 1987   941.082   87-20033
ISBN 0-7099-3363-0

Printed and bound in Great Britain
by Billing & Sons Limited, Worcester.

CONTENTS

for Kathy and Elaine

ACKNOWLEDGEMENTS

The History and English undergraduates who have sat
through our course over the last five years deserve
our gratitude, not least for their forbearance and
their interest as we sorted out our ideas. Peter
Davison, prime mover of that course (on which this
book is based), has contributed more than he knows.
The Open University course 'Popular Culture' has
played a major role in helping us to form a
conceptual framework for this project and our thanks
go to the Course Team, particularly Tony Aldgate, the
General Editor of this series.

We must also thank Alan Rogers of the Computer
Unit, St David's University College, for his help in
preparing this manuscript, and Geraint Davies, Audio-
Visual Technician, for his work in providing us with
the film material we needed.

Last, but not least, thanks to Emily for showing
how films and books can simply be enjoyed.

Peter Miles & Malcolm Smith,
Lampeter.

Introduction

DEFINING TERMS: CULTURE, IDEOLOGY AND SOCIAL PROCESS

'The past is a foreign country', wrote L.P. Hartley,
'they do things differently there'.(1) It is a
comment which serves as a useful corrective to the
view that we can understand and learn from the past
simply by a process of assimilation of historical
facts. It is no doubt comforting to believe that
people in the past shared the assumptions and values
that we hold, and just happened to get it all wrong.
It undercuts the sense of loneliness at being simply
part of one generation, discrete and self-contained,
walking apparently unguided into the future. The
notion that people have passed this way before, that
they have shared the same or analogous problems, even
if they did not find the right solutions, provides
the framework of a popular memory which insists upon
connections across time, connections and judgements
which can guide action in the present for society as
a whole. But to argue along such lines is to
underestimate the depth of the process of historical
change and thus to undervalue the 'foreignness' of
the past. The past was not struggling hard to be like
us. It was living in its own present tense, with its
own short-term problems and its own solutions, and
with its own sense both of the future and of the
past.
    A sense of the past being not altogether foreign
but, rather, proximate and cautionary, informs the
culture of every generation. The interwar period is a
particularly significant case in point for post-war
British generations. This period contributed greatly
to contemporary consciousness, but our view of those
years has begun to change considerably as a new
generation has interposed itself between the
experience of the 1930s and the experience of the
1980s. The generation which learned its politics in
the 1950s and 1960s, which did not have to worry

1

overmuch about unemployment, 'knew' that the 1930s were the 'locust years', and 'knew' too that government policy – be it Conservative or Labour dominated – was based on a rejection of those 'locust years'. The ideal of full employment was deeply embedded in the political culture of the post-war period, as a rejection of what the 1930s were deemed to have stood for. The major argument against the dismantling of the concept of full employment, indeed, has been that it would store up problems for the future in the shape of a generation that would grow up alienated, like the 'forgotten millions' of the interwar dole queues. Yet the revisionist historians of the 1970s and beyond would have us believe that the impact of the Great Depression has been greatly exaggerated, and that unemployment and social distress never really did produce the degree of social friction that was formerly assumed to have played such a dominant role in the interwar political structure.(2)

Media shorthand for the interwar years is switching from the stark monochrome of When the boat comes in and Days of hope to the yellow-filtered nostalgia of Brideshead revisited and Another country; once a symbol of despair and misery, the 1930s are becoming a decadent Golden Age. What is significant about this change in perspective is not whether it is 'right' or 'wrong' as a view of what really happened in interwar Britain; rather it is the fact of the change itself which is important. By challenging the former popular memory of the period, handed down to us by a variety of cultural devices ranging from academic history to journalistic shorthand, the revisionists have challenged the basis on which an opposition to renewed mass unemployment is built. By reworking the popular memory, in effect, they are actually altering perceptions of current events. This is not to say that history is simply a cynically manipulative process, rather to point out that every generation has to rewrite history in terms that contemporaries can understand and to which they can relate. The past is, in fact, simply dead and gone: the real experience of the past cannot be fully recreated; and yet it must still remain true that, as Marx put it, 'the tradition of all the dead generations weighs like a nightmare on the brain of the living'.(3) Assumptions about the lived experience of the past must form part of our lived culture in the here and now; history works for society as a whole as memory works for the individual. It is a major element in shaping the culture of any society, shaping, validating and explaining the present as a function of the past.

History has no past; it exists only as an element in the consciousness of the present. The process of rewriting history to suit the next generation is therefore to some extent inevitable. The key issues are not so much what happened in the past, but how events were perceived at the time and how they have been perceived since; how, in effect, events are mediated by their cultural setting. The documentary record of the twentieth century is immense, but not without its shortcomings. On the one hand, there is the massive written documentation, a function not simply of the vastly expanded role of the state and its consequent need to keep detailed records, but also of a new mass literate society. This material makes up the traditional bread and butter of the historian, sometimes supplemented by new sources like oral history. But, huge as they are, these sources still leave gaps in the record. In spite of mass literacy and oral history, documentation of working-class views of life is still necessarily very partial while, on the other hand, the official record cannot be anything like the full story; on the whole, the official record is more likely to give us only the elite view, and evidence of other views will be at best indirect and at worst simply incorrect.

The major problem, however, is one of absorption: the record is so massive and overbearing that it is very difficult to see the wood for the trees, and the tendency must be progressively to concentrate on increasingly specialized and narrow areas of the historical record in order to make sense of contemporary history. Even when a complete map is made of the inter-relationships between these islands of specialism, a vital ingredient will still be missing, namely the unspoken and unwritten assumptions, the realities behind the realities, the thought processes, the world view of that age and its perception of itself. The past will continue to be a foreign country if we fail to see the significance of placing what happened in the past in the context of the culture, the ideology of that age. It is not just that what happened in the past only took on significance for contemporaries within contemporary culture as a whole, but that culture may also have created what happened in the past, in the sense that it made this fact significant rather than that one. It is this process of backgrounding and fore-grounding, of marginalising and of privileging, of structuring, that makes culture such an important element in dealing with the past, and it is in this area that the foreignness of the past is most conspicuous.

We are concerned in this book with how a society creates and projects an identity for itself in relation to its past and its future. The choice of concerns that informs this book, centring on the complicated issue of the relationship between culture and society, will be familiar to those with a knowledge of mass communications or cultural studies, for it is in these academic areas that critical techniques based on this approach have made their greatest impact. In literary studies, too, and in some areas of social history, the groundwork for such an investigation has at least been laid.(4) Many literary critics and historians, however, will still find this kind of approach boorish and insensitive, if not irrelevant. Literary critics who have grown up in the practical criticism tradition would argue that a poem or a novel exists independently of the circumstances in which it was written, that it is perfectly possible to appreciate the poetry of, say, W.H. Auden, while understanding nothing of the politics of the interwar period. An equally dominant historical school, with a long and respectable record in the British empiricist tradition, would argue that literature and cinema have very little to do with the historical process. Novelists, poets and film-makers, in this view, are by definition extraordinary and atypical, and their work cannot therefore be taken as valid evidence of the views of society as a whole. To hold these positions, however, is to reinforce the view that art and ideas stand autonomously in relation to the society in which they are produced and in which they operate.

It is not so much that literature and cinema may be used as historical evidence as such, nor that historical evidence may be used to elucidate a novel or film, but that text and history must be seen in tandem. There are three points to make here:

(1) It must be true that literature is written to be read and films to be seen, that all texts − be they written, pictorial or 'lived' − imply a relationship between producer and audience, which takes us immediately into the realm of the social, and which is historically specific. Even an unpublished manuscript or an unreleased film implies something directly about the nature of the expected reaction of the audience which can therefore legitimately be taken as part and parcel of the significance of the text. Clearly, W.H. Auden or

Gracie Fields will be re-interpreted by successive generations or by different cultures precisely because the context in which they are encountered changes.

(2) The relationship between producer of the text and its audience also implies an act of articulation, a connection not only between individuals but between ideas as well. A society cannot function simply as a collection of autonomous individuals; it is articulated through its cultural forms in recurrent patterns of themes and ideas. Literature and cinema are just two of the many ways in which an individual's experience of the world is organized and mediated in ways which become common to the cultural group to which the individual is thus induced to cohere.

(3) But, although literature and cinema may be only two of the forms which articulate an advanced society, they are undoubtedly two of the most significant, because of their broad frame of reference and because of their representative status. Traditionally, the question of literacy and of finding the time to read made literature above all the domain of the leisured and the well-off, and while these problems have declined in the twentieth century to the extent that we may legitimately talk about reading as a mass pursuit, nevertheless the concerns of the traditional producers and audience for literature continued to exercise a dominating influence over the mass-reading public. The very acts of writing or reading a novel or a poem, and of subconsciously relating that novel or poem to an established literary canon of what is good and what is bad, in itself implies a certain social positioning. Cinema had no such long tradition and, as part of a new mass culture, was considered to be at daggers-drawn with the literary tradition by dominant cultural theorists. Cinema and literature in the interwar years signify much more than what people did in their spare time; they signify in fact a cultural battleground, a struggle between competing modes of articulation which in turn embodied separate values and assumptions. It was through the perspectives provided by this battle, which was symptomatic of a much wider cultural struggle, that contemporaries acquired consciousness of events that were going on around them, and positioned themselves in relation to those events.

'Culture' is an extraordinarily complicated term, not surprisingly in that some of the definitions of the term take it to the heart of the social process

itself, something which can hardly be described
either briefly or succinctly. For our purposes, there
are two broad ranges of definition which concern us
centrally. On the one hand, the tradition inherited
from Matthew Arnold and Samuel Taylor Coleridge
defines culture as 'harmonised perfection'. Culture
is man at his most aspiring in this tradition;
whether in Art or Learning or Philosophy, it was the
nearest he could come to immortality on earth.(5)
This tradition emphasizes the extra-ordinary as
opposed to the commonplace, the spiritual as opposed
to the material, and the minority as opposed to the
majority. In the period with which we are concerned,
this theory of culture remained dominant, and the
challenge to the conception of Art which it embodied
represented by the development of mass culture was a
central fear.

Conversely, 'culturalists' such as Raymond
Williams, Richard Hoggart and E.P. Thompson in the
1950s and 1960s shared the view that culture was more
than simply the art and the learning of a society,
that these could be included as just one part of an
extended conception of culture which also included
the institutions and rituals of leisure and everyday
life in the fullest sense. More importantly, the
assumptions that underpinned all these manifestations
needed to be teased out. In this view, culture could
be defined as those shared and binding assumptions,
values and aspirations in a group or a society as
they manifest themselves in institutions, habits,
rituals, artefacts and art forms. (5) To move away
from the more traditional definition of culture, as
it had been formulated in Humanities and Arts
faculties in Academe at least, was an important
venture. 'Culture = Art' was a social definition
which directly rendered cheap and tasteless all those
things which the elite which made and maintained that
definition did not consider to be part of 'the higher
things in life'. The culturalists' extended
definition of culture concentrated on culture as a
social function; culture was in fact society at work
being a society, a collection of individuals inter-
relating, articulating, reinforcing or challenging
power relationships between groups. The definition
'Culture = Art' itself was, in this formulation,
merely a cultural manifestation of the fact that, for
long periods of British history, an elite had managed
to arbitrate taste and to make that arbitration stick
for society as a whole. 'Art' was a mystification
which had made ideology transcendent, and in
establishing this very idea of 'Art', the elite had

managed to set itself up as supreme arbiter of the 'structure of feeling'.

'Structure of feeling' was the phrase that Raymond Williams used to describe the shared sets of ways of thinking and feeling which are displayed in a patterned regularity either in a social class or even in a society as a whole.(7) The emphasis of the phrase, however, went beyond a mere description of the form of relationships within a society which may be deduced from its typical cultural forms, for it also hinted at the way in which this process limited the possibility of change within that society. These patterned ways of thinking and of feeling both formed, and were formed by, the whole way of life of the particular class or society in a specific period. At this stage in the development of his ideas, Williams brought culturalism close to structuralism. Culturalism and structuralism are different in many ways but for our immediate purposes, defining culture, they may be taken as similarly opposed to the elitist definition. Structuralism has taken many forms and variations but what underpins the structuralist tradition, as it relates to the role of culture in society, is the view that all the surface phenomena of society – the texts, be they myths, rituals or habits of everyday life – can be analysed and shown to be connected by the similarity of the structures of the rules and codes which govern them in their usage.(8) In the same way that, for example, language is governed by grammatical rules and codes, a structure shared and understood by all in that language group, a structure which must be used if a speaker or writer is to be understood, so all the surface phenomena of society share a repeated structure which guarantees coherence. It follows, however, that fracture of these structures will just as surely guarantee incoherence unless some new structure takes its place and is implicitly accepted and understood. The structures thus both allow communication and also fix identity within a group, by virtue of the fact that they are both familiar and shared. But they also implicitly limit both new communication and new identities by their very inflexibility. Not only are the structures formed by the society, then, but the structures in turn form the society.

If the simplified versions of culturalism and structuralism here presented were the end of the story society would never change, because the inherent conservatism of culture would not give it the wherewithal to do so. But to these analyses of culture must be added the dynamic of Marxism. The extended definition of culture presented by the culturalists, and the socially cohesive function it performed that culturalists and some structuralists identified, brings us within reach of the Marxist concept of ideology. It is basic to Marxism that all the surface phenomena of society are ultimately products of the way in which that society is organized economically. The social formation is composed of classes organized by the relations of production, how they stand in relation one to another as sellers of labour or as owners of the means of production. Class is therefore primarily an economic category but, in that class designates all the relationships in which individuals stand one to another within a class and between classes, it is also a cultural category, describing shared assumptions and values. The ultimate development of the proletarian state depends on the development of a discrete proletarian consciousness. But the connection in Marxism between the economic 'base' of a society and the 'superstructure' of ideas, culture or ideology is a complex and contentious one. The use of the engineering analogy, 'base' and 'superstructure', implies that the latter is directly dependent on the former, and the 'economist' or 'vulgar' Marxist tradition has it that ideas are simply extensions into the realm of ideology of the real relationships within the social formation. In this view, ideology may be seen as something quite ephemeral, in the last resort, in that it will simply change when the economic organization changes with revolution at the grassroots level.

It has been argued, however, that ideology necessarily plays a much more significant role. If revolution depends on the development of working-class culture and solidarity, a reaction to alienation, then a successful challenge to bourgeois ideology becomes virtually a sine qua non of revolution. In this argument, the analogy of 'base' and 'superstructure' is slightly misleading, in that the two are in fact inter-dependent. The Italian Marxist, Antonio Gramsci, was the most prominent of those who, though staying within the classic Marxist concept of class struggle, emphasized the importance of ideology as a legitimizing strategy for the bourgeoisie, adapting to and winning the active consent of subordinate groups by a process of negotiation. Gramsci in effect placed as much emphasis on the role of the working-class intellectual in challenging bourgeois ideology as on the more traditional socialist activities of political organization and unionization. Freedom from ideological thraldom was the primary prerequisite of revolution. Culture, as a major area of exchange between the social classes, was the front line of the struggle in Gramsci's view.(9)

Ideology and culture are in fact virtually interchangeable terms in Gramscian Marxism. Ideology provides us with our perception of the world and organizes or 'positions' us in relation to that reality. Ideology, then, is 'common sense' in this view, taking that phrase in its most literal definition to mean that understanding which is held in common through society and which we do not even bother to question because it is self-evidently the truth. In an important reiteration and extension of this view, the Marxist structuralist Louis Althusser described ideology as a kind of mirror in which we see ourselves apparently reflected; we are constantly 'interpellated' or hailed by this apparent reflection and invited to agree that this is reality. In fact, according to Althusser, this mirror image is no reflection at all but rather a refraction through the 'Ideological State Apparatuses', – the educational institutions, the media and other mechanisms – which produce and reproduce ideology and engender consent among subordinate social classes. In this way, pressure is taken off the 'Repressive State Apparatuses' – the law and the police – which would otherwise simply be overborne by the weight of majority dissent.(10)

Gramsci also placed decisive emphasis on the way in which dominant ideology had to adapt to survive. The concept of hegemony was his explanation of how it occurred that capitalist society still managed to hold together in spite of the reality of class friction. The concept of cultural hegemony describes the way in which a dominant class, as well as having economic primacy, must also generate and maintain intellectual and moral leadership. To maintain this intellectual and moral leadership, the class must be prepared to make compromises with its opponents, to negotiate its continued leadership and thus generate continued consent. Whereas 'economist' Marxism suggested that ideas are imposed by the state in the direct interest of the owners of the means of production, and whereas Liberalism typically argued that ideas are autonomous, free-floating, with no or only a tangential connection with the social formation, Gramsci emphasized the 'relative autonomy' of the ideological struggle, which resulted in the formation of a series of compromise equilibria between competing classes. Hegemony he saw as an active process, never static, forecasting, adapting to and thus neutralizing potential challenges to the authority of the dominant class. Thus, though ideology shifted constantly, as the dominant group continued to articulate the interests of subordinate groups to its own in relation to constantly shifting economic circumstances, the reality of power within the social formation remained unchanged. The implication was that, until the hegemonic process was exposed and fractured and the Ideological State Apparatuses overthrown, the chances of social revolution remained slim.

It is in this kind of interplay of culturalist, structuralist and Marxist approaches to the role of culture that literature and cinema take on significance in a reconstruction of the experience of the interwar period. As two of the most powerful articulators of the structure of feeling of the period – though by no means the only ones – they are indicative of the struggle for hegemonic control that was taking place beneath the surface of events. During the nineteenth century the hegemonic process had worked to transfer the control of ideology from the aristocracy to the bourgeoisie. As we shall see, the process was neither uncomplicated nor complete, and many of the tenets of aristocratic culture survived to create problems of coherence within British bourgeois culture thereafter. Prominent among these survivals was an anti-materialism which remained at odds with the requirements of the burgeoning industrial economy. Yet this anti-materialism itself served the important ideological purpose of providing an apparent disjuncture between superstructure and base in which dominant ideology could argue for its own autonomy as the free-standing tradition of British culture, economically and socially neutral.

Long before 1914, the major threat to this hegemonic compromise between aristocratic and bourgeois ideology, in the shape of a separate working-class culture, had been repeatedly offset by a combination of repressive and concessionary measures. This process continued after 1918. Indeed the main threat was to come not so much from a newly independent working class as such, but rather from a younger generation from within the elite. After the bloodbath of the Great War, and faced with the potentially explosive effects of the Great Depression, this generation challenged the hegemonic authority of its elders. This challenge proved only short-lived, however, as the 'Auden generation' was forced back onto the traditionalists' side of the barricades faced with the offensive of mass culture. Literature was certainly the predominant interest of the hegemonic bloc within the elite, and although attempts were made to break out from the structures and the codings in which literature had become encased, the results of these attempts were to adapt and transform rather than to revolutionize the forms themselves. The emergence of the proletarian novel, for example, or rather the novel about working-class experience, was both moulded and appropriated by dominant concepts of what a novel should be and what it should contain.

At the same time, the anti-materialist tradition of the elite made effective reaction to mass culture a very difficult business, particularly when, as in the interwar period, the new cultural form of the cinema owed so much to American money and American values, not so easily susceptible to the cultural norms of the elite as were the British-owned press or BBC, for instance. At this level, a crisis of hegemony was fought out internationally in the interwar years — not just liberalism against socialism, though certainly that as well — but between two hegemonic styles within Western liberalism: on the one hand, British elite culture, leading from the top; on the other hand, the more actively populist American mass culture, which in the view of the British elite vulgarized and thus jeopardized the cultural inheritance. In the British view, a culture which was not transcendent had little to recommend it. Americanism, just as surely as Fascism or Communism, in its overt attempt to mobilize the masses, was likely to destroy those cultural icons which apparently proved that culture as a whole was autonomous and neutral. To vulgarize culture was to challenge Art, undermining its function within ideology, thus putting the whole question of leadership up for grabs.

Throughout what follows, we have tried to balance discussion of the significance of the threats as they were perceived and met with an awareness of the remarkable resilience of an idea already very old when Orwell gave it articulation during the Second World War, that belief that 'England is one big family'. It was the ultimate hegemonic idea, and it was on the retention of the basic principle that England meant the same to everybody that the success or failure of the struggle of the elite to retain its hegemonic authority ultimately depended. 'Above all, it is your civilization, it is you', wrote Orwell, 'the suet puddings and the red pillar boxes have entered your soul. Good or evil, it is yours, you belong to it and this side the grave you will never get away from the marks that it has given you'.(11) It is on the ability to make such assumptions stick that real power is ultimately built.

NOTES

1.   L.P.   Hartley, The go between, 1953, Prologue.
2.   E.g., see C. Cook and J. Stevenson, The slump: society and politics during the depression, 1977; S. Glynn and J. Oxborrow, Interwar Britain : a social and economic history, 1976; S. Constantine, Unemployment in Britain between the wars, 1980.
3.   K. Marx, 'The 18th. Brumaire of Louis Bonaparte', in Karl Marx and Friedrich Engels, Selected works, 1968, p.97.
4.   See, for example, the journals Literature and History, Journal of European Studies, History Workshop Journal and, for a succinct guide to some difficult material, see C. Belsey, Critical practice, 1980.
5.   J.A. Appleyard, Coleridge's philosophy of literature, 1965; m. arnold, culture and anarchy, 1869 (repr. 1971).
6.   R. Williams, Culture and society, 1961, The long revolution, 1965; R. Hoggart, The uses of literacy, 1958; E.P. Thompson, 'The Long Revolution', New Left Review, 1960, The making of the english working class, 1968.
7.   In The long revolution, 1965.
8.   For a brief and readable guide to the corpus of structuralist writing, see T. Hawkes, Structuralism and semiotics, 1977.
9.   A. Gramsci, Selections from the prison notebooks, (eds) Q. Hoare and G. Nowell Smith, 1971.
10.   L. Althusser, 'Ideology and the Ideological State Apparatuses' , in Lenin and philosophy and other essays, 1971.
11.   G. Orwell, 'The Lion and the Unicorn', Collected essays, journalism and letters, vol. 2, 1968, repr. 1970, p.76.

Part One: 'England, Whose England?'

1. THE POLITICS OF DEPRESSION

Any study of interwar British culture must begin with the most obvious fact of all, that the interwar period was one of prolonged depression. And it was in response to the depression that the mediatory role of culture was, also, most obvious. A study of the way in which culture operated at the sharpest point of possible conflict in this period, however, must involve much more than simply reading off the cinematic and literary images of unemployment and depression as though they were self-explanatory. The representation of the experience of the unemployed worked within a long-developing tradition of cross-class negotiation, of revealing one England to the other. These representations worked, too, within assumptions about the existence of a national family, sharing values and ideals across the class divide. Firstly, however, even the 'obvious' facts of the economic recession are not, any more, that obvious. Recent interpretations of the economic history of the interwar period need to be taken into account simply to contextualize precisely what experience it was that culture was mediating.

The Great Depression of the interwar years was not just an isolated event in British economic history. It had its roots in the long-term and slow relative decline of Britain as an industrial trading power, the first signs of which had already appeared in the years before the Great War. The institution-alized problems of the British economy were made much worse, however, by the effects of a war which Britain simply could not afford to fight, and the after-effects of which created very complicated international trading conditions. The result was the best-documented and the most famous period of mass unemployment in British history, 'the locust years'. Yet, though the period still remains a scar in the

13

popular memory, some historians have recently begun to reconsider the interwar years and to conclude that the effects of the Great Depression have been greatly exaggerated, that unemployment was never more than a localized and minority problem, that contemporary social policy allowed a reasonable standard of existence even for the worse-off in comparison with previous periods. The revisionists contend that the social tension generated by the economic crisis should not be allowed to disguise the much more significant consensus of opinion that dominated the middle ground of British life in the period.

Clearly, however distressing was the experience of unemployment in these years, the effects were nothing like as devastating in Britain as they were elsewhere. All over Europe and in the United States, the effects of the Great Depression changed quite dramatically the forms of politics, whereas Britain carried on relatively quietly with Ramsay MacDonald, Stanley Baldwin and Neville Chamberlain. An explanation of this extraordinary stability that prevailed in Britain must take into account not just the differences between the experience of the Depression in Britain and elsewhere, but also the way in which the experience was mediated by the cultural context in which it occurred.

It is clearly true that the image of the interwar period as simply the years of the Means Test, of the dole queues and of the appeasement of the fascist dictators, badly needs revision. The revisionist historians have pointed out that any satisfactory overview of Britain in this period must also take into account the new economy that, for example, J.B Priestley saw in the environs of London in 1933, when unemployment was at its highest: 'the England of arterial and by-pass roads, of filling stations and factories that looked like exhibition buildings, of giant cinemas and dance-halls and cafes, bungalows with tiny garages, cocktail bars, Woolworths '.(1) The 1930s saw the development of an affluent consumer society as well as the decay of the depressed areas, and the affluence of those who managed to remain in work in the developing consumer economy was a dominating influence on social patterns at the height of the Depression. The truth is that the period presents a paradox economically, of real distress amid relative affluence. It was the sharp division between the 'two Englands' - the England of the South and the Midlands, which were relatively prosperous, and the England of the Depressed Areas in the North, Wales and Scotland - which lent the interwar period its particular complexity.

The basic problem which faced Britain in the economic sphere was that of over-commitment to the staple export industries which had dominated the earlier stages of British industrial development. Britain's industrial revolution had been export-led; the Big Four in the industrial economy - textiles, coal, heavy metals and ship building - all relied overwhelmingly on exports for their continued development. In steel production, for example, Britain already relied on exports to take up 80 per cent of production by the turn of the twentieth century. Such an over-reliance on just four industries, and on exports, proved to be no problem while Britain had the world markets to herself. Already by the 1870s and 1880s, however, the period of the so-called Great Price Fall, Britain was facing increasing international competition from new trading nations. British firms were traditionally only small and under-capitalized, and found it difficult to compete with the huge combines like the German and American steel firms. Then, as the secondary industrialization of the late nineteenth century began to place full emphasis on new industries like engineering and chemicals, Britain soon found herself left behind: British financial institutions were so geared to the servicing of the basic industries that capital was not easily forthcoming for these new and large investments. These problems were temporarily overlaid in the years before 1918 by a number of short-term expedients. First, the expansion of the Empire served as a market for goods that could no longer be sold in the European and American markets. Second, the increasing international friction in Europe created a new demand for armaments and, with the major changes that were taking place in naval technology from the late nineteenth century on, the heavy metals and ship building industries found themselves with fuller order books than ever before. Finally, there followed the unprecedented demand of the Great War itself. The first of the machine wars, with its voracious demand for all that British industry could produce, not only ate up spare capacity but also encouraged the development of further potential. Indeed, in an attempt to maximize production, the State was forced to step in as never before. The mining industry, for example, was taken over by a Ministry of Mines: pits that were unprofitable were kept open, and miners' wages subsidized, in order to maintain the maximum output.(2)

In the years after 1918, the bubble burst, and the problems that had lain dormant since the period of the Great Price Fall came to the fore with a vengeance. Britain was left with massive spare capacity in the middle of a world slump, and with many of her overseas investments sold off to help to pay for the war. The United States, in the period of isolation which had preceded her entry into the war, had effortlessly expanded her economic potential at the expense not just of Britain but of Europe as a whole. Though some of Britain's industries enjoyed a brief post-war boom, the palmy days were over when German industry began to recover in the 1920s. British industrial problems were not helped by a government policy which aimed at 'a return to normality' which meant, in effect, a withdrawal of government control and therefore also of government subsidy from industries which had been artificially stimulated by the national wartime demand. At the same time, the policy of the Treasury was to deflate the economy, cutting public expenditure to allow a return to the pre-war Gold Standard. In fact Britain duly returned to the Gold Standard in 1925, overpricing sterling by somewhere between 2 and 10 per cent, thus creating a further major problem for exporters.(3) One industry, coal, responded to the consequent increase in export price by announcing a cut in wages for its employees, which led directly to the General Strike of 1926.

A central aspect of the problem that resulted was that the major export industries were not only faced independently with extremely difficult trading conditions on the world stage; they were also inter-dependent. Ship-building, heavy metals and coal, for example, were so interlinked that the slump in demand for all three bred a spiralling depression. Significantly, too, these industries had traditionally been very concentrated geographically, with socially catastrophic results for communities like those in South Wales, Lancashire, Yorkshire, County Durham and the Central Lowlands of Scotland. Towns like those in the Rhondda, entirely dependent on coal mining, or Jarrow, where ship-building provided the only employment for men, were particularly hard hit.

The relative prosperity of areas like the South and the Midlands in fact depended on the continuing depression in the North of Britain and in Wales. The depression in the basic industries meant a general fall in prices, but wages and salaries for those who were lucky enough to remain in employment did not fall as quickly as prices, with the effect that

average purchasing power in Britain rose by something
like 24 per cent in the interwar period. It was this
very large rise in real spending power which fed the
consumer boom of the 1930s. In this sense, those who
remained in employment grew more prosperous literally
on the backs of the unemployed. Three million new
houses were built in the 1930s, the large majority of
these being for private sale rather than local
authority use. One million new cars filled the roads
in the decade, and by 1939 advertising for the new
domestic consumer market was a 100 million pound
industry.(4)
    The consumer boom hardly touched the problems of
the distressed areas. The new industries were usually
reliant on new power sources like electricity or oil,
and therefore provided only a marginal stimulus to
the ailing coal industry. Though car production and
house building did stimulate demand for steel, the
demand for new synthetic products was even more
significant. As a result, the consumer industries
tended to develop as a quite separate growth area
within the economy, stimulating other new industries
rather than helping out the failing giants. These
industries also tended to concentrate geographically
near the great consumer centres whose population they
employed; there was little point opening a new car
factory in South Wales, for instance, since there was
little money locally to buy the product and the producer would simply be increasing his transport costs.
All other things being equal, without government
stimulation in the form of financial incentives, the
new consumer economy would do nothing to cure the
problems of the depressed areas.
    Thus, as the depressed areas spiralled downwards,
the consumer industry areas spiralled upwards. A
quite distinct line developed, dividing the South
East and the Midlands from the rest of the country.
Disraeli's notion that there were, in fact, 'Two
Englands' — the rich and the poor — was a
geographical as well as an economic fact.

        Unemployment by Region, 1929 - 1936.(5)
                    (per cent.)

            London   8.8.
            South East 7.8.
            South West 11.1
            Midlands 15.2
            North East 22.7
            North West 21.4
            Scotland 21.8

                        17

Wales 30.1.

Great Britain 16.9
South Britain 11.1
North and Wales 22.8

For the depressed areas, real recovery did not begin until the rearmament boom of the late 1930s. Small wonder, therefore, that there is a temptation to dismiss as the 'locust years ' a period when the economic problems that followed one war were only overcome by preparing for another war, against the same enemy and on basically the same issue. It is difficult to make value judgements about this paradoxical economic situation. As Peter Mathias has noted: 'So much depends on whether the spotlight is turned on Jarrow or Slough, on Merthyr Tydfil or Oxford, on Greenock and Birkenhead or on Coventry, Weston-Super-Mare and the environs of London'.(6) It is clear that the nation as a whole was better off than in Edwardian days. It is equally clear, however, that one section of the community, the section upon which Britain's industrialization had developed and upon which her economic strength had depended for more than a century, was missing out on the relative material progress that the rest of the country was now beginning to enjoy.

This relative deprivation is in fact the key issue involved. Most of Britain was not unemployed, not badly housed and not living in an environmentally deprived area. Most of Britain remained only dimly aware of the problems of the far-away smoky North and the Celtic fringes. It was in this period that the Labour Party built up its large majorities in those areas that were to become its strongholds, but large majorities in single constituencies still only win one parliamentary seat. For the 1935 general election it is possible to draw a line on the map from Bristol to the Wash below which Labour won only a tiny handful of seats. And the contingent from the North, from South Wales and from Scotland found itself in the House of Commons faced with consistent Conservative majorities elected by the other England, majorities which in the elections of 1931 and 1935 proved overwhelming. Whether the radicals liked it or not, the relatively affluent were in the driving seat. The working class was divided between the two economies, between unemployment and employment, segregated by the cultural geography of the 'Two Englands'. Moreover the development of the consumer economy, and of the service industries, brought in their train the huge growth of the lower management and clerical labour goups. The values and ambitions of the newly dominant lower-middle class, 40 per cent of all families in Britain by the 1930s, tending to share the cultural values of the middle class proper though not sharing in the ownership of the means of production, acted as a buffer which altered substantially the traditional structure of class relations in Britain.(7) The question was whether the unemployed could muster the ideological muscle to force themselves upon the attention of the nation.

Clearly, the fact that unemployment was such a localized problem, taking Britain as a whole, made it at least less likely that there would be major social upheaval. In Germany, by way of contrast, as in the United States, unemployment was not a much larger problem, proportionately, but geographically it was much more widespread. There was probably a correlation between the geographical distribution of unemployment and political activism. In the depressed areas everyone was in the same boat; fatalism and apathy were likely to be the result. The Pilgrim Trust certainly found that it was the unemployed in areas which remained relatively prosperous that were the most embittered. Thus the different geographical distribution of unemployment may account, at least in part, for the differing political reactions in different countries. The workforce in the staple export industries in Britain, moreover, had probably become more used to the prospect of unemployment, during the long-term relative decline of Britain, than their counterparts in the recent boom economies in Germany and America. It is also true that the major political parties in Britain during the Depression were acutely aware of the possible problems that might arise from unemployment and, although they followed orthodox economic policies for most of the period, their social policies were adaptive, even progressive in some respects. Unemployment insurance was extended to the large majority of the male work force in successive stages; and the system that had been inherited from the Victorian Poor Law was replaced by a Public Assistance scheme which, by the mid-1930s, was administratively centralized and giving out nationally applicable payments. The 'dole' proper was born in the immediate post-war era to tide over soldiers returning from the war, but became institutionalized as the method by which the gaps between periods of statutory entitlement to unemployment insurance could be filled. The family

Means Test was applied to the dole and to Public Assistance, and a cut was imposed on statutory benefit in the financial crisis of 1931. Distressing though the effects of these cuts and the Means Test certainly were, it is still true that benefits in Britain were larger and given on generally less stringent terms than in other countries.

Stanley Baldwin's Conservatives attempted to blur the harsh edges of class conflict by applying a human face to capitalism. Though the strongholds of Conservative support lay in the relatively prosperous areas of the South and the Midlands, or in the agricultural constituencies, Baldwin was by no means unaware of the problems of the depressed areas. Though the measures that his governments undertook may seem paltry to a post-Keynsian generation, they amounted to a major improvement in the structure of social policy and, in the opinion of some historians, amounted to the real basis of the post-1945 Welfare State.(8) The Labour Party, still struggling to establish itself as the major power of the Left by strangling the remaining support for the Liberal party, found itself in an insuperable quandary because of Baldwin's tactics. Committed to the evolutionary rather than the revolutionary road to socialism, Labour had to attract the votes of more than simply the unemployed if it were to gain power. Labour had to appeal to those middle of the road and relatively prosperous electors who would be scared off by any hint of a really radical solution. As a result, in the public projection of his leadership and of the aims of his party as those of a 'respectable alternative', Ramsay MacDonald sounded distinctly like Stanley Baldwin with a Scottish accent.(9) Yet Labour retained and developed its bedrock support through this period, the far left making very little headway in national terms. The depth of the support for the Labour party, along with the clear tendency of the Conservative party to move to pre-empt the potentially violent consequences of mass unemployment, were both manifestations and reinforcers of a well-constructed stability.

Yet to explain the relative stability of Britain in simply economic, or even in a combination of economic and political terms, is to beg the question to a large extent. After all, though the dole may have kept body and soul together, for former Labour Aristocrats like the miners the experience of living off state charity and being humiliated by the family Means Test was potentially explosive. The dole could alleviate the financial impact of unemployment but not its psychological effects. The understanding that things were not as bad as they could be, which prompted the electorate to cast a typical 80 per cent of its votes for either Conservative or Labour throughout this period, depended on a perception that excluded either the far right or the far left from serious consideration. At what level did this consensus in politics actually begin? Assuming that perception may be taken simply as an alternative term for ideology, it should be borne in mind that the attempt to produce a national consciousness, in place of separate class consciousnesses, had a long history before this period began. Robert Gray, for instance, has shown how a hegemonic bloc operated in Victorian Britain to articulate the interests of subordinate classes to its own, thus heading off the prospect of class consciousness spilling over into overt class action, asserting instead a 'national consciousness'. This is not to say that class consciousness was eradicated, merely contained. Class friction kept breaking through the rhetoric of respectability, Gray explains. Hegemony was therefore a fragile compromise which involved not only the imposition of social discipline from above but, equally, the imposition on the bourgeoisie of working-class interests. Hegemony was not a simple matter of social control but rather of social symbiosis, with the bourgeoisie forced to legitimize working-class interests - such as the development of trade unions or the extension of the franchise - through shifts in its ideology.(10)

Gray's analysis of Victorian hegemony emphasizes the dangers of simplifying what is involved in the hegemonic process. He points out that ideological compromise specifically does not mean ideological assimilation or absorption, that class consciousness still exists even in an 'achieved hegemony'. It is simply that class consciousness expresses itself in terms of interests temporarily held in common with other classes, a national interest. A constant process of ideological shift on the part of the hegemonic bloc is a necessary consequence of working-class consciousness, which is not susceptible to eradication at the level of ideology because it is a function of the mode of production. Here the important point must be reiterated that the Gramscian theory of hegemony implies only a 'relative' and not an 'absolute' autonomy for ideology, that what has been fundamentally fixed at the economic level, the 'base', cannot be fundamentally undone in the 'superstructure'. Gray emphasizes the equally important point that it is misguided to see the theory of hegemony as a conspiracy thesis, to personify bourgeois ideological interests as the shrewd and conscious plot of the hegemonic bloc. When we talk of individuals forming part of the hegemonic bloc, we should constantly be aware that we are simply talking of examples of the way in which wider processes have been channelled into personal experience and outlook. To talk of Baldwinism and of MacDonaldism as being hegemonic in their emphases is not to suggest that they successfully eradicated working-class consciousness, then, nor that Baldwin or MacDonald were conscious conspirators in the ideological contest. As in the Victorian period, so in the interwar period, working-class consciousness kept breaking through. On the other hand, the wide common ground between the two major parties on economic and social matters effectively limited the parameters of political debate to arguments over mere detail and emphasis rather than overall direction. More radical solutions were marginalized as Marxism was lumped with Fascism as totalitarianism, the blind and non-negotiable solutions of sick societies.

Above all, the rhetoric of mainstream interwar British politics was that of pragmatic compromise. As Baldwin put it in a typical newsreel appearance in 1935, explaining why Britain was so stable under a National Government:

... when this country was faced with crisis there were men of all parties who put party politics on one side and united together to pull the country through and take the necessary steps to put our finances once more on a sound footing. But it is also due to the fact that we, true to our old traditions, avoided all extremes, have steered clear of fascism, communism, dictatorship, and have shown the world that democratic government,constitutional methods and ordered liberty are not inconsistent with progress and prosperity.(11)

The assumptions built into this speech are perhaps too obvious to need extended comment, but the connecting structure of the assumptions is very significant. First, 'party politics' are assumed to be only permissible when the national interest is not involved, a kind of game for the good times, and that there exists a deeper national interest and a set of solutions which all patriotic politicians will instantly recognize in a crisis as the only real ones. This hardly does justice to the contortions caused in the Labour party by Ramsay MacDonald's decision to lead the coalition in 1931, as a result of which the Conservatives won a massive electoral majority and maintained that position in 1935. Nor does it faithfully represent the crisis of conscience which the coalition Liberals endured faced with the Conservatives' dictated solution to the crisis in cabinet. The sub-structure of Baldwin's assumption about national interests is an elision of national interests with Conservatism. Second, Baldwin articulates the self-abnegation of all right-minded politicians to the British national character; the 'we politicians' becomes 'we British' united in a centrist approach. By linking chauvinism to notions of compromise and moderation, specifically opposed to the exaggerated and violent politics of foreign countries, Baldwin and his contemporaries in politics reinforced the hegemonic construct that England was one big family united by a common perception of the British national character, and that this national character was broadly conservative in ambition. The bonds of a shared culture, and the need to protect those cultural traditions, were deemed stronger than the claims of class loyalty could break. From the beginning, too, the condensation of 'Britishness' into 'Englishness' was apparent, peripheralizing the separatist cultures of Wales, Scotland and Ireland.

Baldwin's politics depended on more than simply consensus, however. Assumptions about the national political family were aspects of a longer tradition that had begun to dominate leisure activity as well as politics in the late nineteenth century. The corollary of the development of Gray's hegemonic bloc in Victorian ideology had been the development of a hegemonic, 'classless' leisure. Industrialization had meant the separation of work from leisure, a separation which had not existed in a real sense in pre-industrial society. Early industrialization bred few of the cross-class activities that had characterized pre-industrial Britain, such as the fairs or the blood sports. This was a potentially dangerous gap in cultural domination, which produced a need to police the activities of the working class so that it could continue to perform its workday function within the new economy. The development of urbanization had undermined the supervisory functions of the pre-industrial dominant class. In the typical village community, the ever-visible hierarchy of the agricultural economy had meant that the ideological pressures were close at hand. In the developing

23

cities of the second half of the nineteenth century,
however, as the social classes separated into their
ghettoes, this supervisory function was much more
difficult to maintain. Working class pursuits came
under attack precisely because they were expressions
of working-class consciousness, and were potentially
dangerous if left unchecked. The response was a
mixture of repression and appropriation. 'Improving'
pursuits were championed to offset drunkenness and
irreligion, and magistrates often moved heavily
against working-class pastimes deemed likely to lead
to disorder. Football games through the streets, or
specifically working-class blood-sports like throwing
at cocks and bull-baiting, were suppressed by
pressure at local level.(12)

It was, however, the commercialization of leisure
which played the major role in securing control of
the forms of working-class leisure. The profession-
alization of football, for example, took it out of
the streets and into the parks; this no doubt
improved the skills involved but also made it much
more of a spectator rather than a participant sport.
The stars of the game embodied qualities both of
individualism and of co-operation within a team. The
subsequent development of the football league and of
the national teams encouraged both local and national
pride and the competitive spirit. Commercialization
thus both made a profit and reworked the ideological
parameters of the sport. This was 'giving the people
what they wanted', a process repeated in many other
spheres of Victorian and Edwardian leisure. In the
development of the music-hall from the folk- and
work-song tradition, for example, the audience became
literally cut off from the performer once again, as
in the football stadium. Although both football star
and music-hall comedian were no doubt still
expressions of working-class culture - working-class
heroes in fact - the context in which they operated
as stars and as individuals, paid for a performance,
altered entirely their ideological significance. This
change in the ideological significance of
working-class leisure may have taken its place in a
more generalized and fatalistic acceptance of the
existing social order in the decades after the defeat
of Chartism. The skill of the working-class centre
forward or the jokes of the comic offered, to use
Gareth Stedman Jones' phrase, a 'culture of
consolation' for a class whose whole outlook on life
had been effectively transformed. It had become a
defensive rather than an offensive culture, concerned
with protection from as well as survival within the

capitalist structure, rather than its overthrow.(13)
    A similar kind of process was at work after 1918.
Mass   unemployment   could   have   created   the
preconditions   for   a   real   class confrontation. The
fact   that   the   interwar   confrontation was   only patchy
and   sporadic   was   partly   a   result   of   the uneven
pattern   of   unemployment   and distress, and partly a
function of political adaptation to that fact. It was
also,   however,   a function of a continued adaptation
at   the   level   of   ideology,   manifest   in   cultural   forms
such   as   cinema   and   literature   just as much as in
politics.   Rather   than isolating the unemployed as a
forgettable   minority,   both   cinema   and   literature
worked   to re-include   them   in   the   national   family.
    Cinema's   treatment   of   the issues involved, for
instance,   tended   to   concentrate   on   what   the
experience of the Depression for a minority seemed to
prove   about   Britain   as   a   whole,   thus   deftly
translating   working-class   disaster   into   national
valour.   Rather   than being portrayed as victims, the
Depressed Areas were transformed into heroic examples
of   British   fortitude.   Newsreel   rarely covered the
issue,   with   the   result   that   unemployment was not
treated   so   much   as   hard   fact   in the cinema, but
instead   mediated   as   a subject for entertainment in
feature   films. This had an important effect in terms
of   the   presentation   of   the   issue   to   the   mass
audience.   It   was   not   simply   that   the   newsreel
companies   themselves   conspired   to   keep the public
misinformed;   they   saw   themselves   as   part   of the
entertainment   business,   rather   than journalists as
such,   and   probably   saw   in   the   issue   little   to
entertain   an   audience which itself might be largely
unemployed.   Even   if   they   had   wanted to treat the
issue   in   depth,   however,   the   Home Office and the
police   would   not allow film coverage of many of the
major   demonstrations   and marches, for fear that the
mere   presence   of   the newsreelmen would provoke the
organisers   into   staging   a   performance   for   the
cameras.   The belief was that the camera would create
events,   in effect, that news would be staged for the
newsreels   as   demonstrators   made maximum propaganda
usage   of the mass coverage. As a result of this, the
communist-backed National Unemployed Workers Movement
rarely   achieved   media   coverage. On the other hand,
moderate   and   non-violent   marches   organized   by
constitutionally   acceptable organizations did manage
to   secure   a hearing. It is no mere coincidence that
the   relatively   small and probably atypical Jarrow
Crusade   has   become   the   most   famous   of   the
interwar   hunger   marches.   Organized   and   carefully

stewarded by the Labour Party, who gave full co-operation to the police, the Crusade became the symbol of working class stoicism, respectability and pride, when it achieved the mass screening which more violent demonstrations could not. What was significant about newsreel coverage of unemployment, then, was not only that it was so meagre but that what was covered was so tendentiously handled. To foreground the Jarrow Crusade, and to background the activities of the NUWM, was one very significant example of the way that news was structured before presentation to the audience. Coverage of the Prince of Wales' visits to areas of unemployment centred on the symbol of national unity presented by the Prince himself, the real subject of the story, rather than on the socially divisive issues of unemployment itself. In a real sense, what is not covered by the mass media does not happen for those who are not directly involved; consciousness of distant events can only take shape within the terms of reference assigned to those events by the mass media. Unemployment was not only a regionalized and minority problem, taking Britain as a whole, but was also reworked as an item of cinema news to highlight, for employed and unemployed alike, the stiff-upper-lip quality of Britain's national family.

Similarly, feature film rarely dealt directly with the effects of the Depression. When it did dwell directly on contemporary social conditions, commercial cinema projected the problem back to the audience as a question relating not so much to economics as to the British character and temperament. Broadly, two styles of treatment are discernible; first, defusing by means of comedy and, second, by means of moving the context from the social and political to the personal and moral. The two styles were not mutually exclusive, however; comedy depended on recontextualizing the experience of social distress; therein lay the joke. The two great comic stars of the 1930s in Britain, George Formby and Gracie Fields, both made films which at least touched on the issue of unemployment. Their films recruited for the screen and made nationally popular the variety and music-hall tradition of the Lancashire comedians. The sentimentalized and trite expression of Lancastrian working-class identity embodied in the early Formby, with his bowler hat, checked jacket, banjo and gormlessness, was mobilized in buffoonery which both mocked social reality and took its audience into collusion in that mockery. Though 'Our Gracie' was no buffoon, her screen stance as 'Lancashire Britannia' was equally heavily loaded in its ideological significance.

At the beginning of <u>Off the dole,</u> made by Formby in 1931, a working-class man banters and sings with his audience in the dole office in true music-hall style:

Who has to live in houses,
You could cut them with a knife?
Who is it builds you motor cars
That last you all your life?
And who was to the fore
In the Great World War?
Why, the poor old working man!

There is an explicit class consciousness in the words of the song, but it is mediated by the performance. The exaggerated working-class accents, and the sentimental music-hall harmony, close down possibly dangerous interpretations of the song. This is true of the film as a whole, as the experience of social conditions is translated into joke. The combination of nose-thumbing at the establishment ('an MP is a man who gives up your life for his country!') with jokes about workshyness (George wants a job selling leap-year calendars) amounts to a celebration of the resilience of 'the poor old working man' faced with unexplained but traditional adversity. George is pushed off the dole for not actively seeking work, a narrative ploy to send him off for the rest of the film chasing the most unlikely jobs and singing a few songs. The dole becomes just another of those institutionalized difficulties that were the stock-in-trade of the earlier music-hall comedians, like mothers-in-law, rentmen and toffs. No explanation of George's difficulties is either given or needed; his situation becomes a vehicle for reactivating that 'culture of consolation' which the music hall had established for the Victorian and Edwardian working class. The film demands of its audience not simply or even primarily a suspension of disbelief at George's antics in a recognizable crisis, but more importantly a knowingness, a 'nudge-nudge, wink-wink' inter-reaction between Formby and his audience. The film demands understanding and commands laughter because it works within a tradition that had always emphasized stoical and humorous acceptance of inexorable bad times. It is the way in which the generic expectations of the music hall are mobilized, and the way in which these expectations bind Formby to his audience, which make

27

this film typical of the British mass culture of its time. The contemporary experience was recontextualized, re-placed in a well-known and ideologically-neutralized cultural terrain, where it still remained an expression of working-class identity but, just as importantly, where it was not an expression of class friction.(14)

A most important element in Formby films was the role of the partially invisible community in resolving the complications that George, in fact, set up for himself. Formby was characterized above all by his incompetence, be it in the face of the problem of finding a job or getting a girl. He won through in the end of his films not because of his own actions but rather because right was on his side. In Formby films, the community as a whole was the hero. George's gormlessness meant that he could not solve problems on his own, but in Formbyland the incompetent still survived and prospered finally, as long as they were in the right, because the community turned out to help, whether visibly or invisibly, ensuring that it would 'turn out nice again' in the end. Formby films were themselves in fact part of a developing tradition in British films which celebrated the concept of the community as hero, culminating in the Ealing comedies of Michael Balcon after the war, notably Passport to pimlico and Whisky galore.(15) This partially invisible community is an important identificational link between the screen-plot and the audience, reflecting the audience's will that things should indeed 'turn out nice again'. The community is in fact the audience's collective sense of right and wrong as an audience, a neat self-congratulatory strategy to confirm the British sense of fair play and to reaffirm the audience's commitment to the innate values of their national family.

Gracie Fields was a more individualist 'star' than Formby, in the sense that in her films she actively moved the story towards its resolution, rather than assuming the role of victim and relying on community support. But her cinematic role was to defuse tension with humour, to salve rather than to change things. Largely, this is due to the fact that the structure of the films rarely even admits the possibility or even the relevance of change. In Sing as we go the closing of the mill at the beginning of the story provides a chance to demonstrate British working-class pluck rather than bemoan a social disaster. The reaction of Gracie is still cheerful: 'if we can't spin, we can still sing': she leads the workforce out of the mill in good style, singing as they go. It is also made clear that the closure of the mill affects everybody, irrespective of class; the bosses will also have to find new jobs. Unemployment, however, is not really the point; it soon becomes clear that this is simply a narrative ploy to set Gracie off on her bike to find work in Blackpool, providing the seaside setting for some laughs and some songs. While the narrative certainly relies on the initial issue of the closure of the mill, and the resolution depends on the mill's reopening, the connection between the initial disequilibrium and the final resolution is musical, comical and moral, never economic. Finally, a magical resolution is offered; the mill reopens for no reason other than that mystifyingly referred to as 'technological innovation'. Gracie is symbolically rewarded for the role she has played as mediator of all personal crises by being given the job of Personnel Manager. She leads the workforce back into the factory, as she led them out, arm-in-arm and waving flags. As the workforce marches past behind her, she stops to sing directly to camera the last strains of Sing as we go, cutting to a fluttering Union Jack behind the final credits. The connection between Gracie's cinematic qualities and those of the nation as a whole is thus explicitly drawn, and left sitting heavily on the viewer's retina at the very end of the film.(16)

As Jeffrey Richards has pointed out, the popularity of the song Sing as we go made it the anthem of the Depression.(17) It is true to say too that Gracie herself moved from on-screen working-class stoic to embody those same qualities in her 'off-screen' image. She was even recorded by cinema newsreel as star guest at the gala opening of a new factory. Such an event was rare enough in the 1930s, and treated as a sign of returning good times by the newsreel. The appearance of Gracie at such an event was presented, in effect, as a case of virtue rewarded after the stoical reaction of working people to the Depression, much the same as in the film Sing as we go, the Queen of Lancashire leading her audience in yet another rendition of the famous song.(18) It was an example of the way in which the process of cinema culture constantly sought to break down the distinction between big screen and real life. In the cinema of the 1930s, escapism had a distinct habit of re-appearing as realism: 'stars' were also 'news'. The ephemera of cinema culture, with movie magazines contending that the stars were

the same people in real life, and star guest
appearances such as those of Gracie Fields on
newsreel making the same point, worked to take
cinematic ideology out of the cinemas and into the
streets.

By embodying supposedly national characteristics
of conciliation and moderation, the films of Gracie
Fields developed an ideological strategy similar to
that of the British cinematic social dramas of the
period. In all of these the narrative revolved around
linked discourses on moderation, law and order and
community. Proud valley, for example, produced by
Michael Balcon in 1939, found Paul Robeson as the
unemployed merchant seaman drifting into the mining
community of Blaenau in South Wales. There is a mild
problem caused by the fact that he is black, quickly
disposed of by the reminder that all men are black
down the pit. Another and more serious difficulty in
assimilating the Robeson character, David Goliath,
into the community is the jealousy felt by some
members of the local male voice choir at the power of
Robeson's voice. This difficulty is in turn set aside
as a pit collapse draws the village together in
shared tragedy. The accident causes not only the
death of the choir-master but also brings
unemployment to the community as a whole. The rest of
the plot involves the attempts of the villagers, with
David as friend and mentor, to get the pit re-opened.
Thus the potential racial issue is registered only to
be immediately resolved while still leaving David as
an outsider in the community. David functions to
reinforce those sympathetic characters in the story
depicted as moderate, constitutionalist and
non-violent. He accepts their plight and keeps their
peckers up by bursting into yet another hymn at the
least hint of crisis: 'they can't stop us singing'.
The two great traditions of negro gospel singing and
Welsh male voice choirs, with their embodied cultures
of consolation, are thus brought into ideological
partnership: David, though remaining an outsider,
functions to emphasize the moderation of the
community by linking it to another similar tradition.
It is eventually decided that a deputation should
march to London to argue with the owners. During the
march, however, war breaks out and the meeting
between the deputation and the owners ends in the
decision to re-open the pit as the joint contribution
of owners and workforce to the national war effort.
As one of the miners puts it: 'Coal in wartime is as
much a part of the national defence as guns or
anything else. So, why not let us take our chance

down the pit?'. The mining engineer considers 'it would be an honour to lead' the men in the dangerous operation of clearing the shaft. During the resultant near-disaster, David is killed saving the group of men, the community and, thus, the national coal production.(19)

The real issues of the depressed areas are sidestepped by the narrative. The unemployment is caused by the danger to life posed by explosive gas after the accident, rather than the failing world demand for coal, and it is the danger of Hitler which finally resolves the problem. At the same time the concept of community, signified both by the common plight of the miners and the apparently instinctive harmony of their singing, is linked to the concept of the national family in the resolution. The role of Robeson-Goliath in all this is complex. Robeson is, in fact, just too big for the part he plays. On one level, as an international and major star, the only black actor of real status in the period, Robeson represents the dignity and aspirations of downtrodden humanity in general. At one point in the film, as he sings 'Deep River', his persona almost bursts out of the ideological confines of the film. Yet, as David, he represents the good friend who can never join the community. There is at least a little of the 'faithful Mtumbe' or Gunga Din syndrome in Goliath's virtual suicide to save the other men. As the first coal comes to the surface after the long closure, the village inevitably bursts into another hymn; the camera sails up from the village to the valley, then to the hills and finally to the sky. The soundtrack switches to 'Land of My Fathers', a celebration sung by Robeson, partly as a major star embodying a wider sense of international brotherhood, and partly as Goliath, the lonely outsider, leaving the community stronger behind him by his presence and by his sacrifice. The outsider, simply by being an outsider, throws the sense of community into stronger relief. The tension between Robeson the star and Goliath the film character is thus finally resolved in a celebration of unity in wartime, with hints of a wider international unity to follow in the fight against Fascism.

Carol Reed's The stars look down, also made in 1939, similarly homed in on the themes of moderation and of community, but it did so indirectly. Its emphasis was not so much on the assumption that contemporary social problems proved the resilience of the national character; it was rather more that the national character was threatened by these problems, posed in turn as an incipient threat to law and order. The film was not only unusual in that it was one of the small number that dealt with social problems at all, it was also virtually unique in dealing with resultant physical violence. During a strike a butcher refuses to give meat on tick to a striker. The violence that follows is in fact started by the villain of the story, Joe, who has no sympathy for the miners' cause. The moderate and non-violent leader of the strike tries to intervene to stop the wrecking of the butcher shop, only to be arrested by the police. The instigator of the looting then walks away with the takings from the till, to the accompaniment of the local bible-thumper forecasting Apocalypse. While neither the tradesman nor the police are treated particularly sympathetically during the incident, the violence is portrayed as simply criminal, and the strikers as a dangerous and irresponsible mob. Constitutionalism is portrayed as the only possible solution to a situation created by the collusion of selfish union leaders and employers whose irresponsibility borders on the criminal. This malevolent conspiracy pervades the whole fabric of the narrative; the wife of the hero, Davy , is seduced by Joe, with the result that the campaign Davy launches against Joe's skulduggery is labelled as simply personal animosity. At the end of the film, with five men dead down the pit because of the greed of the mineowner, the Labour MP diverts Davy's bitterness: 'the world is like a wheel', he says, 'your turn will come'. The impact even of this fatalistic appeal for evolutionism is muted by the anodyne words of an off-screen commentator as, once again, the camera sails off into the sky:

And so, out of the darkness of the world that is, into the light of the world that could be, and must be, a world purged of its ancient greeds, a world in which dreams are not empty or sacrifices in vain, a world full of infinite promise which the unconquerable spirit of man will some day forge into fulfillment.

The film does not patronize; it does not project the working class as happy, singing idiots. It is a campaigning film rather than an essay in national self-congratulation. Yet it does personalize the issues to such an extent that the problem becomes one of morality rather than economics or politics, and the solution offered is couched in terms of a moral regeneration rather than a distinct and specific set

of social changes. True, Davy does find his roots
again, after a period of seeking his own
self-interest, signified sexually by his chasing a
clearly vapid and unfaithful woman. His regeneration,
however, is pictured specifically in terms of a move
from self-seeking to seeking justice for the
community, and it is the moral aspect that assumes
most significance - a morality, moreover, encoded in
patriotic terms. The impassioned plea for the
nationalization of the mines, made by Davy in a
university debate, is couched in terms which link a
resentment at the personal greed and mass
exploitation involved with private ownership with a
straightforward nationalism: 'I resent it as I would
resent a foreign flag on the Cliffs of Dover'. While
the idea of a national family characterized by mutual
respect and moderation is not proclaimed quite as
shrilly in this film as in the others discussed, the
idea is still implicit; 'real' values still exist;
they need only to be regenerated and allowed to
resume their command of the national scene, in place
of self-interest and disloyalty.

It was an idea with which George Orwell had a
great deal of sympathy in his writing. Carol Reed's
film appealed explicitly for what Orwell would have
called 'decency', a talismanically English word. The
similarity of approach is significant because of the
very different audiences assumed by a film like The
stars look down and a book like The road to Wigan
pier. No doubt many were drawn to a film like The
stars look down by their knowledge of Cronin's book
on which it was based, and the use of an actor like
Michael Redgrave surely gave the film a rather more
up-market appeal than the others that have been
discussed. Nevertheless, a feature film has to be
made for a mass audience simply to recoup the large
financial outlay involved, while the editions of the
Left Book Club can hardly be said to have had mass
appeal on quite the same scale. Reed's film does
signify a much more sophisticated assumption on the
part of the film-maker about the nature of the
audience. This involved a move towards copying some
of the strategies of the literary commentators, but
adapting them specifically to cinematic techniques.
In particular, rather than imposing the themes of
moderation, law and order and community on the plot,
the film invited the audience to make its own
judgement along these lines, presenting them with a
situation in which moderation and community were
clearly in trouble and asking the audience why this
had happened. The audience could only make sense of

the plot if it were implicitly understood that moderation and community were the features that needed to be defended. In this way, the audience was taken into an active and participatory role in decoding the film, a rather more sophisticated strategy than the stolidly propagandist technique of many other films. The British national character continued to be the hero, but Reed's film proved that cinema was maturing as a hegemonic instrument, becoming more clearly an area of exchange and negotiation rather than a patronizing instrument of ideological coercion. (20)

The literate audience of the 1930s had a wealth of material to choose from in confronting the problem of the 'Two Englands'. The 1930s was par excellence the period of the social survey. The bulk of this material was a great deal more critical of existing conditions than anything produced for the cinema screen, The stars look down excepted. A number of reasons account for this. First, published books were never subjected to the same degree of censorship as was film in this period, an indication of the depth of the class bias which inflected the gap between literary and cinematic culture in this period. Nevertheless, cinematic treatment of contemporary social conditions remained a matter of 'us' looking at 'them', founded upon a rock-hard expectation of the triumph of consensual values. Time and again, the opening shot takes the viewer literally down into the city and the closing shot takes the viewer literally up into the clouds; the narrative loop that comes between depends upon a 'pleasure of closure' which will confirm the values of the British national character. A second reason for the more critical stance of so many literary commentators is that government itself had not yet fully developed the social service network which would need to conduct its own surveys and compile its own statistics of social problems. As a result, the work was left largely to those outside government likely to be interested, which meant almost by definition those who were opposed to government policy to a greater or lesser degree. Finally, because book publishing did not need quite such a large audience to survive financially, it could afford to be more selective in its audience appeal, and publish for those with special interests. The thoroughness of the detail of the surveys, and the fact that so many of them were published, is evidence enough of their success in forcing recognition of one England upon an interested section of the other England.(21) Nevertheless, the charitable or religious intentions of groups like the Carnegie or Pilgrim Trusts and Barnett House, or of individuals like B.S. Rowntree, clearly constricted their politics. This was equally true of writers who professed more radical intentions, who proved themselves constricted in the very act of selecting and positioning the audience that would read their work.

It is, for example, the selection and positioning of his audience in relation to the England of the Depressed Areas that makes Orwell's The road to Wigan pier such an important book in demonstrating both the strengths and weaknesses of contemporary literary radicalism. In many ways it is a highly embarrassing book, and is surely meant to be so. Orwell exposed his own prejudices and assumed that his reader would see in them a reflection of his or her own secret views. Orwell constructs his reader as a southern middle-class liberal: his description of the miner's journey to the coal face, for example, is couched in terms that only the London commuter will fully understand: '...you hardly feel yourself deeper down than you would at the bottom of Piccadilly Tube ... I had not realised that before he even gets to his work he may have to creep through passages as long as from London Bridge to Oxford Circus'.(22) In the unmasking of his own physical revulsion at the working class experience, Orwell attempts to take his audience into self-denigrating complicity. Not only in his famous admission that he had been brought up to believe that the working class smells but in a crowd of other small physical winces, Orwell aims to expose the depth of the class gulf, and its irrationality. All this is by way of preparing his reader for an expression of the need for a common front, a cross-class solidarity, to face contemporary foreign as well as domestic problems. Yet there is no question in Orwell's argument of the liberal middle class he is addressing surrendering its privileges, only of losing its aitches. The doubt he has about his intellectual superiority when watching miners at work is, after all, only 'momentary' (23), though certainly he does concede that it is only because miners sweat their guts out that he can remain superior.(23) Yet the view of socialism for which Orwell appeals in Wigan pier is clearly one to be dominated by Orwell and his readers. Socialism, however, should be shorn of the faddists and ideologues of the cosmopolitan eccentric Left - those 'who take their opinions from Moscow and their cookery from Paris' - for the sake of attracting working-class support, and also for the sake of keeping English decency at the forefront of the struggle. 'We can bring an effective socialist party into existence', he concludes, but:

> We can only get it if we offer an objective which fairly ordinary people will recognise as desirable. Beyond all else, therefore, we need intelligent propaganda. Less about 'class consciousness', 'expropriation of the expropriators', 'bourgeois ideology' and 'proletarian solidarity' ... and more about justice, liberty and the plight of the unemployed ... All that is needed is to hammer two facts into the public consciousness. One, that the interests of all exploited people are the same; the other, that socialism is not incompatible with common decency.(24)

Having argued that class differences are immutable, because they are physically encoded among other things, Orwell simply dismisses rational attempts to explain class distinctions as the eccentric efforts of 'shock-haired Marxists chewing polysyllables', implicitly concluding that 'we', (Orwell and his readers) know best anyway. His view of the liberal middle class remains arrogant and his view of 'fairly ordinary people' remains patronizing. He offers a revolution controlled by the liberal middle class with the working class stuck in an Edwardian after-glow where 'Father, in shirt sleeves, sits in the rocking chair at one side of the fire reading the racing finals, and Mother sits on the other with her sewing, and the children are happy with a pennorth of mint humbugs'. For Orwell, ultimately, nostalgia for a mythical prewar world of order and dignity substitutes both for radical solutions and for material progress:

> ... it is not the triumphs of modern engineering nor the radio nor the cinematograph ... but the memory of working-class interiors ... especially as I sometimes saw them in my childhood before the war – that reminds me that our age has not been altogether a bad one to live in.(25)

It is the combination of this attitude with his rather trite imaging of working-class heroism in the face of adversity that might have crippled the very argument Orwell seeks to make about the possibility

of cross-class collaboration. He reveals one England
to the other in terms which end up simply confirming
the values of the England to which he belongs and for
whom he writes, confirming the right of the liberal
middle class to control the future of the nation,
with some working-class support. It was to take the
foreign developments of the second half of the 1930s
to provide Orwell with the factual equipment for a
radical reorientation of his thinking. Even then, the
radicalism was to be short-lived.

At the end of his English journey, J.B. Priestley
concluded:

> You have only to spend a morning in the dole
> country to see that it is all wrong. Nobody is
> getting any substantial benefit or any
> reasonable satisfaction out of it. The Labour
> Exchanges stink of defeated humanity. The whole
> thing is unworthy of a great country that in
> its time has given the world some nobly
> creative ideas. We ought to be ashamed of
> ourselves.(26)

Yet the dole queues had been only part of what
Priestley had seen; there had also been Suburbia and
Merrie England among other 'Englands'. He was clearly
not that ashamed of England either, but rather filled
to bursting with patriotism, as he himself admitted.
Only for those who lived through the Slump in the
Depressed Areas was the unemployment a 'lived
culture'. For the rest, unemployment was worked into
the English landscape as a stain which served only to
throw the real English values into stronger relief:

> It is for us to find the way out again, into
> the sunlight. ... rather than live on meanly
> and savagely, I concluded, it would be best to
> perish as the last of the civilised peoples.
> Warmed a little by my peroration, I noticed
> that a lamp was cutting the fog away from a
> charming white gate. Doors were opened. Even
> the firelight was familiar. I was home.(27)

And the door closed quietly behind Priestley, and the
dole queues merged with 'the inner glowing tradition
of the English spirit'.

What all these refractions of the experience of
the Depression held in common – and they are
representative of many others, from Ellen Wilkinson
to T.S. Eliot, was the overdetermining charge of
meaning that the word 'England' held for them,

irrespective of their political point of view or
their social class. The book or the film about the
Depression became part of a new genre, operating
within conventions and rules which governed their
development as texts. Above all was the complicity
between audience and author, clearly underlying all
the examples here discussed, that 'England' stood for
certain moral precepts which could not and should not
be jarred by the experience of the Depression.
Indeed, the Depression was contextualized and given
significance in such a way as to reinforce these
precepts. With different emphases, depending on the
angle of approach, 'England' mobilized and
articulated discourses on tradition, resilience,
self-restraint and, above all, community. Though
socialist, conservative and liberal might struggle
for control of these precepts, and differ radically
on how they should be applied to the contemporary
problems, nevertheless the fact that this idea of
'England' was shared and pleasurable amounted to a
major hegemonic influence. In turn, this view of what
'England' stood for was articulated to a parallel
view of the English landscape which relegated the
problems of the urban areas to secondary importance.
Pastoralism and 'decency' went hand in hand.

NOTES

1.   J.B. Priestley, English journey, 1934,
Penguin ed., 1977, p.375.
2.   See D.H. Aldcroft and H.W. Richardson,
The British economy, 1870-1939, 1971.
3.   See G. Glynn and J. Oxborrow, Interwar
Britain: a social and economic history, 1976.
4.   See J. Stevenson and C. Cook, The slump -
society and politics during the depression, 1977.
5.   Extrapolated from S. Constantine,
Unemployment in Britain between the wars, 1980.
6.   P. Mathias, The first industrial nation,
1971.
7.   See G. Crossick (ed.), The lower middle
class in Britain, 1977.
8.   B. Gilbert, British social policy
1914-1939, 1970.
9.   See D. Marquand, Ramsay MacDonald, 1977.
10.   R. Gray, 'Bourgeois Hegemony in Victorian
Britain', in J. Bloomfield (ed.), Class hegemony and
party 1977.
11.   Gaumont British, 'The Prime Minister
Speaks Out', November 1936 (Visnews).

12.   R. Malcolmson, Popular recreations in English society, 1973.
13.   H. Cunningham, Leisure in the industrial revolution, 1980; G. Stedman Jones, 'Working-Class Culture and Working-Class Politics: Notes on the Remaking of the Working Class', Journal of Social History, 1974.
14.   Off the dole, no director credited, 1935. (Not available for hire at time of writing.)
15.   C. Barr, Ealing studios, 1977.
16.   Sing as we go, dir. B. Dean, 1935 (EMI); J. Richards & A. Aldgate, The best of British, 1983.
17.   J. Richards, 'The Lancashire Brittania', Focus on Film, December 1979.
18.   'Our Gracie - Our Guest at Monster Gala at Chorley', Pathe News, August 1938; N. Pronay 'Newsreels in the 1930s', History, 1971, pp. 411-8; 1972, pp. 63-72.
19.   The proud valley, dir. P. Tennyson, 1939 (EMI).
20.   The stars look down, dir. Carol Reed 1939 (BFI).
21.   The Pilgrim Trust, Men without work, 1938; Carnegie Trust, Disinherited youth, 1943; B.S. Rowntree, Poverty and progress, 1941.
22.   G. Orwell, The road to Wigan pier, 1937, repr. 1977, p.22.
23.   Wigan pier, p.31.
24.   Wigan pier, p.24.
25.   Wigan pier, pp.104-5.
26.   J.B. Priestley, English journey, 1934, repr. 1977, p.385.
27.   English journey, p.390.

2. SUBURBAN PASTORAL

The disunities and the paradoxes of the interwar
years are clear enough; in particular, the stark
contrast between the Depressed Areas and the new
economy of the South and the Midlands. These
disunities can not simply be forgotten, for they
played a very major role in shaping perceptions in
the interwar period, generating a creative friction
which produced some of the best-known literary and
cinematic material of the period. Love on the dole or
The road to Wigan pier would not have been written in
a country where everyone was unemployed, or where
nobody was. Yet to concentrate entirely on these
disunities and paradoxes is to miss the significance
of the underlying unities and, in particular, the
extraordinary tenacity across the political spectrum
of the concept of the national family. In exploring
the strength of this notion in interwar Britain, it
becomes quickly clear that much of its subtlety as an
act of persuasion lies in its relationship to the
pastoral/urban opposition. In Britain, pastoralism
was articulated historically to the myth of the
pre-industrial Golden Age, a time of supposed harmony
and progress. Time and again, the village community
is represented as a microcosm of the national
community. In the interwar years, much of pastoral
England was in fact being eaten up by developing
suburbia, yet the myth only grew stronger
ideologically as the physical reality began to fade.
    Pastoralism implied not simply a love of the
countryside but also a range of assertions about the
history of pre-industrial Britain, centring on the
development of the rights of the 'free-born
Englishman'. It was not simply a conservative
strategy to bemoan the loss of the links with the
land, though conservatives certainly did see the
development of industrialization and mass society as

40

a chaotic blow to the English tradition. Few British radicals, however , would have accepted Marx's strictures on 'the idiocy of rural life'. While mainstream European socialism depicted industrialization as an exploitative but necessary and, finally, liberating phase in human development, British radicalism was prone to deplore industrialization and urbanization as a reversal of the supposedly inexorable rise to freedom and equality that characterized Britain in the agrarian age. Blake's 'Jerusalem' has always remained a more potent anthem for British socialism than the 'Internationale'. All over Europe, pastoralism was appropriated by the political right, and especially by the fascists. In Britain, uniquely, mainstream left and right could combine in a common despair at the implications of the materialist age.

Pastoralism is perhaps the strongest and longest-lived tradition in British culture. It became particularly important to a country which industrialized as early and as thoroughly as did Britain. Pastoralism predates industrialization by many centuries, of course, but the potency of a major tradition already associated with Chaucer, Shakespeare, Herrick, Milton, Cowper and so many others took on a particular poignancy in the industrializing setting. The Romantic ideal, and particularly Wordsworth's development of the theme of Nature as a clarifying and restorative force, became the yardstick by which it was possible to measure just how much had been lost in the traumatic shift from the fields to the factories. Along with the idea of nature as a restorative force, in so many formulations - particularly among nineteenth century liberals and liberal radicals such as Cobbett, Carlyle, Ruskin and Morris - went some specifically political associations. For the first liberals in the industrial generations, pre-industrial England had seen the development of that personal liberty and natural justice which were the natural birthright of every Englishman. The ideals of Magna Carta of the thirteenth century, the unshackling of the links with Rome in the sixteenth century, the fight against absolute monarchy in the seventeenth, and the proto-socialism of the Levellers and the Diggers, suggested a political tradition of developing liberty unique in Europe. England, it seemed, had modernized politically before it modernized economically: the stout yeoman farmer John Bull stood in sharp contrast to the downtrodden European peasant. It was this concept of freedom and self-reliance which was most

closely threatened by the strict time code and the
cash nexus of factory life. As Raymond Williams has
accurately pointed out, 'real' values continued to
reside in the countryside rather than in the town:
'the townsman envies the villager his certainties ...
and has always regarded urban life as just a
temporary necessity. One day he will find a cottage
on the green and "real values"'.(1) In this
formulation, 'Merrie England' was neither reactionary
nor impoverished: rather, it was a mode of life which
guaranteed liberty and independence, whereas
industrialization was a sinister and shackling force
which created exploitation and , thus, rifts in the
national family, the enlarged village community.

During the second half of the nineteenth century,
something like three millions moved off the land and,
with the population explosion in the towns, Britain
was overwhelmingly urbanized by the time the Great
War broke out. A generation had grown up knowing
nothing but the horizons of the industrial city. It
was still true, however, that for most of the
nineteenth century the land remained proximate in a
physical as much as in an ideological sense. Not till
1851 did more people live in towns in Britain than in
the countryside. Often the industrial workforce
maintained its links with the land long after
migration, returning for the annual harvest, for
example: hop-picking in Kent remained an annual event
for many East End Londoners until well after the
Second World War. Within living memory of the
generation just too old to fight in the Great War,
heavily urbanized though that generation was, the
rhythms of agricultural life had been as real as the
harsher time code of the factory. Political power had
also been remarkably slow to slip out of the hands of
the agricultural class. Not until the third Reform
Act did the landowning class lose its absolute
majority in the House of Commons, and even then
retained a remarkable political clout in the
House of Lords, until it was reformed shortly before
the Great War. The imperial expansion of the late
nineteenth century also tended to reinforce rather
than to undermine the ideal of the countryside as
'home'. Of the colonialists, Raymond Williams has
noted: 'the images of home are of an ideal of rural
England: its green peace contrasted with the tropical
or arid places of actual work; its sense of
belonging, of community, idealized by contrast with
the tensions of colonial rule'.(2)

This idealized, sentimentalized view of rural
England – England as Arcadia – became a dominant and

recurrent image in late nineteenth century Britain. From Thomas Hardy to the 'rural radicalism' of the Liberal party or the country seats of Lords Derby and Salisbury, from the setting of the English public schools to William Morris and the Socialist Labour League, the future of England's 'green and pleasant hills' was the real context of cultural debate. Pastoralism as a unifying myth,however, took on a new significance as a result of the experience of the Great War. The popularity of Rupert Brooke's poetry made rural England a constant point of reference. For trench poets, for writers of popular songs and designers of postcards alike, rural England became the touchstone of stability and tranquillity in the first of the machine wars. Paul Fussell has pointed out the enormous range of pastoral imagery that the war threw up, an apparent paradox considering the unprecedented destruction wrought on the countryside in the war zones by the available military hardware during the Great War.(3) The uses to which pastoral imagery was put, moreover, were intriguingly contradictory. It might be used, for example, as a comfort in itself, a dream of home, as in Brooke's 'Grantchester', or as in the popular song 'Roses of Picardy', the quintessentially English rose symbol linking the specifically French context of the war with a nostalgia for home. Just as easily it could be used by maudlin postcard designers to be sent home to Mum from the trenches.('The roses round the door\ Make me love Mother more').(4) Pastoralism was used, very frequently, as shorthand imagery of what England stood for in the patriotic songs and verses of the war. Equally, however, it could be used by the anti-war poets to make an exactly opposite point:

Pale flakes with fingering stealth come
      feeling for our faces,
We cringe in holes, back on forgotten
      dreams and stare, snow-dazed,
Deep into grassier ditches.
So we drowse, sun-dozed,
Littered with blossoms trickling
      where the blackbird fusses.
Is it that we are dying?.(5)

Pastoral tradition was thus used for very different objectives, but the point remains that it was the tradition itself which provided an underlying structural unity. The values of rural England could be used as a point of reference for virtually any point one cared to make about the Great War. In this

sense, the unity implied was more significant than
the disunity implied by its varied use; the struggle
was for the control of the implications of
pastoralism. For those raised in the pastoral
tradition, the calm, tranquil English landscape had
itself become a site of struggle, but the struggle
itself was limited in its implications by the fact
that pastoralism came down to the interwar generation
ideologically precoded; it was by definition an
anti-materialist tradition, and the experience of the
Great War encouraged nostalgia for a lost Arcadia,
closing down possibilities of a new beginning.

Moreover, in interwar Britain, the countryside
was threatened as never before. The migration into
the cities of the nineteenth century was followed by
an equally massive migration of urban dwellers into
the suburban sprawl that was one of the most marked
social changes of the period. The development of
metropolitan transport at the turn of the century had
begun to make it possible for the middle class to
move out of the city centres almost as fast as the
labourers were coming off the land into the inner
cities. Ribbon development occurred along the
out-of-town railway lines which provided easy access
to the city. The attraction of living in semi-rural
bliss, after working in the teeming city all day, was
obvious. Dormitory boroughs developed as islands
beyond the London boundary, along the lines leading
out from the termini at Euston, King's Cross and St.
Pancras, but especially Waterloo and Victoria, which
offered access to the pleasant rolling countryside of
Surrey. The role played by the availability of
transport in this process was crucial. In London,
competition between forms of transport was a major
stimulant. By 1914, the motorbus was taking over much
of the short-haul commuter traffic, and the
underground railway began to reach out further beyond
the City of London looking to create new markets. The
railways in turn began developing longer suburban
lines deeper into the surrounding countryside.(6)
Thus, the long-term drift into the cities of the
agricultural working class, which created such
pressure on public utilities and on the quality of
life in the inner cities, in turn bred a migration
out of the cities of the middle class, stimulated by
the competition between the forms of urban and
suburban transport.

This process continued at an accelerating rate in
the interwar years, with the result that the urban
area of England and Wales rose by nearly 26 per cent
between the wars while the urban population rose by

only 15 per cent. The gaps between the suburban
islands formed before 1914 were filled, and new
islands were formed further afield as the better-off
struggled to distance their private lives from their
place of work. The population of Middlesex rose by
nearly 31 per cent between 1921 and 1931, and rose by
the same proportion again before 1938. West Surrey
saw similar growth, with seven new railway stations
opening there between 1920 and 1937 alone.(7) The
upper-middle class pushed on into the Surrey
countryside, to Woking and all stations to Guildford,
to avoid the throng of lower-middle class and working
class who followed them out of the city. The typical
urban-suburban pattern of concentric rings of class
ghettoes was formed most clearly in this period.
Though the development of transport, and competition
between forms of transport, clearly played a major
part in the formation of suburbia, the process was
also helped by the housing policies of the
governments. Lloyd George had promised 'homes fit for
heroes to live in' during the Great War and, though
few of these materialized during Lloyd George's term
of office, a commitment to major spending on housing
was a prime feature of the social policy of both
major parties in the interwar period. Housing
subsidies given to Local Authorities made it possible
to take some of the pressure off the inner cities by
developing huge exurban estates like those at
Wythenshawe, to take the overspill from Manchester,
and at Kirby outside Liverpool.(8)

While the priority in spending these subsidies
was to rehouse the working class in council-owned
property, Local Authorities and County Councils were
also able to offer cheap mortgages. In the period of
low interest rates that followed the 1931 financial
crash, banks and building societies were also able to
cash in on what became a giant housing boom. This was
especially noticeable in the South East and in the
Midlands, the areas of the consumer boom. The social
class to benefit most from this process was almost
certainly the lower-middle class, the fastest growing
of the social classes in this period, comprising 40
per cent of all British families in the census of
1931. While many of the working class in heavy
industry were affected by long-term unemployment, and
while sections of the upper-middle class were
affected by the decline in profits in large sections
of the economy, the lower-middle class seems to have
sailed through the Depression years relatively
unaffected. There was to be none of that
radicalization of the lower-middle class that

inflation produced in Germany, for example, which generated so much support for the Nazis. Neither owners of big capital nor sellers of obsolescent manual skills, the white-collar workers emerge as the class least at risk in the particular circumstances of the Depression in Britain. The consumer boom was primarily their boom; they fed it with their sub-managerial and clerical skills, and they fed it by buying their suburban houses, their cars and their electrical goods. Suburbia threatened pastoralism, and thus the British cultural tradition, but suburbia was also the domain of the lower-middle class, a principal stabilizing sector in the British population in this period. In the disguise of this paradox lay a major success of conservative ideology in this period.

The emergence of the lower-middle class was a function of the rationalization in the organization of industry in advanced capitalism. The formation of much larger conglomerate firms, needing a much larger and more complex management system, entailed a vast army of lower management, clerical and sales staff. This division of labour within the middle class was accelerated by the development of the service industries, banking and the consumer economy. Recruited largely from the working class, yet committed to management, they functioned as a shock-absorber of class friction. The lower-middle class might be defined as a separate social grouping in two ways; first, by their economic function, which made them neither decision makers nor owners of capital but servicers of management; second, by their self-perception, their concept of status. For the lower-middle class, the home-ownership offered by the changing circumstances of the interwar period gave the typical family 'a shelter from the harsh realities of the world', and a 'controllable, predictable environment' in which to shelter.(9) In lower-middle class suburbia, the full flavour of the notion that 'an Englishman's home is his castle' was allowed full play. Everything about the design of the neo-Georgian or mock-Tudor self-contained, owner-occupied, semi-detached may be read as signifying both the desire for privacy and the desire for status. The development of the mortgage system of house purchase in this period was the first phase in the formulation of the concept of 'the property-owning democracy'. It created, in effect, a class of industrial kulaks, relatively satisfied economically and deeply committed to the status quo. They were the target of working-class activists and intellectual snobs alike. 'Boring bumsuckers' they may have been, as Orwell's George Bowling described himself and his kind, but they were not insignificant. Their sheer numbers and their attitude to life gave them a crucial stabilizing role to play in the development of British society between the wars. The problem, however, was that their very environment was a threat to the traditional roots of British culture.

Though suburbia threatened rural Britain by destroying it at the rate of 60,000 acres a year in this period, suburbia developed its own blend of pastoralism, the 'rus in urbe' of Elm Groves and Laburnum Avenues which was to reach its climax in the Garden City projects after the Second World War. This vulgarization of the pastoral tradition was savagely attacked by the popular novelist as much as by the intellectual elite. H.G. Wells laid into the lower-middle class cruelly; so too did Evelyn Waugh, George Orwell, D.H. Lawrence and Walter Greenwood. In cinema, too, they played an indeterminate and sulky role between upper-middle-class glamour and working-class chirpiness. Only Alfred Hitchcock treated them in any sense seriously as a film subject, and then only for dramatic effect. The typical Hitchcockian use of a lower-middle class setting was to present a very mundane and boring context into which something distinctly unboring intruded. The life-style of the lower-middle class was the most common complaint, most famously in the relatively gentle vein of John Betjeman's 'Slough':

Come, friendly bombs, and fall on Slough.
It isn't fit for humans now,
There isn't grass to graze a cow
Swarm over, Death!

In labour-saving homes, with care
Their wives frizz out peroxide hair
And dry it in synthetic air
And paint their nails.
Come, friendly bombs, and fall on Slough
To get it ready for the plough.
The cabbages are coming now:
The earth exhales.

Nevertheless, suburban pastoral was clearly good business, a constant theme in the advertising of the estate agents and the transport industry. Even more problematic than the suburban estates, which were at least planned, was the unplanned sprawl of the 'weekend' bungalows, retirement homes, those

converted railway carriages, wooden prefabricated
structures and assorted asbestos houses,
aesthetically monstrous, which appeared all over
rural Britain. John Lowerson notes in particular the
case of Peacehaven on the South Downs, where the
population increased from 400 to over 3,000 between
1920 and 1924, the result of brilliant financial
speculation: 'with over seventy-five types of
bungalow available, and its own "Peacehaven Song", it
marked the steady growth of an English "Costa
Geriatrica"'.(10)

Along with the threats to the countryside which
these developments necessarily involved, went a
renewed interest in country pursuits, a demand that
the countryside should be protected, and that access
to that countryside should be guaranteed to the urban
population. The Town Planning Act of 1932 and the
Ribbon Act of 1935 were foretastes of the more rigid
controls that were to come after the Second World
War. The London and Home Counties Act created a Green
Belt, and local authorities were sometimes prepared
to buy sites of natural beauty, Beachy Head for
example, to prevent their development. If moves such
as these presaged more careful and purposeful action
to prevent the towns spilling into the countryside,
the question of access to privately owned
beauty-spots brought out the old spirited radicalism
of the pastoral tradition. The boom in interest in
hiking and camping brought the urban working class
into direct confrontation with not just the farming
community, but also the hunting, shooting and fishing
fraternity. The result was a series of conflicts with
landowners for access across farming or shooting
preserves, described by John Lowerson as 'a conflict
over the use of land unmatched since some of the
protests against the alienation of common rights by
eighteenth century Parliamentary enclosures ...'(11)
Mass trespasses onto the Duke of Devonshire's grouse
moor on Kinder Scout, organized by the British
Workers Sports Federation, seem to have excited as
much media interest as anything organized by the
National Unemployed Workers Movement. The Youth
Hostels Association, the Ramblers Association, the
National League of Hikers and the Pedestrians
Association all flourished. So too did the motoring
organizations. All of them, in different and
sometimes contradictory ways, contributed to the
growing feeling that the national heritage needed to
be saved, but saved so that it could be related more
thoroughly to the needs of an overwhelmingly
urbanized and industrialized society.

Shell Oil, for example, early associated itself with the conservationist lobby. During the 1920s, it advertised the fact that it did not spoil the countryside with advertising, and in the 1930s it began to produce the Shell Country Guides. Their 'lorry bills', moreover, which replaced the hoardings, employed contemporary artists such as Paul Nash, Graham Sutherland and Ben Nicholson, featuring the sites of national heritage in the countryside in terms descibed by Michael Bommes and Patrick Wright as 'conventional unrealism'. Painted in an assertively modernist style, they linked 'the unfamiliarity with which the countryside appears to the city-dweller with the strangeness of what ... is normally accepted as proper to modern art. The evocation may still be nostalgic and pseudo-pastoral in many cases, but like motoring it is also stridently modern'.(12) Thus Shell caught the countryside between a traditionalist display of nature, in choice of subject matter, and a stylized celebration of the machine in the form of the presentation of the subject matter, a neat bridging strategy between pre- and post-technology which translated pastoralism into modernism for a mass society. 'You can be sure of Shell', even though motoring was still confined to a small and wealthy faction, precisely because of its hegemonic construct of an organic link between the unchanging, cyclical time of Nature and the progressive time of the machine age.

For cultural commentators less willing to make such a daring compromise, however, mass civilization was quite simply a threat to the countryside, whether this threat appeared in the guise of a new housing estate or a group of working-class lads from Liverpool tramping across Snowdonia. To this extent, the debate over the countryside may certainly be seen as a manifestation of class conflict, but overlaying the conflict was the common assumption, with its more traditional and hegemonic implications, that the roots of British identity lay in the countryside. With the creeping problems associated with the mechanization of life and the social problems of industrial depression, the pastoral tradition offered roots, a fundamental stability. But how could such a view, comforting though it might be, square with the simple physical disappearance of the traditional countryside?

The lower-middle class was an easy target for the anti-materialist intellectual elite, and its very ordinariness also made it a very suitable vehicle for prophetic warnings of the dangers of deracination from the rural traditions. George Orwell articulated the hopes and fears relating to the suburban lower-middle class to the myth of the agrarian Golden Age in Coming up for air. What made the novel so frightening, in the circumstances of the late 1930s and the approach of a war likely to be even more devastating than the last, was that Orwell suspected that there was in fact no return to the past: the salving comfort of the pastoral tradition was over. Trying to recapture the bliss of a prewar rural childhood in Lower Binfield, Orwell's George Bowling interpellates the reader in the most strikingly direct way, coming out of the page at the end of a chapter to grab lapels and ask: 'Is it gone for ever? I'm not certain. But I tell you it was a good world to live in. I belong to it. So do you.' For Bowling, however, it was the distance between what was real at an ideological level, and what had physically happened to Lower Binfield, that was the cause of despair. The mechanized and threatening contemporary scene intrudes with a bump when the RAF drops a bomb on Lower Binfield by mistake as he is visiting it. The event leaves Bowling exposed to the future, a complete rejection of all the values that he associated with prewar rural England. In its place, there was totalitarianism and the technology of mass destruction. Images of the future crowded into his mind:

> It's all going to happen. All the things you've got at the back of the mind, the things you're terrified of, the things that you tell yourself are just a nightmare or only happen in foreign countries. The bombs, the food-queues, the rubber truncheons,the barbed wire, the coloured shirts, the slogans, the enormous faces, the machine-guns squirting out of bedroom windows. It's all going to happen.(13)

Orwell used the common strategy of linking the threat to the pastoral tradition to the threat of war. To contextualize the horrors of a bombing war in the near future in terms of a rootlessness caused by the death of traditional values was a particularly telling and frightening ploy. To represent the ashes of pastoralism as suburbia and its inmates, increasingly the typical British home and the typical British citizen and probably the typical target in a bombing war, was to present a boundlessly depressing view of the world. On the other hand, although Orwell was certainly going through a period of intense depression and fear for the future after his return from Spain, all was not lost. By presenting the problem as one caused by people not caring ('why should a chap like me care?'), he implicitly left alive the possibility that hope could be regenerated. During the war that followed, Orwell was to re-mobilize the pastoral tradition for a British social revolution with all the punch of a pre-1914 xenophobe. In effect, Orwell was not actually arguing that the pastoral tradition was dead, merely that it had been submerged.

In invoking a nostalgia for pre-1914, moreover, Orwell reinforced that part of the myth of the rural Golden Age which implied that the Industrial Revolution had suddenly happened on August 4, 1914. The reason is perhaps obvious: if divorce from the land = death, then the first of the machine wars included some of the best available iconography to give substance to that idea. Orwell was only employing a linkage between the Great War and the threat to pastoralism that had been used many times before. Lawrence had used it in Lady Chatterley's lover and, even earlier, in England, my England. For Lawrence, the Great War was the epitome of the way in which industrialization and mechanization destroyed the old realities. For Egbert in England, my England, death in the Great War comes, however, simply as an almost inevitable consequence of the fact that he and his wife were already living out of sorts with Nature, townies trying to return to the land: 'That was Crockham. The spear of modern invention had not passed through it, and it lay there secret, primitive, savage as when the Saxons first came. And Egbert and she were caught there, caught out of the world'.(14) The war was simply being used by Lawrence to throw the threat of deracination into stronger contrast. But the implication of linking the threat to the pastoral tradition with the threat of war was to effect an ideological displacement as well, for it disguised the internal threat as an external one. This helped to make both Orwell's and Lawrence's work somewhat muted as strict social commentary. Though both despised the lower-middle class for what it represented, the link with the threat of war left the problem rather ambivalently posed as something external and faceless – the machine men – rather than something internal and politically definable. The solution seemed to lie in a moral regeneration, a return to the common English spirit, rather than in confronting latent internal fissures.

The pastoral tradition could also be used, however, by apparently ignoring it. While the trench poets, Orwell and Lawrence all used the pastoral tradition as a point of contrast with the present, poets like T.S. Eliot simply inverted it. The startling impact of The waste land to a generation brought up with pastoralism was that that tradition was turned completely on its head:

What are the roots that clutch, what branches
                           grow
Out of this stony rubbish? Son of man
You cannot say, or guess, for you know only
A heap of broken images, where the sun beats,
And the dead tree gives no shelter, the cricket
                          no relief,
And the dry stone no sound of water.(15)

To convert one of the most sacred icons of the pastoral tradition - Keats' nightingale - into the dirty little creature of 'Sweeney Among the Nightingales' could only be a deliberate and conscious slap in the face for that tradition. Its impact, however, relied on there being a pastoral tradition to invert. Without the implicit understanding between writer and reader that Eliot took for granted, without the underlying cultural unity that the pastoral tradition supplied in other words, Eliot would make no sense at all. The same is true of the desert limestone landscape of Auden's poetry or the suffocating, claustrophobic atmosphere of Greenwood's Hanky Park in Love on the dole. There can be no escape from Hanky Park because there is no way in for 'real' values. The characters are literally stuck in a vicious circle - the book begins and ends with virtually identical scenes - because the city is cut off from the renovating force of Nature. Rural = life, and urban = death; this is a recurrent binary opposition in interwar British culture.

Thus even when reference was not being made specifically to the pastoral tradition, it was still significant, because a contrast was immediately implied for the reader, consciously or unconsciously: the cultural context negotiated a contract between writer and reader. The relationship of these texts to the whole structure of pastoralism, and the values that were validated by that structure, demonstrates an underlying unity in interwar culture, a commonly-held set of assumptions about the 'real' England. This sense of the 'real' England, rural England,

fading away as the contemporary problems of
industrialization bore more and more heavily on the
development of English culture, predisposed so many
different shades of opinion to approach those
contemporary problems from broadly the same
direction. This is not to suggest that there were not
differences of opinion which were apparently serious,
simply to argue that the wider unities in outlook
limited the possibilities of really radical
confrontation. Clearly, this had directly political
consequences. Stanley Baldwin, the most enduring of
all interwar politicans with an ability to withstand
crisis after crisis to lead the Conservative party in
its domination of interwar politics, owed a great
deal to the public projection of himself as the
kindly, paternalist English squire guiding a society
in which industrialization was just a headache.
Baldwin fed on the same cultural roots as the
radicals and the ultra-conservatives. A constant
theme in his public speeches was the soundness of the
English tradition, which he associated specifically
with rural life and, in particular, Worcestershire,
'the heart of England', where he was born:

> The wild anemones in the woods of April, the
> last load at night of hay being drawn down a
> lane as the twilight comes on ... and above
> all, most subtle, most penetrating and most
> moving, the smell of wood smoke coming up in an
> autumn evening ... they are the chords that
> with every year of our life sound a deeper note
> in our innermost being ...These are the things
> that make England, and I grieve for it that
> they are not the childish inheritance of the
> majority of the people today in our country ...
> but nothing can be more touching than to see
> how the working man and woman after generations
> in the town will have their tiny bit of garden
> if they can ... It makes for that love of home,
> one of the strongest features of our race ...
> It is that power of making homes, almost
> peculiar to our people, and it is one of the
> sources of their greatness. They go overseas,
> and they take with them what they learned at
> home: love of justice, love of truth, and the
> broad humanity that are characteristic of
> English people.(16)

Baldwin's cliched image of rural England was one that
could be found in so many instances of popular
culture, from Country life and Field to the holiday

postcard. It was prominent also in cinema newsreels.
The annual Armistice Day ritual, for instance, was
always covered by all the major newsreel companies,
the accompanying commentary reminding the audience
what had been fought for. The Gaumont British edition
dealing with the 1936 ceremony was typical of them
all: 'liberty' said the commentator and the visual
image to accompany that word, to give it concrete
meaning in cinematic shorthand, was a whole series of
shots of rural England - a ploughman and a shire
horse in a huge field, the South Downs, and the Lake
District. This was also the year that the old King
died; the newsreel made much of the double mourning
shared by royal family and the nation at large on
this particular Armistice Day. By intercutting,
during the one minute's silence, shots of the royal
family on the balcony in Whitehall (the new King
having 'shared with his generation the test of
battle'), the wreath-carrying politicians, the crowd
and the country churchyards, the newsreel constructed
a powerful image of the national family, linked by
the pastoral tradition, 'communing with those who had
marched into the Great Beyond' in the Great War.(17)
    Baldwin was, in other words, tapping a rich vein
in the post-war period. In fact, he began the tweedy
squire image which was to stand leaders of the
Conservative party in good stead until the 1960s.
This no doubt accounts for at least part of his
appeal. He offered the dream that there was safety in
the old values, that the nation was sound at heart;
the paternalist squirearchy was still guarding the
nations's future. But he also managed to articulate
these values to those of the lower-middle class. In
the late nineteenth century even so patrician a
politician as Lord Salisbury had seen the potential
value of 'Tory Villadom' as it developed; it was
during the Baldwin era that the decisive capture took
place. In many ways, it was a foregone conclusion:
the lower-middle class was, by economic and cultural
definition, on the Tory side of the fence. What
singled out Baldwin's achievement, however, was the
bridging strategy between traditional and progressive
conservative values. The constant emphasis on his own
ordinariness and on the trust that could be placed in
him, gave him the aura of a man who displayed the
common sense of the man in the street. 'I give you my
word', he said in an election newsreel in 1935, 'and
I think you can trust me by now'.(18) In this stance,
he belied his establishment background, earning
himself the contempt of patricians like Lord
Birkenhead or Lord Curzon, but enjoying immense

political success.

Though suburbia never produced the rich high cultural vein that fed on the anti-industrial tradition, nevertheless it had its own hallmarks centring on privacy, the search for status and the primacy of respectability. Above all, however, it was the economic function of the lower-middle class which helped to create the possibility of a new hierarchical rather than class-based society, in which individual hard work could bring the joys of property ownership down from the social heights to relatively humble families. It was in this sense, the development of the lower-middle class as an industrial peasantry, that suburbia in effect pastoralized British urban society; the village community was being transformed into the property-owning democracy; the New Jerusalem was being built by the speculators. Anti-materialism continued to dominate high culture but its ideological core was being swamped by the invasion of urbanized culture which redefined the countryside as a kind of consumer durable, significant for the role it played in relation to urban culture rather than in its own right. Pastoralism and anti-materialism remained major elements in the national consciousness, but a massive section of the population was now locked into the national family for quite different reasons. The position of the elite was further complicated by the fact that the Great War could be blamed for so much; it was a unifying explanation of what had gone wrong which offered a comfortable nostalgia rather than credible solutions.

NOTES.

1.   R. Williams, The country and the city, 1973, p.51.
2.   The country and the city, p. 64
3.   P.Fussell, The Great War and modern memory, 1977
4.   The Great War and modern memory, p. 245.
5.   W. Owen, 'Exposure', in D. Hibberd (ed.), Wilfred Owen: war poems and others, 1973, p.91.
6.   A. Jackson, Semi-detached London, 1973.
7.   Semi-detached London, Ch. 1.
8.   J. Lowerson, 'Battles for the Country-side', in F. Gloversmith (ed.), Class, culture and social change, 1980, p. 258.
9.   Semi-detached London, Ch. 10.

10.   'Battles for the Countryside', p.260.
11.   See Lowerson, pp.262ff.
12.   M. Bommes and P. Wright, 'Charms of Residence: The Public and the Past', in R. Johnson, G. McLennan et al. (eds), Making histories, 1982, pp. 253–302.
13.   G. Orwell, Coming up for air, 1939, repr. 1971, pp. 223–4.
14.   D.H. Lawrence, England, my England, 1922, repr. 1979, p.11.
15.   T.S. Eliot, 'The waste land', 1922, Collected poems, 1974, p.6
16.   S. Baldwin, 'England', On England and other addresses, 1926, pp. 7–8.
17.   Gaumont British, 'Armistice Day', November 1936 (Visnews).
18.   Gaumont British, 'Prime Minister', October 1936 (Visnews).

3. 'THE HEART OF ENGLAND': THE PUBLIC SCHOOLS AND
THE GREAT WAR

In 1933, Vera Brittain remembered the pre-war world
as a long rural summer. The War destroyed, in her
view, not simply millions of men but also the English
landscape. It was to be a constantly reiterated theme
in interwar culture that Arcadia had died with the
Lost Generation:

> I remember Kingswood very clearly as it
> looked twenty years ago, with the
> inviolate Downs stretching away to
> Smitham, and the thick woods unbroken by
> the pink and grey eruption of suburban
> villas ... I have never heard the nightin-
> gales there since the War, and the once
> uninterrupted walks have long been spoilt by
> barbed wire and notices drawn up for the
> intimidation of stray trespassers.(1)

Together, the pastoral tradition and the Great War
cut like a knife across the experience of the
interwar period, complicating in many areas the
possibility of a clear and unequivocal class response
to the problems caused by the Great Depression. Like
the pastoral tradition to which it was so closely
articulated, not just by Vera Brittain but by so many
others, the shared memory of the slaughter created
another bond in the national family, even for those
who had not been directly involved, which offset the
class tensions that might have been caused by the
mass unemployment that followed. For public-school
writers and intellectuals in the interwar years, the
experience was particularly acute. The Depression
hardly touched their daily lives – they were not
prominent on the dole queues, though they could
hardly fail to be aware of the problems which beset
other social classes – but the enormous casualty list
of the trenches haunted the interwar public-school

generation, to the extent that it constituted a threat to the public-school code. In the final analysis, however, it is not clear that the changes which the experience of the Great War brought to public-school culture were actually fundamental. The majority of men from this background seem to have found no reason to change their ideas radically. What did occur, however, among those articulate enough to be prominent among writers, thinkers and film-makers, was a transmutation of old loyalties, an adaptation to the changing circumstances which, in effect, actually ensured the survival of the elite. Flexibility and adaptability were the keys to the public-school code, and the generators of hegemonic adaptation in interwar Britain.

It is, of course, simply stating the obvious to point out that almost all of the 'recognized' artists and intellectuals of the interwar period had been to public schools. For most of the few who had not been through such an education, moreover, university had a similar programming effect. The auto-didactical tradition of the working class may or may not have produced thousands of 'village Newtons' but, with the exception of Walter Greenwood, none found their way into the canon of the elite. Obvious though the point may be, its significance should not be under-estimated. The very obviousness of this fact disguises its significance, the role that public-school culture played in inscribing class and gender inflections in the hegemonic process. The self-perpetuation of the elite involved the perpetuation of their ideals as well, though in adapted form, and even their very self-questioning involved an extraordinary degree of self-advertisement as the shamans of their age. It is in this sense that the role of the public schools as an Ideological State Apparatus, adapting the parameters of debate in the period under discussion, is an essential key to the self-perception of the interwar generation. If the Depression posed a threat to the authority of the more prominent among the products of those schools, the Great War had posed an equally major challenge to their self-confidence in dealing with such a threat. A new credo, or at least a new rationale for the old credo, had to be found.

The anti-materialist theme in public-school culture turned from the optimistic vein of pre-1914 to the pessimism of the interwar period. No longer did the public-school men stress 'England's Mission' to rise above materialist self-interest to show the world how to live the Christian life; rather there

emerged the cynical theme that now that the higher
ideals of pre-1914 had been snuffed out, materialism
could hardly help but flourish all around in a
consumer society. The interwar period was
characterized by a search for new loyalties, though
the old values could not easily be discarded. A large
section of the public-school elite, the traditional
guardians of high culture, sought relief in
ridiculing popular culture and the social pretensions
that accompanied it. In place of the muscular
Christian tradition of the public schools, the belief
that it was a duty to go out into the world and give
a moral lead from the front, there emerged a tendency
to retreat into insularity. Perhaps the most extreme
example of this was the conversion of Evelyn Waugh to
Catholicism, from which privileged position he could
scorn materialism and all its works. Graham Greene
went through a similar conversion, though he leaned
as hard as he could to a familiarity with, and a
comprehension of mass culture. Another section turned
to socialism. Orwell, Auden, Spender and many others
embraced socialism with all the enthusiasm of the
convert, if only temporarily in most cases. The
problem of the public-school socialist was that the
anti-materialism basic to public-school coding
remained a major element in their make-up, creating
incomparable difficulties in accepting a materialist
credo. There were to be all kinds of curious
contradictions in the writings of the public-school
socialists, many of whom were finally to give up the
struggle to rid themselves of public-school values
and retreat into neutrality.

Nevertheless, it was the impetus to adapt which
was important, rather than whether adaptation was
successful in individual cases. In this period, among
writers as different as Waugh, Greene, Orwell, Auden,
Spender and Isherwood, there was an awareness of the
fact, which would never have occurred to their
nineteenth-century predecessors, that there was
something anomalous about their social background, a
self-consciousness about being a public-school boy
which pervades their writing. Yet in their search for
new absolute truths, they helped to adapt and thus to
reinforce the very social values that they appeared
to be questioning. In this sense, the changes that
occurred in public-school ideology were deeply
hegemonic, and they helped to retain the central role
of the public school as an Ideological State
Apparatus, educating and training an elite for the
changing needs of society. In effect, this meant that
the elite would maintain its domination as the result

of a process of negotiation and compromise that continued to generate general consent.

Before 1914, the public-school system played a crucial role in bringing the middle class to dominance in an almost seamless transfer of cultural authority. For most of the nineteenth century, in spite of the incursions of liberal anti-oligarchic ideas and legislation, the major institutions of the state were still in effect in the patronage of the aristocracy. It was basically to secure aristocratic patronage to enter the armed forces, parliament, the civil service and the law, that the public schools came into being to serve the sons of the middle class. As Imperialism expanded in the late nineteenth century, the major institutions of the state were faced with a manpower shortage; it was the development of the public schools which filled the gap. The public schools performed their role by teaching the values that came naturally to the aristocracy by virtue of their wealth and social position. The replacement, through the boarding system, of parental control by the spirit of loyalty to the house and to the school was reinforced by an elaborate system of pupil autonomy, with the senior pupils themselves administering the day-to-day affairs of the school outside the classroom. It was this system which produced that enormous group solidarity, the freemasonry of 'the old school tie'. The glorification of the manly virtues, not just the famous games cult of the late nineteenth century but primarily the accent on moral and intellectual integrity, combined with this emphasis on group loyalty to give the system an extraordinary vitality and self-confidence. The curriculum gave the pupils access to the most prized possession of all, namely the guardianship of the cultural tradition of the aristocratic age. Thorough grounding in the Classics and the Humanities may not have given the pupils a suitable education for the technological realities of the industrial age (2), but it did give them something equally useful in intellectual and cultural terms, namely an understanding of the development of Western culture since the Renaissance. They alone among the younger generation had access to that understanding, and it became of priceless value in establishing and maintaining their cultural domination. What made the elite the elite was the fact that the anti-materialist tradition disguised the role they played in legitimizing the burgeoning economic domination of the social class from which they emerged.(3)

The great secret of the relatively painless modernization of Britain in the nineteenth century, painless in comparison with other modernizing nations at least, was that there developed an educational system that permitted the transfer of power through a process of cultural assimilation rather than confrontation. The public schools geared themselves for power by absorbing the culture of the aristocracy. Meanwhile, the group loyalty imbued at the schools ensured that the major institutions of the state would continue to inter-relate as successfully as they had before. Politicians, soldiers, civil servants, artists and academics held broadly the same social and cultural values, whereas the separate and separating vocationally-oriented educational systems in other countries stored up problems of inter-relation between what were in fact different elites. And from the time of the 1870 Education Act on, the public schools were established firmly at the top of the educational structure, an example and unquestioned model for the whole educational system.

It is fashionable and easy to condemn the public-school values of Victorian and Edwardian Britain but, unless one understands the strengths of this system of education, it is difficult to appreciate the framework of the national culture of pre-1914, nor is it easy to understand the impact of the Great War in producing the self-doubt and the self-analysis which characterized the intellectual and artistic elite of the interwar period. Kipling's 'Recessional' or Newbolt's 'Vitae Lampada' embodied values which helped to make the Great War possible, but the slaughter in turn made those values foreign to those who have come after. They were, it is clear, deeply committed poems which mythologized England's Mission, proclaiming her manifest destiny to rule the world in the name of God rather than Mammon. It was the way in which the ideal of service overdetermined and thus disguised the economic dynamic of Imperialism which produced the particularly gruesome form of nationalism which dominated late nineteenth-century Britain. In carrying over the anti-materialism of aristocratic culture into the industrial era, moreover, public school culture created an apparent ideological disjuncture from the economic structure, an apparent autonomy for the realm of ideas from that of economics. What is more, Kipling and his contemporaries were able to mobilize the cultural rationale for Imperialism in cross-class terms. As Orwell shrewdly noted, having seen the processes both of Imperialism and of writing from the inside, Kipling's power as a popular writer lay primarily in his ability to evangelize Empire, to portray it as a religious duty, and also to articulate this sense of religious responsibility in what Orwell called 'snack-bar wisdom' terms, which could have populist appeal. Kipling despised the 'flannelled fools at the wicket and the muddied oafs at the goal' which the public schools turned out to administer the Empire. At the same time, he sympathized with the British Tommy sent out to clean up other people's messes. It was a neatly populist tactic to portray Tommy Atkins as the downtrodden hero of Empire, with parallels in the culture of consolation provided by contemporary music halls and popular press. Kipling thus vigorously expressed a world-view which could find a national rather than simply a sectional response.

Without the harnessing of the hegemonic influence of the public schools to the apparatus of jingoism, it is almost impossible to believe that Britain could have survived nearly two years of total war without even introducing conscription. Rupert Brooke's '1914' is, like the poetry of Kipling or Newbold, so well-known and now so often laughed at for its outmoded values that it is easy to underestimate its relation to contemporary 'common sense', yet it remained one of the most popular poems of the war, long after Owen and Sassoon began to try to undermine the jingo fervour. Brooke portrayed the war as a release from a monotonous and soul-destroying materialism. The volunteers, 'as swimmers into cleanness leaping' were prepared to 'pour out the red sweet wine of youth'. He meant, of course, that they were prepared to bleed: the Keatsian tradition had turned sado-masochist when allied to nationalism. Bleed the volunteers certainly did, in their thousands. The prefects of 1913 and 1914 were the young subalterns of 1915 and 1916. With their conspicuous uniforms and their conspicuous bravery, they took worse casualties proportionately than any other group involved. Britain mobilized six million men between 1914 and 1918; twelve per cent were killed. Eton sent 5,687 to the front, presumably virtually all of them officers; over twenty per cent were killed. One in 10,000 British soldiers won the VC, but one in 380 Etonians.(4) So much of the poetry of the Great War, however, tended to anaesthetize the experience by concentrating on 'lads' (not men) 'falling' (not dying). The blood-red poppy imagery reinforced the macabre sensuality of the slaughter, the homoerotic overtones owing a great

deal no doubt to the all-male group solidarity, the
displaced homosexuality, of the public school.(5)
     The languid sado-masochism of the early cultural
response to the casualties prompted Owen and Sassoon
to a bitter response, which also involved throwing
over the literary style that Brooke had established
as the norm for war poetry. It was, potentially at
least, a radical move, based upon the implicit
understanding that to destroy an idea it is also
necessary to destroy the form in which it is
expressed. Sassoon, for example, took up the ironic
tone of the soldiers' songs, but while the soldiers'
songs parodied the jingo music hall, Sassoon parodied
the public pronouncements of the establishment. Yet
Sassoon never could quite pick up the idiom of the
working-class soldier credibly; the soldiers of his
poetry were products of Kipling's Tommy Atkins
freshened by the music-hall comic, the patronizingly
chirpy cockney sparrow with a wry comment on his
lips. Owen did not live long enough, either, to break
away more than in part from the poetic forms, and the
ideological imprints which they brought with them, of
the previous period. Pastoralism and homoeroticism in
particular, two of the motifs previously captured by
the jingos, remained latently significant in much of
his later poetry, though he certainly tried to
contest the nationalist connotations of these themes.
     It took, in other words, a great deal to break
down the structures of authority, and the cultural
forms they had appropriated, which the public schools
had established for the 1914 generation. The
reaction, moreover, took a long time to break through
into cultural acceptance. The bitterness of the
anti-war poets like Sassoon and Owen did not really
attract literary notice until after the war was over,
and it was not to be until the end of the 1920s that
anti-war prose began to get published in significant
quantity in Britain. Even at the end of the anti-war
publishing boom which followed, a pacifist and
feminist such as Vera Brittain, remembering 'the
unmelting bitterness into which I had been frozen by
the ... tragedy of my experience', could still write
liltingly of the summer Speech Day in 1914 when she
had heard the Headmaster of Uppingham issue the
prophetic words, followed by a breathless silence,
'if a man cannot be useful to his country, he is
better off dead':
     ... roses with velvet petals softly shading
     from orange through pink to crimson foamed
     exuberantly over the lattice work of an old
     wooden trellis ... it was the one perfect

summer idyll that I ever experienced, as well
as my last care-free entertainment before the
Flood. The lovely legacy of a vanished world,
it is etched with minute precision on the
tablets of my memory.(6)

One after the other, in tragic procession, all the
men closest to her were killed in the war which
followed. Throughout that period, however, it was the
poetry of Rupert Brooke, as well as of her fiance
Roland Leighton, which seems to have consoled her:

> Between 1914 and 1918, young men and women
> ... were continually rededicating themselves
> ... to an end that they believed, and went on
> trying to believe, lofty and ideal. When
> patriotism 'wore threadbare', when suspicion
> and doubt began to creep in, the more ardent
> and frequent was the periodic re-dedication,
> the more deliberate the self-induced conviction
> that our efforts were disinterested and our
> cause was just ... To refuse to accommodate
> this is to underrate the power of those white
> angels which fight so naively on the side of
> destruction.(7)

For the four boys who left Uppingham in the summer of
1914 and went into uniform, the image of the school
was all-important. The way in which the group loyalty
of the school, the urge to die if necessary in order
to ensure group survival, had replaced the duty to
family to survive was one clear way in which the
public schools of pre-1914 succeeded in sustaining
the war effort for four years. Even those who loathed
the war and denounced it, either privately or
publicly, went on fighting, so powerful was that
loyalty.

The loyalty to the old values was, moreover,
reinforced by new loyalties learned as the war
progressed. The 'fellowship of the damned' which is
said to have united Great War soldiers
internationally also united them in cross-class
terms. In other countries, the process helped to
produce fascism, but in Britain it worked itself out
in more liberal forms. For those officers who
survived the slaughter, the effect was traumatic in
more than the merely physical sense. In the trenches,
traditional paternalist ideas were given a new
dimension, a new emotional basis. John Keegan has
noted the significance of the relationship between

officers and men, quoting one officer's picture of
the idealized 'Beloved Captain':

> The fact was that he had won his way into our
> affections. We loved him ... If anyone had a
> sore foot he would kneel down ... and look at
> it ... If a blister had to be lanced, he would
> very likely lance it himself ... There was
> something almost religious about this care for
> our feet. It seemed to have a touch of the
> Christ about it.(8)

For most young platoon commanders, the appalling
conditions of the trenches were also their first
close cross-class experience. This much is also
evident from the poetry of Sassoon, Owen or Herbert
Read:

> In many acts and quiet observances
> You absorbed me:
> Until one day I stood eminent
> And I saw you gathered round me
> Uplooking,
> And about you a radiance that seemed to beat
> With variant glow and to give
> Grace to our unity.(9)

The Christ-like relationship that often developed
between young officer and men, be it considered
touching or patronizing, was to predispose an
important section of the elite, those coming to
political maturity in the 1930s, to react
sympathetically to the problems posed by the
Depression. It is no mere coincidence that the prime
architects of the Welfare State were public-school
officers on the Western Front in the latter stages of
the Great War: Major Clement Attlee, Haileybury,
University College Oxford, South Lancs. Regt and Tank
Corps; Captain Anthony Eden, Eton and Christchurch,
King's Royal Rifle Corps; and Captain Harold
Macmillan, Eton and Balliol, Grenadier Guards. Though
he never fought in the trenches, it was to be John
Maynard Keynes, Eton and Balliol, who gave the
politicians-to-be the theoretical wherewhithal to
translate their emotional commitment to social
betterment into legislative reality. This was to
produce the new 'middle way' in politics which first
emerged on the right wing of the Labour Party and the
left wing of the Conservative Party in the 1930s.
    As a factor in producing an adaptive ideology,
this new paternalism may well have been a crucial

catalystic factor. Gramsci noted that an intellectual could not be 'distinct and detached from the people-nation', that he had to feel 'the elemental passions of the people, understanding them and thus explaining and justifying them in a particular historical situation, connecting them dialectically to the laws of history'. In Gramsci's view, an emotional bond between intellectual and people was essential, otherwise the relationship between the two would become 'purely bureaucratic' and the intellectuals would become simply 'a caste or priesthood'.(10) The trauma of the trenches may well have forged an organic link between social groupings in Britain, leading to an adapted social conscience among those who survived to come to the centre of political power in the 1940s and 1950s, achieving massive political consensus in the process. One of the crucial cores of this new consensus was to be the construction of the myth of the Depression years. The dynamic which motivated this section of the elite in adapting traditional values was not, then, simply and self-consciously that of self-preservation; the hegemonic process is not that cynical. It was rather a question of an emotional commitment to a continued leadership for the good of society as a whole, a transformed paternalism, negotiating a new class alliance without actually conceding anything real in terms of ultimate cultural authority.

The war had an equally traumatic effect on those in the public schools who were just too young to fight. Standing in chapel, week after week, the experience of listening to the lists of names of old boys killed at the front began to undermine the formerly impregnable armour of group loyalty. There may never have been any serious doubt that future recruitment would be in jeopardy, but many headmasters talked of an incipient bolshevism among their pupils in the last months of the war and in the few years after. This was, no doubt, a gross exaggeration, but there clearly was a growing cynicism about the prosecution of the war in view of the heavy casualties. Orwell later remembered how at Eton in the latter stages of the war, it became the done thing to sneer at the traditional values of the public school, and 'to be as slack as you dared on OTC parade'.(11) Christopher Isherwood, too, in Lions and shadows described the sense of foreboding that hung over a sixth form prepared for the 'brief and violent career of the trenches'. Yet, for this generation in the public schools, the sense of having just missed the experience proved to be a telling point in defining their future attitudes. Though they helped to make it fashionable to condemn the pre-1914 values, and turned frequently to fairly radical politics, they were also guiltily aware of a dereliction of duty with the Armistice. 'You felt yourself a little less than a man', Orwell later remembered, even explaining his decision to go to fight in Spain partly as an expiation of his sense of guilt at not having fought the Great War.(12) Isherwood, haunted by his sexuality, erected the Great War as a personal 'Test':

I was obsessed by a complex of terrors and longings connected with the idea 'War'. 'War', in this purely neurotic sense, meant The Test. The Test of your courage, of your maturity, of your sexual prowess: 'Are you really a Man?'. Subconsciously, I believe, I longed to be subjected to this test; but I also dreaded failure ... I was rapidly forgetting the inconveniently prosaic truth about my old school. I was deliberately forgetting, because 'war', which could never under any circumstances be allowed to appear in its own shape, needed a symbol – a symbol round which I could build up my daydreams about 'The Test'. Gradually, and in the most utter secrecy, I began to evolve a cult of the public-school system.(13)

Thus, from a neurotic elision of themes of violence, sexuality and authority, emerged the Mortmere fantasy, a private world into which Isherwood, Auden and their clique could withdraw, a solidarity myth which was implicitly opposed to the solidarity myth of the public schools themselves. Yet, in the very need for a solidarity myth, they remained unmistakably public school in outlook. Mortmere was a compound both of public-school cliquishness and of an anti-public-school conspiracy theory.

Much of the more outrageous behaviour of the Auden-Spender clique must be read as a deliberate nose-thumbing at the establishment from which they had emerged. Their homosexuality, though they kept it secret for years, was an opening-up of what had always been repressed and silenced in public school culture. Their socialism never seems to have been more than skin-deep, on the other hand; the nearest either Auden or Isherwood seems to have come to the working class was in a series of slightly sordid sexual encounters. Orwell, too, though his socialism was clearly more of a commitment than it was for Auden or Isherwood, could never get away from the fact that he was, obviously, a gentleman slumming it, as in The road to Wigan pier among other works, Orwell and Isherwood even adopted fake cockney accents in an attempt to win more credibility. The socialism of the artistic coterie associated with the Auden-Spender group was something of a weapon in a struggle within a class, rather than a real commitment, a generational dispute resulting from being just too young to fight the Great War. They railed against 'the old men' - a phrase that comes up repeatedly in their writings - rather than against the social structure as a whole, for what had happened to the boys just older than themselves and what had so nearly happened to them too. They wrote distinctly difficult poetry, which cut them off not only from their social and cultural peers, but also from the masses they professed to champion. In fact, their work might be described simply as an elaborate code virtually designed to be impenetrable to all but the small clique to which they belonged.

What applied to Auden and Isherwood applies, though with lesser force, to many of the other public-school socialists of the interwar years. We are dealing here with a generational dispute within the elite as much as with a deep intellectual division. Many toyed with communism, but few became committed. Naturally, Soviet civilization was an enticing alternative to a generation of fellow travellers who no longer believed 'dulce et decorum est pro patria mori', who saw the Five Year Plans producing employment while capitalism languished in the Depression, who saw Russian intellectuals and artists accorded a role and position denied artists in Britain, and who saw in the notion of the Popular Front the only way of stopping fascism short of another war. What held them back might be described either as bourgeois squeamishness, self-protection or simply moral integrity; whichever it was, it is clear that, even for them, the public-school code was not that easy to break. Orwell, calling on the middle-class intellectuals to throw in their weight with the working class, wrote 'we have nothing to lose but our aitches'; he was drastically oversimplifying, in fact; there was a lot more to being public school than having a posh accent. This much the Spanish Civil War was to prove. Forcing intellectuals to take sides, the War was to create a major moral crisis in the minds of many middle-class socialists. It was to bring into even sharper relief the struggle between

minority culture and mass civilization and force them
either to accept or to renounce those prejudices
which lay still just below the skin.(14)
        While public-school socialists sought, unhappily
most of them, to marry-up the anti-materialism with
which they had been programmed with socialism, the
escape of writers such as Graham Greene into
Catholicism allowed them to approach the
juxtaposition of the deracinated man in an uncultured
world in moral rather than social or political terms.
Anthony Farrant, in Greene's England made me, is a
sham, a public school boy but not the Old Harrovian
he claims to be, drifting listlessly through a series
of unwholesome jobs, kept going only by his innate
charm. Minty is a real Harrovian, but a shabby and
impoverished journalist, whose only real pleasure and
hope of status is to relive his school days: 'They
hadn't the resources to hold their places, but the
world had so contrived that they hadn't the vigour to
resist'.(15) Against them are ranged Krogh, the
unscrupulous financier, and the ferocious Hall,
carrying with him 'the atmosphere of third-class
Pullmans to Brighton, the week-end jaunt, the whisky
and splash, the peroxide blond'.(16) The opposition
between the two pairs of men is set up in class terms
which assume also that culture has no money and that
money has no culture. Between them comes Kate,
Anthony's twin sister and Krogh's lover, symbolically
bridging the two worlds but quite unable to bring
them into harmony. Anthony buys Krogh's ties for him
and Krogh gives Anthony money for just being there.
Who exploits whom? In the last resort, though, there
are things that Anthony will not do, though he might
leak the dirty work to Minty in an underhanded stab
at maintaining decent values and restoring his
personal integrity before he drifts off again: 'you
need money to have scruples', Kate had once warned
him.(17) Anthony ends up with a week in cold water
and a friendless funeral. It is a very bleak world
which Greene depicted, of a culture represented by
Anthony which has descended into mere style and
questionable stance, and also of a culture 'not young
enough to believe in a juster world, nor old enough
for the country, the king and the trenches to mean
anything'.(18) On the other hand, there is a violent
and boorish materialism, fascinated by the style and
deferential to it, but unable to risk its little
moral idiosyncrasies, which show up as simple
disloyalty.
        If England made me (like the collection of essays
Greene edited on the subject of The old school) was

the work of a public-school educated writer
questioning his public-school education while being
unable to escape its influence, the novel was also
the work of an Oxbridge-educated author.(19) The
writer who had Anthony Farrant expose Krogh's lack of
culture could also patronize elements of
public-school philistinism in Anthony, his
willingness to deploy the term 'highbrow', his
favouring of the fun-fair and pleasure-gardens over
opera and Shakespeare. Yet, beyond this, Greene also
broods on the complicity of high culture and an
amoral high finance. The poetry-writing ambassador
('beastly aesthete' in Minty's public-school patois)
is by no means averse to insider-trading on the stock
exchange; sculpture and theatre benefit from Krogh's
patronage. This double-edged quality of Greene's (not
surprising, in itself, from the socialist-inclined
Catholic convert and anti-materialist film-critic) is
only one symptom, however, of responses to Oxbridge
education in the period.(20)

Oxford and Cambridge provided the final phase in
the education of the elite, filtering an intake from
the public schools as the public schools filtered
their intake from the preparatory schools. If the
public schools provided the mass of servants of the
state, the soldiers and the administrators, Oxford
and Cambridge assembled the leaders of society and
established a powerful social bonding between them.
As a consequence, the cultural meanings of the old
universities permeated the apparently disparate
fields of writing, publishing and film-making on the
one hand, and politics (of all shades) and mandarin
administration on the other; today's undergraduates
were inevitably to figure as tomorrow's leaders in
all those fields. It was not that such embryo-leaders
had undergone an analogous kind of education, but
that they underwent the same education. This had deep
effects on political and cultural life in Britain.
Allegiances and bonding established at the old
universities may link individuals across apparent
boundaries of political difference. T.E.B. Howarth
has highlighted one of the more bizarre modulations
of such deep structures of loyalty – Guy Burgess,
following his flight to Moscow, still refusing to
betray the secrets of the Cambridge Apostles (his
student society) to Tom Driberg.(21) Less
theatrically, British consensus politics has long
been reinforced by such a heritage. For those outside
the prioritized patterns of education in British
society, the most astonishing aspects of the postwar
spy scandals involving Burgess, Maclean, Philby,

Blunt and others, have been less concerned with the
fact of treachery (although clearly this has its
implications for any assessment of the reliability of
Oxbridge as an instrument of dominant culture), than
with the degree of interpenetration of the spy-rings
with elite leadership across the board. Martin
Green, writing a narrative of literary decadence in
Children of the sun, and Andrew Boyle, pursuing the
spies in The climate of treason, end up tilling
precisely the same ground.(22) Yet for those within
the prioritized patterns of education such
overlapping and intersection is inevitable and
demands for the naming of non-spies (Hollis,
Rothschild) go hand in hand with the naming of spies.
Alec Waugh, author inter alia of a novel entitled A
spy in the family, observed in 1975:

> The average Englishman of my generation who was
> brought up in the Galsworthy pattern had by the
> time he was twenty-five met most of the people
> that he wanted to; at his 'prep', his public
> school, his university; when, in the early
> twenties, he embarked on his profession he knew
> the men with whom he would be working, his
> colleagues and his rivals ... We had heard of
> those of our contemporaries whom we had not
> met, so that when we did meet them we could
> quickly establish our identities ... We did not
> need to make any particular effort to keep up
> with our old friends. We would rely on the next
> meeting, which would surely take place if not
> this year then the next, and if not then, well
> then within four years.(23)

Alec Waugh isolates this commonsense expectation of
the Oxbridge-educated as the central dynamic of
Anthony Powell's The music of time (and inevitably
the legibility of that novel-sequence must vary
according to the reader's sharing of that
expectation). A similar principle is observable in
the phenomenon of recurring characters in Evelyn
Waugh's oeuvre. Certainly Russian interests in the
1930s appreciated the social logic of an Oxbridge
training. The undergraduate converted to espionage in
his early twenties might have had no immediate
usefulness; but the risk of his not becoming (as it
were) Keeper of the Queen's Pictures or Head of M15
or a Washington diplomat, was small enough not to
endanger the cost-effectiveness of recruitment. The
very success of Oxbridge in the training and placing
of the elite guaranteed the success of subversion in

high places, and the sense of social solidarity that both public schools and Oxbridge fostered made it certain that they would be very difficult to uncover. Moreover, as Martin Green has explored, tensions of allegiance and identity apparent in the personal psychology of the spies echo those of Oxbridge's literary leaders of the same generation who shared with the spies a memory of the Great War, and experiences of political instability and economic depression. Graham Greene, whose first published novel was entitled The man within, has long been recognized as exploring in himself and in his fictional characters variations of the theme of 'the divided man';(24) Greene's respect and admiration for Philby (under whom he worked in MI5), attested in numerous writings, has led to the writer taking the attitude towards the spy-scandals of 'there but for the grace of God go I', an observation which may well be taken as having a literal force. In terms of espionage, Greene would not appear to have attracted the interest of the secret service (beyond MI6 considering whether to suppress Our man in Havana for breaching the life-long silence rule imposed on MI5 employees), but the divided consciousness, what Green has called 'the virtue of disloyalty', remains in common.(25)

Greene, with his sense of division, is the central point in the spectrum of responses among the Oxbridge-educated to the values of their training. Greene's co-religionist Evelyn Waugh remained wholly impervious to the sirens of socialism and to the seductions of mass culture. The potentially radical questioning of the establishment in Waugh's early fiction found its justification not in the logic of social and political alternatives but in that of his Catholicism, in an outlook sub specie aeternitatis which could, however, happily recollaborate with his conservatism. The Scone College of Decline and fall (where dons beg God to cause riotous students to attack the chapel and increase the fines likely to arise out of the disturbance) gives way to the Oxford of the wartime Brideshead revisited, an Arcady, a Lyonesse which co-operates with high art and the country house in those divine, if tortuous workings of grace which bring Charles Ryder to the faith.(26) In turn, Brideshead revisited, as university pastoral, has subsequently entered dominant culture, remodulating analogous articulations of value in, for example, Milton's 'Lycidas' (where Camus joins St. Peter in King's funeral procession), Ackerman's prints and Arnold's 'The Scholar Gypsy'. This valorization is echoed in Vera Brittain's early experience at university when her English tutor invited the student to see her Milton manuscripts; initiation to the university and high culture stand cognate.(27) When in English journey Priestley aligned the colleges of the universities with 'the Old England', the England of cathedrals and the old landscape painters, he indicated the extent of acceptance of such conjunctions through a society mainly only familiar with the universities through Boat Race Day.(28) Waugh, John Fowles has suggested, found a 'safety valve' in his humorous writing which allowed him to persist in his Tory psychology which otherwise might have been subject to more de-stabilizing influences.(29) Only forced into a somewhat theatrical conservatism, Waugh is found in postwar Britain celebrating the virtues of Catholic hagiography as an antidote to a cultural decline perceived in Leavisite terms.(30)

Others such as Auden and Isherwood took up clear stances of commitment. Yet in many cases such declared political movement towards the left hardly survived the decade, the 'apostacy' of Auden and Isherwood (or 'Parsnip and Pimpernel' as Waugh repeatedly mocked them) being representative of such disembarkations of fellow-travellers.(31) John Cornford understood the difficulty of eliciting a lasting commitment from the Oxbridge educated, phrasing his advice in terms of a strategy to 'Keep Culture out of Cambridge'; the ideological formation of the Oxbridge undergraduate was too deeply founded for anything but a root-and-branch approach.(32) If such as Burgess and Maclean did not disembark (even while maintaining a quaint impress of their Oxbridge personalities), the loneliness of their particular form of commitment may be seen as only emphasizing how Oxbridge may have teetered, but never toppled. It may be seen as the exception which shows how in general Oxbridge fulfilled its ideological function within the period and even eventually twitched so many of its less contented sons back upon the thread, or else projected them into non-combatant states of division and paralysis. From the outside the institution looked solid enough. For Gwyn Thomas, the working-class undergraduate from a depressed area confronted at university an ideology which was just as unified as it was alien:

In the valleys you see just one side of it. You see the large majority oppressed and conscious of oppression, primed with anger and ready for

revolt ... As far as I can see at present,
these people are the real strength of society.
We protest with words. They would answer back
with forms of violence we would never dream of.
Even when our hatred of unemployment, want,
insecurity and avoidable disease is at its
angriest and most violent, we have doubts about
how far our anger and violence can go, and how
best to direct them. These people have no
doubts. Their cause, in their eyes, is
sacredly, unquestionably just, and exclusive of
all fears and hesitations ... It makes them
invincibly strong ... It makes me afraid and
draws my horns in.(33)

If so many writers were acutely aware of being
public-school educated, and felt anomalous as a
result, cinema sought to familiarize its audience
with the outlook of the ruling class with a mixture
of nostalgia and bonhomie. Tell England, one of the
earliest of British talkies, was made by Anthony
Asquith and Paul Barkas in 1930. It was based on a
novel by Ernest Raymond, published in 1922, but it
reflected the very different climate about war which
permeated the 1930s. The novel, subtitled A study in
a generation concentrated on the years at school
leading up to 1914, the growing relationship between
two boys, and their hero-worship of the young master
Radley, a Middlesex county batsman. A contemporary
re-reading of this section can hardly fail to note
the originally unconscious masochistic and homosexual
overtones; it is ironically called 'Five Gay Years at
School". The story continues in a highly ritualized
vein; the period of apprenticeship at school is
followed by a long sea passage to Gallipoli in which
the two boy-officers, coming under the influence of
the regimental padre, come to see life as the pursuit
of the perfect religious beauty in self-sacrifice.
The novel ends on the hill of Cape Helles on
Gallipoli, a kind of Calvary on which two of their
shipmates are killed before Edgar Doe makes the
supreme and beautiful sacrifice of himself at the end
of a doomed campaign.(34) There is not a hint of
anti-war sentiment in the novel: it is a public
school fantasy of homoerotic sado-masochism,
unwitting testimony of the darker side of public
school culture. The film, however, was much more
ambivalent. The section at school was cut to a
minimum, to be replaced by heavily nostalgic
flash-backs to the summer of 1914. It is this image
of England which Doe finally decides he would rather

die to save than allow to be changed. Throughout the
film, as in the novel, Doe is struggling to find a
good translation of the doomed Spartan's message from
Thermopylae and finally arrives, just before his
death, at:

Tell England, ye who pass this monument,
We died for her, and here we rest content.

A question remains at the end of the film, however,
whether the audience is expected to accept the values
implied in the epitaph either at face-value or
ironically. There can be no question that the film is
anti-war in its implications. The sequence of the
landing on Gallipoli with hundreds of men being cut
down in swathes by Turkish machine-gun fire is
strikingly handled, and referred back to in one of
the crucial sequences of the film. Doe has cracked
up, under the strain of daily bombardment, and shouts
at his friend Ray that he wants to 'tell England
...tell England ... ', interspersed with flashbacks
to the slaughter on the beach. Nevertheless, the code
is still confirmed at the end of the narrative. Doe,
in spite of doubts about the war, does go off and get
himself killed in a heroic gesture, redeeming his
previous cowardice. On the other hand, it is equally
possible to interpret the story in a very different
way; the point of the attack in which Doe made his
heroic gesture was to cover a British evacuation of
the area, as his friend learns to his revulsion after
Doe's death; here the point seems to be that the
idealism of the public-school code was being
exploited by the circumstances of the horrific war.
    Either way, the film is ambivalent in its
treatment of pre-1914, its nostalgia in soft focus
for a supposedly idyllic age when the attitudes which
were actually to lead Doe to his death were
unquestioned. There is a tension between the film's
apparent basic loyalty to the traditional values of
sacrifice and honour, and its awareness that those
very values produced and sustained the war effort.
This tension is never fully resolved in the film.
Tell England is at its most revealing as a film in
its assumptions about its contemporary audience. The
cut-glass public-school accents must have been
extremely hard going for working-class audiences in
the North, for instance, and its treatment of
working-class characters was even more embarrassingly
stereotyped than was usual in British films of this
period. With its intercutting, superimposition and
other editing devices, it was also a very 'arty'

film, which seems to have been made with a 'cultured'
audience in mind, one which would be able to
associate with the two young officers fairly readily.
The film was, in effect, the cinematic equivalent of
a _Times_ obituary, an epitaph for the lost generation
of public school boys, made by the man whose father
had presided over the disaster; Anthony Asquith was
the son of H.H. Asquith, Prime Minister at the time
of the Gallipoli campaign. It reworked Ernest
Raymond's public-school fiction but it remained, like
the anti-war literature of the same genre, unhappily
caught up in an ideological bind, unable either fully
to undermine or fully to accept the implications of
the public-school code.(35)

In contrast to _Tell England_, _Goodbye Mr Chips_
offered no such tell-tale insight into the soul-
searching and the contradictions of contemporary
public-school culture. It offered a rosy and
comfortable view of the public school as an
institution in which all tensions were mediated and
resolved. Released just a few months before the
outbreak of the Second World War, it constructed for
a cinema audience which had never been anywhere near
a public school a sentimentalized projection of the
schools as a microcosm of 'Englishness'. The film
concentrates not so much on the children, but rather
on the pleasantly eccentric figure of Chips himself.
Clearly, Chips could be anyone's grandad, almost
classless; but he is also a fantasy image of the
ideal schoolmaster, and the fact that he is actually
the teacher of the leaders-to-be is used to reinforce
his calling as a teacher. The film offers a view of
the English upper class based on an educational
system which is both informed by and protector of
traditional paternalist values, which Chips himself
personifies. Chips stands for anti-materialism; he
accuses the reforming new headmaster of trying to
turn out 'materialist little snobs with fat bank
balances'. The school, 'the heart of England' we are
told at the beginning of the film, is like Orwell's
England, one big family. This time, however, there is
no question whether the right members of the family
are in control. Indeed, there is no control as such,
because the school has a separate and objective life
of its own, its own unchangeable process, in which
headmasters come and go and the boys flow through in
an unending series of register parades. It will even
go on after Chips. The Great War intrudes as a major
event in the life of the school, and Chips is brought
back to keep things going because so many teachers
are away at the war. Chips returns not, as a

visiting general suggests, to train more subalterns for the trenches, but because the school must go on to train and fashion young men for the future. The class question in Chips is reduced to a fight between one of the boys, Colley, and the grocer's roundsman, which Chips intervenes to stop. The grocer's boy then becomes Colley's batman when he goes off to the war, and Colley is actually killed trying to save him after he has been fatally wounded. The film thus manages to articulate a number of different ideological discourses in its construction of the public school as the epitome of decent English values. It links family to education through the grandad figure, Chips himself, who as a teacher finds a huge surrogate family, and it links that family to the idea of the nation, for these are no ordinary children, but the cream of society. The film ends on an optimistic note, with yet another generation of the familiar family names beginning the pattern of assimilation into the school with a rendition of the school song, and yet more cakes and tea at Chips' lodgings.(36)

Chips in fact relates to a wider stratum of popular culture and it acts, intertextually, with the kind of material that Orwell analysed in his study of 'Boys' Weeklies'. Orwell found the survival of the public school story in boys' comics somewhat startling, particularly when the setting of the Famous Five or Billy Bunter yarns had frozen some time round 1910. Yet the school stories clearly provided a comfortable and familiar context for those 'tens and scores of thousands of people to whom every detail of life at a "posh" public school is wildly thrilling and romantic. They happen to be outside that mystic world of quadrangles and house-colours, but they yearn after it, day-dream about it, live mentally in it for hours at a stretch'. Orwell could trace the tradition back to Tom Brown's schooldays and Stalky and co., and believed that it succeeded because it managed to offer a careful grading of characters so as to give almost every reader someone with whom to identify, even if that character might in fact be the type of 'monocled idiot who made good on the fields of Mons and Le Cateau'.(37) Long before the modern semiologists, Orwell was able to understand the ideological consequences of the fact that popular culture was an area in which socialist ideas had hardly even begun to permeate. The public school functioned in popular culture as a comfortably unchanging context in which none of the new ambivalence of the public school men themselves was allowed to intrude. It was always 1910, Bunter's postal order was always on its way, the problem of sex did not even arise, and Chips was always there to turn to. The two films discussed here spoke differently to different audiences, and they worked within different genres. Tell England articulated the self-doubt of the elite itself, articulated equally in contemporary literature, while Chips continued to thump out the Old School Song as if nothing had happened. Yet both Tell England and Chips accept equally that the old values remain worthwhile. Tell England ambivalently, and Chips more certainly, were both structured by assumptions about the the ruling elite, convictions that that elite was sound at heart and that that heart was in the right place.

Public school men continued to dominate British culture and society at least in part because the public school was not seen as a threatening institution to any but that small section of the elite itself which rebelled in the aftermath of the Great War. The self-confidence and the vigour of the previously homogenous public-school culture may have been temporarily undermined but, even in its fissures, public-school culture remained hegemonic: wherever there was a position to defend there was a public school man to defend it, and to attempt to articulate it to the debate on what had been lost from the 'real' England of traditional values. But it was to be in their ability to form a new mainstream, to shed the extremes and to shape a new national culture, that their significance ultimately lay in this period. The Great War, and the materialism of a consumer society, brought problems for public-school culture just as severe as the test posed by the Depression. But these problems bred their own panacea solution. To go on regretting the passing of some Golden Age, as did so many of the elite theorists or pessimists was to risk being left altogether high and dry with no role to play at all in contemporary society. On the other hand, to move directly to the opposite pole, to socialism, was too great an ideological shift to accomplish. Gradually, as the Depression wore on, the variety of responses was to be honed down, partly by the flow of events but especially by the deepest preconceptions of the public school men themselves. Men like F.R Leavis and John Maynard Keynes were to modify traditional values at the critical levels of artistic discrimination and the theory of the state. Those who survived the ravages on the left, like George Orwell, were to become the strident mouthpieces of the political centre. Between them, they were to present a manifesto for a new hegemony.

NOTES.

1.   V. Brittain, Testament of youth 1933, repr. 1978, p. 37.
2.   M. Wiener, English culture and the decline of the industrial spirit, 1850-1980, 1981.
3.   For the history of the public schools in the nineteenth century, see J. Honey. Tom Brown's universe, 1977; B. Simon and I. Bradley, The Victorian public school, 1975; D. Newsome, Godliness and good learning, 1961; J. Gathorne Hardy, The public school phenomenon, 1977; J.B. Mangan, Athleticism in the Victorian and Edwardian public school, 1981.
4.   See P. Stansky & W. Abrahams, The unknown Orwell, 1966.
5.   See P. Fussell, The Great War and modern memory, 1977.
6.   Testament of youth, pp. 90-1.
7.   Testament of youth, p.370.
8.   Cited by J. Keegan, The face of battle, 1978, p.281.
9.   H. Read, 'My Company', repr. in J. Ellis, Eye-deep in hell, 1977, p.1.
10.   A. Gramsci, Selections from the prison notebooks, Q. Hoare and G. Nowell Smith (eds), 1971, p.418.
11.   G. Orwell, 'My Country Right or Left', CEJL, vol. 1, 1970, p. 589.
12.   Ibid.
13.   C. Isherwood, Lions and shadows 1938, repr. 1968, pp. 46-7.
14.   See Part Three, 1.
15.   G. Greene, England made me 1935, repr. 1979, p. 180.
16.   England made me, p. 161.
17.   England made me, p. 150.
18.   England made me, p. 180.
19.   G. Greene (ed.), The old school, 1934.
20.   See G. Greene, The pleasure dome, John Russell Taylor (ed.), 1972; 'Subjects and Stories', in C. Davy (ed.), Footnotes to the film, 1938, pp. 57-70.
21.   T.E.B. Howarth, Cambridge between two wars, 1978, p.51.

22.   M. Green, Children of the sun, 1977; A. Boyle, The climate of treason, 1979.

23.   A. Waugh, A year to remember: a reminiscence of 1931, 1975, pp. 16-17.

24.   See e.g. K. Allott and M. Farris, The art of Graham Greene, 1951, Ch.2, 'The Divided Mind'.

25.   G. Greene, The tenth man, 1985, repr. 1986, p.17.

26   E. Waugh, Decline and fall, 1928, repr. 1937, p.10; Brideshead revisited, 1945, rev. ed. 1960, repr. 1962, p. 23.

27.   Testament of youth, p. 154.

28.   J.B. Priestley, English journey, 1934, repr. 1977, p.372.

29.   J. Fowles, 'The Enigma', in The ebony tower, 1974, repr. 1975, p.238.

30.   E. Waugh, The holy places, 1952, pp. 5-6.

31.   See P. Miles, 'Improving Culture: The Politics of Illustration in Evelyn Waugh's Love among the ruins', Trivium, 18, 1983, pp. 7-38.

32.   Cambridge between two wars, pp. 212-13.

33.   G. Thomas, Sorrow for thy sons, 1986, pp. 187-8.

34.   E. Raymond, Tell England, 1922.

35.   Tell England, dir. G. Barkas and A. Asquith, 1931 (British Film Institute).

36.   Goodbye Mr Chips, dir. S. Wood, 1939 (Harris Films).

37.   G. Orwell, 'Boys' Weeklies', CEJL, vol. 1, 1970, pp.505-39.

Part Two: Elite and Mass Culture

1.'THE EMBATTLED MINORITY': THEORISTS OF THE ELITE

In the mid-1920s the arch-conservative Wyndham Lewis
wrote wearily of the oppressive respectability of the
word 'revolution'. '"Revolution" today', he observed,
'is taken for granted, and in consequence becomes
rather dull'.(1) In Black mischief, the increasingly
conservative Evelyn Waugh, recently received into the
Roman Catholic church, could satirize the whole idea
of political revolution through the vehicle of a
mythical African state.(2) It is salutary to
encounter such attitudes and warnings in writings of
the interwar period, even while acknowledging that
Lewis and Waugh are extreme and colourful voices, for
their writings may be aligned with other
articulations of conservative political and cultural
strategies which took more persuasive, developed and
influential forms.
    Study of such privileged institutions as the
public schools and Oxbridge, and their accommodation
of social change dating back to the nineteenth
century, shows an elite continuing to be created into
and during the interwar period for service in
government, civil service, church, military,
education and the arts. What is also important to
recognize, however, is the extent to which there was
a living and influential articulation of ideas within
the period supporting a principle of elitism which
was to a greater or lesser extent identifiable with
real state institutions. Moreover, while such ideas
may be fairly termed a body of conservative argument,
it also needs to be recognized that they often
appeared to be voiced from oppositional standpoints,
and hence in context were capable of being read as
radical critiques of society and culture rather than
as bland endorsements of the status quo. Energy,
spirit, urgency - even an aura of banditry - could
certainly accompany the presentation of the

desirability of an elite and shape its appeal; one man's conservative argument becomes the next man's crusade against vested interests. Also complicating the reception of elitist arguments was the fact that elitist principles were being defended against the background and stimulus of the growth of mass culture. The 'shiny barbarism' of modern Britain, as Richard Hoggart was to term it in the 1950s, could offend both the anti-materialism of the public-school and Oxbridge tradition and those sectors of left opinion which saw mass culture as a debased substitute for popular culture or indeed as a conservative form of social control governed by capitalist production. In consequence, cinema, newspapers and chain coffee-houses were capable of being denounced within different perspectives either as symptoms of social decline and the spread of materialism, or as the new opium of the masses. This meshing of attitudes on the left and right gave elitist arguments the advantage of widely-conceded premises as far as opposition to mass culture was concerned.

It is, after all, not just in the writings of Eliot and the Leavises that a hostility towards mass culture is found, but, for example, in the neutral orange marmalade and streamlined eating-house of Orwell's Coming up for air and in the cry of 'nothing but films, films, films' in the frankly populist J.B. Priestley's English journey.(3) The Graham Greene who leans as far to the left as he dares in It's a battlefield creates his modern wastelands out of the artefacts of a consumer society, the half-built housing-estates of A gun for sale and the seaside entertainment world of Brighton rock.(4) Ralph Fox's scepticism about cinema as a medium is echoed not just by Lewis Grassic Gibbon but by Aldous Huxley. Writing on the subject of radio, Lewis Grassic Gibbon and Q.D. Leavis are curiously of one mind:

> And you'd listen to talks on ethics and cocktails and how to go hiking on the Cote d'Azur, minding the baby, copulation in catkins, and the views of Jacob P. Hacken-schmidt on Scotland and her Ancient Nationhood; and you'd switch the thing off, lost, that was better, worth paying a licence to keep the thing quiet ...(5)

The British Broadcasting Company reports that in 1930 every home had a wireless set, which in practice means not that a nation of music-

lovers has sprung up, but that in any town two
out of three houses one passes in the evening
are reading and talking with the support of a
loudspeaker.(6)

Social and historical analysis focusing on the
competition of elites is recognized by social
scientists as a late nineteenth-century development,
principally in Europe, and one having its impact on
Britain and America in the 1930s, particularly
through the dissemination of the work of Pareto. More
than this, study of elites as an academic tendency
has also been regarded as in part a response to, and
implicit refutation of, Marxist analyses of history
and society. The assumption of such study is that
societies comprise distinct groups of the rulers and
the ruled, and that the history of any society is
necessarily inscribed in the competition for power of
warring elites. The corollary of this, in T.B.
Bottomore's words, is that such analysis 'formed part
of a political doctrine which was opposed to or
critical of, modern democracy, and still more opposed
to modern socialism', and he emphasizes that Pareto
'reserves his most scathing comments for the modern
notions "democracy", "humanitarianism" and "progress"'.(7) The dynamic of history being assigned
wholly to elites, this category challenges the
Marxist construct of a classless society (in which
elitists' necessary concepts of rulers and ruled are
absent). Interwar British discourse on culture and
society was demonstrably coloured in the writing and
reception by aspects of this school of thought, and
that consideration says much about the way in which
traditional and native terms of argument on the
subject take on more extreme overtones during the
interwar period. While, for example, T.S. Eliot was
inclined to present his drawing on continental
theories of elites in the spirit of an impartial
consultation with academic theory, his movement
towards such sources for intellectual support leaves
it open to interpretation as an act of association
with a specifically anti-Marxist school of thought.
The parameters of continental debate fd into an
interwar discussion of elitism, notably pursued by
men of letters and literary critics, which at the
same time inherited a native discourse with its own
history and meanings. That native tradition has been
seminally explored by Raymond Williams in his study
Culture and society.(8) It is a tradition of debate
running through the nineteenth century and serving as
a commentary on the growth of industrialization and

of the social organization which supported it. It is a commentary on the elevation of means - exemplified in the idea of the machine - at the expense of ends. The ends at stake are seen as human fulfilment, the expression through living of the best of human potential, to which the social organization of men, justifying its claim to constitute a 'civilization', should be geared. Seen in another perspective, it is also a record of the displacement of literature away from the centres of power in society, of the poet's role as legislator being unacknowledged.(9) Coleridge provided a central statement of the perceptions of the debate in opposing the idea of 'culture' to the idea of 'civilization'.(10) In the separation of these ideas there had occurred, it appeared, a split in the national life. It seemed no longer possible to see the project of society as an organization of men striving for excellence in human activity or for self-fulfilment, striving to live the good or religious life. Instead, society had to be viewed merely as an instrument for the production of wealth. If at some point in the past there had been a whole society, an organic society, a unified culture, then what had replaced it was the fragmentation into individualistic bourgeois society in which, in Wordsworth's terms, 'getting and spending we lay waste our powers'. In his principal contribution, Culture and anarchy, Matthew Arnold set up the value of culture against a utilitarian society preoccupied with coal and machinery and indeed against a society which he saw as consciously concerned to define the terms of its greatness by the measure of its prowess in production.(11)

The culture and society debate, then, had two main cutting edges. On the one hand it was a continuous tradition of criticism of bourgeois, laissez-faire, industrial society; a searching of the middle-class conscience. On the other, it was a tradition of various treatments for the reversal of the tendencies diagnosed. The greatest continuity in the tradition lies in the diagnoses, the greatest variety in the treatments proposed. However, one continuing thread in the proposals for healing the split between culture and civilization lies in the idea of an elite. In a situation in which culture is perceived to be under threat, many writers in the tradition turn to the idea of gathering the like-minded and creating an enhanced role of cultural guardianship for them. The juggernaut of materialistic society may roll onwards, but those individuals who retain a respect and capacity for culture, together with a desire to see its reintegration with civilization, may be given an institutional weight within society which will overcome the problem of their powerlessness, which in turn stems from their dispersal and the fact of their being a minority.

Coleridge's strategy was to call for a body he termed the 'clerisy' or the 'National Church' (terms to influence Eliot). This clerisy would comprise the 'learned of all denominations, ... the sages and professors of all the so-called liberal arts and sciences' and would provide the moral, spiritual and intellectual bases of a unified culture.(12) Carlyle, though his frustration with contemporary conditions on occasion led him to look for more baldly authoritarian solutions, also pleaded for an organized literary class accorded privilege, place, and appropriate reward. Taking his stand on the ground that the spiritual always determines the material, Carlyle described the man of letters as 'our most important modern person ... The world's manner of dealing with him is the most significant feature of the world's general position'.(13) In Culture and anarchy, Matthew Arnold recognized the stratification of English society by class, but specifically rejected the possibility of any single existing class serving as the nucleus of a renewed cultural order. Instead he proposed an elite made up of a saving remnant from all classes, a body of class-misfits whom he termed 'aliens', and called for them in a language of cultural revivalism. Arnold's strategy aimed to sidestep the cauldron of class divisions and class interests; his anxiety was to dissociate his aliens from any suspicion of 'class interest'. However, for any reader there must remain questions about the ideological bases of Arnold's concept of culture and about the composition of his aliens as a group. The membership of the latter must inevitably reflect the privilege structures of the existing society. Arnold presented his project as ultimately an egalitarian one ('Culture seeks to do away with classes'), but it was a 'true' egalitarianism that he offered, an egalitarianism of enlightenment. However, this spiritual and mental egalitarianism leaves many questions unanswered about the degree of change in society and its institutions which Arnold's programme involved. Certainly it involved some, such as widening access to the universities and changes in the organization of education in general. But at the same time Arnold's satire of short-term political reform gives the reader little confidence in the author's commitment to structural changes in society. Arnold sought to win his case by appearing combative but actually trod on the toes of existing material interests as little as possible.

Elitist remedies, as Arnold's words demonstrate, need not be presented as a project to wrest the benefits of culture away from some broader social base in order to restrict them to a minority. On the contrary, such remedies can be presented as a strategy to secure, on behalf of all and from a defensive position, the guardianship of a disappearing culture among at least a few. The newly-refined consciousness of purpose among those few, and their new strength deriving from the support of institutionalization, promises a bulwark against the forces undermining the value of culture. The elitist remedy can, then, present itself as a way of securing a breathing space, an assurance of the survival of values and standards in a society which is judged to be moving too fast and too destructively for those benefits to be ensured in any other way. Tonally, elitist remedies are apt to be presented as guerrilla tactics against the effects of industrialism, a banding together of Davids against the Philistine giant, looking forward, perhaps, to some future process of dissemination which can however only occur after the consolidation of the elite.

By the interwar period the main terms of the debate, because of the perceived accentuation of crisis in an era of technological advance and monopoly capitalism, have become those of culture versus mass culture. The root enemy may well still be an industrial, utilitarian and materialist spirit with its consequent impoverishment of value, but the symptom spawned by that process - mass culture - is now perceived as so virulent and aggressive in its posture towards traditional high culture, towards 'highbrow' art and values, that mass culture itself becomes the enemy to be faced sword in hand. The very existence of such a term as 'highbrow' testified to a fracturing of cultural wholeness, and, as the term was usually used with pejorative overtones, a fracturing which worked to marginalize the high, the difficult, the traditional and the serious. The situation perceived was a compounded version of that described by Wordsworth in the dawn of industrial Britain when he charted not just the invasion of British culture by 'frantic novels, sickly and stupid German tragedies, and deluges of idle and extravagant stories in verse', but their effect of driving into neglect 'the invaluable works of our elder writers, I had almost said the works of Shakespeare and Milton'.(14) In the 1930s, for the Leavises in particular, there was no longer any place for such diffidence as Wordsworth showed: the Gresham's Law principle in cultural process worked unswervingly to substitute a false cultural currency for a true in the valorization of both the works of the past and the works of the present. Indeed, the title of Leavis' 1930 pamphlet 'Mass Civilization and Minority Culture' can be viewed as a grim reformulation of Arnold's title Culture and anarchy, the nature of the revision announcing Leavis' assessment of how far the situation had deteriorated since Arnold's time. 'Culture' shrank to 'Minority Culture', both in frank recognition of the increasingly defensive posture of its acolytes, but also in an uncompromising attempt to turn defence into attack through the position that culture had always depended on a minority for its existence and development. Turning the embattled minority into a confident elite constituted the necessary strategy. In turn, 'anarchy', the symptoms of which Arnold had found in the Hyde Park rioters, could now be clearly identified with the essence of mass civilization and the consequent generation and elevation of the middlebrow and lowbrow. As Leavis explicitly observed, the increased pressure on culture was indicated by the Daily Telegraph's being the newspaper with the largest circulation at the time of Culture and anarchy (a consideration which had caused Arnold great unease); but as Leavis put pen to paper the newspaper with the largest circulation was The News of the World. While Arnold thought himself hard-pressed in having to contend with the Telegraph, Leavis saw himself as having to do battle with the whole intervening revolution of Northcliffe's in journalism, not to mention developments in advertising, cinema, pulp fiction, book clubs and the BBC. Moreover, he could be less assured of support. He had also to deal with cultural fifth-columnists, renegades, those who while having a capacity for intelligent discrimination had sold their souls to the mass cultural machine and its debased systems of value, and those whom Leavis judged as simply too woolly-minded to recognize the scale of the cultural disaster he perceived. The enemy was not just at the gates but making converts inside the walls; it was installing its own furnishings and its puppet officers while the castle's treasures were being thrown on the midden. Such metaphors come readily to mind in attempts to capture the nature of Leavis' enterprise, and do so in response to his rhetoric and its inherent sense of crisis. The 1932 manifesto of Scrutiny is typical in charting disarray and in simultaneously insisting on there being a way forward:

> The general dissolution of standards is a commonplace. Many profess to believe (though fewer seem to care), that the end of Western Civilization is in sight. But perhaps even the Spenglerian formula, in its deterministic non-chalance, represents an emotional as much as an intellectual reaction: and if optimism is naive, fatalism is not necessarily an intelligent attitude. Intelligence has an active function.(15)

Criticism, for Leavis, was the service owed civilization by intelligence. The centrality of the literary-critical intelligence which he preached was justified in the activity's involvement with language, civilization's common intellectual currency. The mind capable of making fine, informed, sensitive judgements in the area of literature and language was equipped to serve civilization by aiding the survival and refinement of that language in which such judgements were made - and indeed in which judgements in any area of civilized human activity were made. Leavis thus sought to mobilize intellectuals on a broad front, not on the grounds of a crisis in critical discrimination within English Studies, but on the grounds that such a crisis was central to, and symptomatic of, the whole crisis in civilization. The historian, the economist, the philosopher, the psychologist, the educationalist, the biologist, chemist and physicist - all fell, for Leavis, within the range of his address. In jeopardy was a tradition of living which fostered individual human fulfilment, 'the culture that transcends the individual as the language he inherits transcends him', 'a sense of relative values and a memory - such wisdom as constitutes the residuum of the general experience'.(16) No surprise, then, that it was the biologist Joseph Needham who was called in to review Brave new world in the pages of scrutiny. the worrying implication of I.A. Richards' 'practical criticism' experiments in Cambridge in the 1920s, experiments which had served to demonstrate a perceived looseness, inconsistency and idiosyncrasy of response to poetic language among its guinea-pigs, was precisely that the students concerned came from a range of faculties in the University.(17) Scrutiny's contributors were drawn from a spectrum of disciplines, and Leavis himself could take particular satisfaction in the testimony of one contributor to the decisive effect of the experience of English in the Scrutiny school to his development as an anthropologist. This broad front of resistance echoed the dimensions of the threat Leavis perceived. The elevation of science from means to end ('Wellsian' or 'neo-Wellsian') interacted with materialistic values to form new constellations of forces('Techno-logico-Benthamism') and to provide a fertile environment for mass culture.

Within the specializations of modern life Leavis sought the 'common' or 'cultivated' reader whose existence was a precondition of cultural stability. The very idea of such a reader, itself a testimony to Leavis' faith in the possibility of a common culture, was mythicized in the form of an organic community of pre-industrial England, a world in which the rich language of Shakespeare was essentially the language of the people and in which the same cultural artefact spoke to all levels of society. Fracture of this common culture had begun in the seventeenth century, but crisis was now. In this context the literary critic did certainly have a central and special function, and one which put out of court any stereotypes depicting him as necessarily lost in recondite academic activity. Such academicism represented a new trahison des clercs, an activity divorced from acts of judgement and valuation, divorced from a concern with lived experience and cultural health. The Leavisite critic was faced with challenges and duties which he could not decline. Leavis' characteristic rhetoric, his uncompromising and apparently ungentlemanly attitudes towards scholars of less highly-energized schools of thought, itself enacted those challenges and duties. The critic, Leavis asserted, if he took his function seriously (and 'seriousness' was a keyword in Leavis' redefinition of the scope and tenor of critical activity), had to be '"impossible", "puritanic", an apparent enemy of social amenity; there is certainly a social code that he must defy and to the best of his powers discredit'.(18)

Most typically, Leavis' dramatization of himself as outsider took the form of the conflict between himself as guiding figure of 'Cambridge English', of the effective achievement of the University in that discipline, and the monolith of the institutional Cambridge which failed to offer him appropriate

recognition and position. If such concerns risk
appearing parochial at a distance, they can also be
recognized as just the intimate aspect of his stance
on the larger map of British culture. As he was
outside Cambridge, so he was outside the British
Council, the Times Literary Supplement and the BBC,
and so he also challenged what he saw as those
falsely-constituted cultural guardians for the
authority they had illegitimately appropriated from a
true centre of authority. In short, it was the
question of authority within the culture which was at
issue. Indeed, it may now seem a paradox that in
laying his own claims to authority Leavis should have
continued to attract so many anti-authoritarian
spirits to his support. But in the reaction against
Leavis which has occurred in recent years it has been
easy to forget just how liberating his stance could
appear at earlier stages of cultural tension. To, for
example, the university-educated grammar-school
product of mid-century Britain Leavis meant the
possibility of participation in authority through a
route which seemed dependent on mind and sensibility
rather than class, inheritance or institutional
background.(19) If the elitist aspects of Leavis'
thought were apparent, they could be outweighed by a
sense of the urgency of a situation in which the
evident malignity of the elites Leavis sought to
displace made the issue of elitism a secondary one
beside the dimensions of the immediate cultural
crisis. That grudging acknowledgement of the
liberating in Leavis is apparent in even such
assessments as Perry Anderson's and Francis
Mulhern's.(20)

Behind Leavis' writings there lay the seminal
work of his wife, Q.D. Leavis, in her
'anthropological' research into the history and
contemporary state of reading in Britain. In Scrutiny
Leavis frequently referred to her studies in terms
which suggested their embodying the fundamental
motivating perceptions fuelling his own work and the
journal's function. Q.D. Leavis' Fiction and the
reading public also deployed a rhetoric of crisis and
constituted a call to action. Her conclusion deploys
language of remarkable, even astonishing, force:

I have here isolated and shown the workings of
a number of tendencies which, having assumed
the form of commercial and economic machinery,
are now so firmly established that they run on
their own and whither they choose; they have
assumed such a monstrous impersonality that

individual effort towards controlling them or checking them seems ridiculously futile. This is probably the most terrifying feature of our civilization. If there is to be any hope it must lie in conscious and directed effort. All that can be done, it must be realized, must take the form of resistance by an armed and conscious minority.(21)

The specific programme of action she envisaged included the 'training of a picked few who would go out into the world equipped for the work of forming and organizing a conscious minority', and the establishment of 'an all-round critical organ and a non-commercial Press'. With such a programme of training and dissemination the seductive appeals of the journalist, the middleman, the bestseller, the cinema and advertising might be countered. From the vantage point of the late twentieth century it is particularly revealing that in stressing the feasibility of her programme she should have instanced the success of the community of British Honduras in resisting American cultural influence; citing as a model the success of one imposed culture in resisting another testifies to a significant ideological blindness and, moreover, one which may have its counterpart in the Leavises dealings with the structures of British culture. Even in the 1960s, when measuring the achievements of Scrutiny, F.R. Leavis observed:

We had a great influence - and not the less because Scrutiny was known to be an outlaw enterprise - on generations of Cambridge students from the Indian sub-continent who now form key elites in India and Pakistan. How measure the effect of such influence? And who will pronounce it negligible?(22)

Fiction and the reading public records Q.D. Leavis' outrage at the kinds of appropriation of cultural authority she detected in interwar Britain, and not least in terms of the displacement of literature by cinema. This is observed within a situation where fragmentation of the reading public has occurred and where that public in general is at risk of acquiring 'the habit of reading while somehow failing to exercise any critical intelligence about its reading'. Representative of her fears and of her assessment of the mechanics of cultural overthrow is this account of the 'Reader's Library' series of books distributed by F.W. Woolworth:

> The editor started off by choosing the popular
> classics (Uncle Tom's Cabin, The Last Days of
> Pompeii, Pilgrim's Progress, Westward Ho! etc)
> and writing a critical introduction to each;
> but soon a new principle became apparent:
> whenever a super-film was released - Love (film
> version of Anna Karenina), Ben Hur, His Lady
> (film of Manon Lescaut), The Man Who Laughs
> (film version of L'Homme Qui Rit) - the 'book
> of the film' was published too (and advertised
> as such on the dust-cover with photogravures
> from the film inside). ... the next stage was
> to produce an eponymous book of the film or
> play, when none existed, put together by a
> hack. The latest stage is the appearance of the
> Readers' Library Film Edition.(23)

Other signs of the same insidious process at work
were evident in the 'Novel Library' stopping
'publishing Wells and Galsworthy for the masses'
(which was presumably bad enough, but a retrievable
situation), and now producing 'the book of the
talkie'. Clearly, editors complicit in such reshaping
of literary projects were corrupted guardians as well
as self-appointing ones. Literature was insisted upon
as a discrete category, although one which was now to
be found displaced by books nestling among (and
presumably tainted by):

> cheap crockery, strings of beads, lampshades,
> and toffee, toys, soap, and flower-bulbs, and
> under the stimulus of 6d. gramophone records
> filling the air with 'Headin' for Hollywood'
> and 'Love Never Dies'.(24)

While in the eighteenth century James Lackington
could remember poor country people with Tom Jones,
Roderick Random and Pamela on their kitchen shelves,
Q.D. Leavis saw their modern equivalents as likely to
have a book with a title page running:

> 'The Girl from China'
> Novelized by Karen Brown.
> Adapted from John Cotton's
> DRIFTING
> Universal Pictures
> Starring Mary Nolan.(25)

Had the peaceful co-existence of such publications

with traditionally-valued - or appropriately-valorized - works been a possibility, then Q.D. Leavis' tone might have been different. But again, the process she describes involves driving valued writings into neglect, both as a direct consequence of reader choice and indirectly as a result of the restriction of channels of distribution within the culture. Such an example as Girl from China pointed the finger directly at the influence of cinema and, with a degree of helpfulness she could never have anticipated, one of the best-selling novelists she quizzed in her researches provided explicit evidence for the complicity of the cinema and the best-seller in the erosion of the audience's mental faculties:

It has been discovered through repeated experiments that pictures that required thought for appreciation invariably have been box-office failures. The general public does not wish to think. This fact, probably more than any other, accounts for the success of my stories. I have evolved ... a type of fiction that may be read with the minimum of mental effort.(26)

The utter mindless passivity of the cinema audience was taken for granted by the Leavises (as it was by Huxley) in spite of more objective evaluations made at the time. Cinema in their eyes was anathema to the active intelligence they sought to cultivate. At times Scrutiny reviewers did flirt with the possibility that film, the democratic art, might indeed have potential as an artistic medium, but it remained flirtation only. So clear-cut and self-evidently beyond contest were such matters to the Leavises (who seem not to have seriously attempted to contextualize cinema-going within the lives of cinema-goers) that, as F.R. Leavis put it, 'all this seems so obvious that one is diffident about insisting upon it'. Cinema might have to be reluctantly conceded as the main leisure activity of the western world, but that was precisely the problem, for cinema involved 'surrender, under conditions of hypnotic receptivity, to the cheapest emotional appeals' resulting in indisputable 'serious damage to the "standard of living"'.(27) And when Q.D. Leavis had an opportunity of contrasting the cultural harmony of Elizabethan London with the degenerate present, there could have seemed no reason for her to withhold her most baldly authoritarian sentiments:

For a penny one could hear Marlowe's mighty line and the more subtle rhythms of his successors. And to object that most of the audience could not possibly understand the play and only went to the theatre because the alternative to Hamlet was the bear-pit is beside the point for the student of cultural history; the importance of this for him is that the masses were receiving their amusement from above (instead of being specially catered for by journalists, film directors, and popular novelists, as they are now). They had to take the same amusement as their betters, and if Hamlet was only a glorious melodrama to the groundlings, they were none the less living for the time being in terms of Shakespeare's blank verse ...; to argue that they would have preferred Tom Mix or Tarzan of the Apes is idle. Happily they had no choice ...(28)

Q.D. Leavis' definition of cultural harmony was founded, then, upon a denial of choice to the majority and the imposing of canons of taste upon them - in short the denial to subordinate classes of opportunites to construct themselves through their own art and thus challenge for dominance. But this is the most extreme version of the Leavises' position. Benevolent paternalism is another tone: in the mid-1960s Leavis, reflecting on the British working class in the toils of consumerism, was still expressing concern and apprehension 'at the way our civilization has let them down' (our italics).(29) Most familiarly, Leavis offered something far more flexible than simple conservatism, and this is particularly evident in the actual transformations he worked upon the detailed perception of literary tradition - the aspect of his work with which professional literary students are most familiar. The elite with which Leavis was concerned was 'the minority capable not only of appreciating Donne, Baudelaire, Shakespeare, Dante, Conrad, but of recognizing their latest successors'.(30) This is clearly an adaptive capacity, and it manifested itself in the revaluations (a key word in Leavis' vocabulary) of past works (for example upgrading Jane Austen and George Eliot; downgrading Milton and Shelley), and in the vital task Scrutiny set itself of evaluating new writing, of identifying the latest successors who deserved to join the Great Tradition. In some respects this involved an expansion of the central literary heritage. By appropriating to the tradition such writers as John Bunyan and D.H. Lawrence Leavis was a critic who asserted the participation of non-conformist and working-class experience within English culture - something which T.S. Eliot effectively found harder to swallow, Lawrence being one of the heretical subjects of After strange gods. Similarly, Leavis' changing attitude to Dickens over the long term amounted to an appropriation in the interests of hegemonic adaptation. Early on, Leavis had seen Dickens merely as a popular entertainer rather than as a serious novelist to be placed in the company of George Eliot or Henry James, but in time - swayed particularly by the attractiveness of the anti-utilitarian theme of Hard times - Leavis was to concede Dickens a significant position. In his adaptation of the boundaries of a select tradition of English literary culture, Leavis demonstrated the adaptive capacity of the hegemonic process to assimilate challenges to the dominant culture rather than to concede the possibility of a counter culture. To that extent Leavis was effectively engaged in renewing and revitalizing conservative traditions by adapting them to changed cultural traditions. Perhaps there was a conscious irony which Leavis missed in an early review for Scrutiny by W.H. Auden, where the poet commented on how 'unconsciously the liberal becomes the secret service of the ruling class: the most powerful weapon against social revolution'.(31)

The Leavises' success was bound up with an active concern for education, educational institutions and educational methods, from the primary school through to higher education. 'The life of a country' observed Scrutiny, 'is dependent upon its educational ideals'. Certainly the dissemination of the Leavises' views, the pages of Scrutiny and the books that grew out of that enterprise, resulted in their stance influencing a whole generation of teachers. They gave back to the intellectual and artistic elite, communicated through crusading tones of debate, the self-confidence necessary to confront the crisis head-on. The function of the critic was one 'commanding enthusiasm' and supported by a network of reassurance regarding value. Leavis once summed up the process of making critical judgements as a repeated exercise in asking 'This is so - is it not?' The statement and question seem to involve a process of free interchange and modification of views, but the rock-hard assumption behind that formulation was that a consensus view founded upon a traditional and self-evidently validated sense of standards must inevitably emerge. Given the trained teachers, such an educational method must inevitably promote the multiplication of the 'common reader' through the state's own educational institutions. The centre of value established and echoed in the sensibility of those readers could for Leavis represent no dictatorship or unreasonable imposition of taste since that taste would be organically related to the essential continuities of British culture leading from the past into the future. But the homogeneity of culture Leavis projected stemmed, in a circular fashion, from his assumptions about the homogeneity of intellectuals and of tradition itself. In a situation where his question 'This is so - is it not?' were to have been met with the response 'It most certainly is not', then his project would have had nowhere to go. Ultimately that project depended on the ideological recognition of questioner and interlocutor.

By the side of Leavis, T.S. Eliot's style of promoting elitist principles was very different. While his writings communicated a similar perception of crisis within the culture, Eliot cultivated a tone of urbanity and detachment which contrasted with the aggression of the Scrutiny school. Moreover his Toryism was an avowed and foregrounded value in his work in contrast to the more fluid, indeed sui generis, patterns of allegiance of the Leavises. Eliot frequently declared an uncertainty about how much the intellectual, the clerc, should become involved in action as opposed to performing his role as thinker - and his response to the Left Review's questionnaire on Spain is typical in that respect. Such diffidence, however, was hardly borne out in the provocative implications of his social criticisms in such texts as The idea of a Christian society and Notes towards the definition of culture. (While the latter was published after the Second World War, it drew together essays written in the early 1940s and evolving out of his engagement in Christian discussion groups and publications in the late 1930s).(32)

At the heart of Eliot's social criticism, as arguably at the heart of his literary criticism, was a quasi-medieval idea of the civilization of Christendom, of a supranational European civilization unified in spirit through its common foundation in Christian values and beliefs. This was underlined by his personal stance as Anglo-Catholic, permitting him on the one hand to be more British than the British in matters of religion (the Royalist and the Anglican, the enthusiast for the English parish system), while simultaneously sustaining contact with the long traditions of European thought, classical and Catholic. It is within such dimensions of cultural geography and history that Eliot habitually positioned himself and located the sources of his values both in his social and his literary criticism. So, in his seminal essay 'Tradition and the Individual Talent' he stressed how his sense of history contributed to a transhistorical perception of literary order:

> The historical sense compels a man to write not merely with his own generation in his bones, but with a feeling that the whole of the literature of Europe from Homer and within it the whole of the literature of his own country has a simultaneous existence and composes a simultaneous order.(33)

The reader discovers this sense of a 'simultaneous order' enacted in Eliot's tendency to speak of past writers in terms which involve little recognition of their pastness. (It is the living writer who is the anomaly, singled out by the title 'Mr') It is literature and history seen through God's eyes, a vista of centuries where occasionally an adjustment in valuation may be required.

The theocratic elements of Eliot's criticism gave it a quality distinct from the Leavises', but his different angle of approach led as inevitably to elitist propositions. Eliot started out from the threat to religion, the continuing corrosive threat posed by an increasingly secularized, democratic and materialistic society, and by the more immediate threats within Christendom of Communism and Nazism. Such a stance was shared by the Catholic apologist Christopher Dawson, and Dawson significantly saw such threats as equally dangerous: Nazism, Communism and Western Liberal Democracy were for him 'parallel paths to the same goal, which is the mechanization of human life and the complete subordination of the individual to the state and to the economic process'.(34) Indeed, anticipating movement towards a welfare state, Dawson observed:

> The apparatus of the social services – universal secondary education, birth-control clinics, ante-natal clinics, welfare centres and the rest – may become instruments of a

collective despotism which destroys human liberty and spiritual initiative as effectively as any Communist or Nazi terrorism.(35)

For Dawson, spiritual reality stood above the contemporary world 'like the snow mountains above the jazz and gigolos of a jerry-built hotel', and such imagery is consonant with his persistent suspicions of mass culture as an implement of the secular state:

> We have already gone a long way towards the nationalization and public control of Broadcasting, and I believe the time is not far distant when similar methods will be applied to the control of the Press, and the Cinema ... Hollywood today forms the taste and influences the thought of millions all over the world ... Do people go to the cinema or to church? Does not the cinema take the place that was formerly occupied by church and chapel? Has not Hollywood got a distinct ethic of its own which influences the mind of its audience? Is this ethic in any sense Christian? ... The greatest danger that threatens modern civilization is its degeneration into a hedonistic mass civilization of the cinema, the picture paper and the dance hall, where the individual, the family and the nation dissolve into a human herd without personality, or traditions, or beliefs.(36)

For Dawson, as for Eliot, a response to this situation had to be based upon a faith in the workings of a select minority, bearing in mind that what was at stake was 'not the literary culture of a privileged minority, but the spiritual life of the people' - a people deprived of orthodox leadership and the religious supports of a displaced popular culture.(37) In After strange gods Eliot spoke with contempt of 'the number of the half-alive' subjected to the 'buncombe and false doctrine' of the modern press. Greeting the appearance of Fiction and the reading public in the Criterion he had reflected on the sorry fact of 'the labour of the few at the top' being 'largely in vain' as far as most members of society were concerned.(38) As David Craig has shown in relation to The waste land, Eliot's lack of faith in human nature and human capacity was a distinctly class-stratified one.(39) While 'the number of people in possession of any criteria for discriminating between good and evil is very small', 'a mob will be no less a mob if it is well fed, well clothed, well housed and well disciplined'.(40) Not surprisingly, Eliot's reflections on education included disapproval of educating beyond capacity or social station (a view shared by Middleton Murry in The price of leadership), and recommending the reduction by two-thirds of the number of people attending university. In The idea of a Christian society Eliot elevated the minority into a 'clerisy' who would provide the directing force of an English Christian State. This 'Community of Christians', occupying the higher levels of the nation's institutional structures, would be the conscious Christians, the remainder ('the Christian Community') living unconsciously and ritualistically within the parameters set from above. Eliot described his 'Community of Christians' as a body 'of indefinite outline', but certain features of the elite firmed up considerably in Notes towards the definition of culture. Here Eliot's elite slipped into an identity with class and, as he developed his points in more detail, into an identity with existing class. Given the environment in which Eliot's views took shape, the transition is hardly surprising. In his hopefully entitled book Beyond politics, Christopher Dawson had singled out the public school as a bastion of freedom and a model of ideal cultural institutions, 'an organized cultural institution which is neither the creature of the State nor the servant of the financial powers that dominate democratic society'.(41) In Notes towards the definition of culture Eliot similarly found his way to ideal cultural structures which turn before the reader's eyes into a mirror-image of existing dominant structures. The position he accords the family in the transmission of culture is only coherent in the context of an aristocratic or upper-middle class social pattern. The position he accords the regions (particularly Wales) underwrites existing English paternalism. Oxbridge provides the model for the educational transmission of culture:

Culture - distinguishable from knowledge about culture - was transmitted by the older universities: young men have profited there who have been profitless students, and who have acquired no taste for learning, or for Gothic architecture, or for college ritual and form. I suppose that something of the same sort is transmitted also by societies of the masonic type: for initiation is an introduction into a way of life, of however restricted viability, received from the past and to be perpetuated in the future.(42)

It is perhaps a measure of the ideological division of interwar Britain that Eliot and Lionel Britton should have come to similar conclusions about the transmission of dominant culture and yet have presented them as respectively, and self-evidently, ideal and iniquitous. It is also a measure of the strength of that dominant culture that Eliot's texts found a mode of existence within the culture whereas Britton's did not. While, at this distance, the theocratic quality of Eliot's thought lends his social proposals a utopian air, the elitist social structures he recommended to Christians and those who do not just 'pay lip service to culture' were eminently practical because they largely existed. The road to Jerusalem still led via Eton and Oxbridge.

NOTES

1.   W. Lewis, The art of being ruled, 1926; see E.W.F. Tomlin (ed.), Wyndham Lewis: an anthology of his prose, 1969, p. 101.
2.   E. Waugh, Black mischief, 1932.
3.   G. Orwell, Coming up for air, 1939, repr. 1962, p. 12; J.B. Priestley, English journey, 1934, repr. 1977, p. 118.
4.   G. Greene, It's a battlefield, 1934; A gun for sale, 1936; Brighton rock, 1938.
5.   L.G. Gibbon, Grey granite, 1934, in A Scots quair, 1936.
6.   Q.D. Leavis, Fiction and the reading public, 1932, repr. 1979, p. 56.
7.   T.B. Bottomore, Elites and society, 1964, repr. 1967, p. 56.
8.   R. Williams, Culture and society, 1780-1950, 1958.
9.   T. Eagleton, Literary theory, 1983, pp. 18-20.
10.   S.T. Coleridge, On the constitution of church and state, 1830, J. Barrell (ed.), 1972, pp. 33-4.
11.   M. Arnold, Culture and anarchy, 1869.
12.   On the constitution of church and state, p. 36.
13.   T. Carlyle, On heroes and hero-worship, 1841; see 'The Hero as Man of Letters', in A. Shelston (ed.), Thomas Carlyle, Selected Writings, 1971, pp. 235-6.

14.   W. Wordsworth, 'Preface to the Lyrical ballads', 1800, rev. 1802, in R.A. Foakes (ed.), Romantic criticism, 1800–1850, 1968, p. 29.
15.   F.R. Leavis, 'Scrutiny: A Manifesto', Scrutiny, 1, i, 1932, p. 2.
16.   F.R. Leavis, 'The Literary Mind', Scrutiny, 1, i, 1932, pp. 30–1.
17.   I.A. Richards, Practical criticism, 1929.
18.   F.R. Leavis, 'The State of Criticism', Essays in criticism, 3, ii, 1953, p. 232.
19.   See M. Green, A mirror for Anglo-Saxons, 1961.
20.   P. Anderson, 'Components of the National Culture', in A. Cockburn & R. Blackburn (eds), Student power, 1969; F. Mulhern, The moment of Scrutiny, 1979.
21.   Fiction and the reading public, p. 213.
22.   F.R. Leavis, 'Scrutiny': a retrospect, 1963, p. 17.
23.   Fiction and the reading public, pp. 27–8.
24.   Ibid, p. 29.   25.   Ibid.
26.   Ibid, p. 52.
27.   F.R. Leavis, Mass civilization and minority culture, 1930, in Education and the university, 1943, rev. 1948, repr. 1979, p. 149.
28.   Fiction and the reading public, p. 78.
29.   F.R. & Q.D. Leavis, Lectures in America, 1969, p.5.
30.   Mass civilization and minority culture, p. 144.
31.   W.H. Auden, 'Private Pleasures', Scrutiny, 1, i, 1932, p. 193.
32.   See R. Kojecky, T.S. Eliot's social criticism, 1971.
33.   T.S. Eliot, 'Tradition and the Individual Talent', 1917, repr. in Selected essays, 1917–1932, 1932, p. 14.
34.   C. Dawson, Religion and the modern state, 1935, p. xv.
35.   Ibid, p. 106.   36.   Ibid, pp. 153, 55–6.
37.   C. Dawson, Beyond politics, 1939, p. 31.
38.   T.S. Eliot, After strange gods, 1934, p. 61; T.S. Eliot's social criticism, p. 117.
39.   D. Craig, 'The Defeatism of The Waste Land', in C.B. Cox & A.P. Hinchcliffe (eds), T.S. Eliot, 'The waste land', 1968.
40.   T.S. Eliot, The idea of a Christian society, 1939, p. 21.
41.   Beyond politics, p. 30.
42.   T.S. Eliot, Notes towards the definition of culture, 1948, p. 43.

2. ALDOUS HUXLEY: THE ART OF LIFE AND THE THREAT OF LEISURE

Among British literary intellectuals of the interwar
period, Aldous Huxley was conspicuous for the degree
to which his writings assessed the growth of mass
culture and the significance of the development and
extension of leisure in British society. In his
essays and in his fiction, notably in <u>Brave new
world,</u> he combined a commentary on those topics with
an often insightful discussion of the nature of
culture and the conditions which underpinned
political domination. This writing took place within
an awareness of broad political tendencies at home
and abroad, and engaged with the existence of Soviet
Russia, the rise of Mussolini and Hitler, and the
threat to European civilization of consumerist,
materialist and egalitarian democratic values termed
'Americanization'. Huxley provides, in fact, a
significant instance of an intellectual's
construction of the cultural tensions of the interwar
years, an analysis which is susceptible to
ideological analysis in its own right.

The Aldous Huxley concerned with mass culture and
leisure may require extrication from the more
familiar versions of the writer. Certainly, it must
be acknowledged that at the centre of his writing is
a consideration of 'timeless' high cultural forms,
through which Huxley has generally been acknowledged
to move with the easy confidence of the polymath.
Thus, for example, a typical value-laden statement
from 1929:

I've been reading little recently except the
Great Authors and have come to the conclusion
that it's really rather a waste of time to read
anything else. The Odyssey, for example - what
a marvel! I'd no idea it was so incredibly good
- and such a lot to be learnt from it about

Aldous Huxley

> Life: Shakespeare, and recently the Paradiso of
> Dante, which is really staggering and, like
> everything by a sufficiently big man, quite
> dateless, completely actual and to the point.

In a crude transformation, the vigour of his position
is even less mistakable: '99.8% of the literary
production of this age - as of all other ages, for
that matter - is the purest cat-piss'.(1) Such
artless enthusiasm for the great and the dateless is,
however, counterpointed by instances of a more
considered recognition of the larger parameters of
culture and of the intimate connections between the
arts and their social context. It is this drive
towards the social contextualization of art, this
perception of art as integrated within a broader
concept of history and culture, which can dispose
Huxley to move beyond the bounds of a synchronic high
culture to a more panoramic awareness of the
conditions and implications of cultural production.
    Huxley's writings reveal an acquaintance with the
products of mass culture which is by no means remote.
In his essays the Hollywood film, popular fiction,
jazz, motor cars, the fashion industry and the design
and decoration of hotels and places of entertainment
are dealt with in the concrete detail registering
with a consumer and a participant, and are not simply
sketched with dismissive contempt from the
battlements of ivory towers. Though he may never have
been in serious doubt as to where his cultural
allegiances lay, Huxley was quite willing to present
a corner of his sensibility regretting in himself
'that intellectual snobbishness, that fastidious
rejection of what is easy and obvious, which is one
of the most melancholy consequences of the
acquisition of culture'. Typically, however, the
cultured mind reasserts itself against the pleasures
of the crowd and Huxley turns from them 'as a ceno-
bite of the Thebaid would have turned from dancing
girls or a steaming dish of tripe and onions'.(2) In
this essay, 'Democratic Art', both the temptations
and the narrator's vulnerability are somewhat wryly
staged to enhance the wisdom of the return to
cultural conformity, but the concessions made are
greater than would be entertained, even as a tactic,
by Leavis or Eliot. Huxley's intellectual interest in
cultural choice is shot through with an awareness of
tensions, an unwillingness simply to range 'us'
against 'them'. This alone would make the case of
Huxley interesting as an instance of the writer
trained in minority culture confronting the

experience of life in mass society.

Huxley's treatment of politico-cultural topics was much shaped by circumstances of publication. Through the 1920s and 1930s Huxley did not write his essays from a university nor for the social-scientific journal, nor for some campaigning cousin of Scrutiny, but for the broad audiences of such publications as The Athenaeum, Vanity Fair, London Mercury, Harper's Magazine, Vogue, House and Garden and the Chicago Herald and Examiner. Many of those essays reappeared in collections composed to fulfil a succession of challenging publishing contracts agreed during the 1920s and 1930s. Something of the manner and address of those essays is caught in the title under which they appeared in The Athenaeum, 'Marginalia'. The snapper-up of unconsidered trifles reaches out to the periphery for some minor subject - a copy of McGlennon's Pantomime Annual, say, or a book on community singing - and elegantly and surprisingly conducts the reader to the centre, contextualizing the trifle as a facet of a central cultural issue. This typical insistence on going to the margin, on being the trifler, the jesting Pilate, while being symptomatic of a larger tradition of English essay-writing with which Huxley is identifying himself, is also a defensive tactic, a form of under-bidding. It adds up to a quiet confidence that the margins are worth visiting because there is a centre to which to return; the margins, indeed, confirm that the centre is indeed the centre.

Huxley's attitude became more urgent and direct, however, as he associated himself more directly with the peace movement in the later 1930s. With this change in Huxley's tone went a parallel development in his fiction which has been described as a progression from the 'dramatization' of ideas to the 'exposition' of them. The playful detachment of the early 'novels of ideas' gave way to a more thorough-going didacticism.(3) Brave new world occupies something of a transitional stage in this development - still playful, mercurial, but also written out of an increasingly gelling set of attitudes to cultural change. The early Huxley saw society as a loose structure made up of competing claims which in themselves had no inherent priority or authority over their competitors: 'There are no such things as "Natural rights". There are only adjustments of competing claims'.(4) In this argument, however, civilization is made possible by such conventions as a theory of justice, expressed by Huxley in the

familiar liberal maxim: 'What I have at your expense
ought not to be more than what you have at my
expense'. This involved a powerful ideology of
individualism and a basic mistrust of the interests
of groups. Indeed, Huxley's persistent abhorrence of
the idea and fact of groupings of people is
disproportionate for his intellectual position, and
at times appears almost a psychological obsession. In
Jesting Pilate he anticipated Orwell's reflections in
The road to Wigan pier on the middle-class citizen's
education into physical revulsion from the lower
classes, and, especially, crowds of them:

> We, who were brought up on open windows,
> clean shirts, hot baths, and sanitary plumbing,
> find it hard to tolerate twice-breathed air and
> all the odours which crowded humanity naturally
> breathes. Our physical education has been such
> that the majority of our fellow-creatures,
> particularly those less fortunately
> circumstanced than ourselves, seem to us
> slightly or even extremely disgusting.(5)

This response is clearly recognized as a condemnable
class-prejudice, but the studied appeal to 'we', 'us'
and 'our' through the passage invites justificatory
sympathy, and robs the term 'fellow-creatures' of
anything beyond an ironic meaning. Indeed, even his
quasi-scientific concern in his later years with
world overpopulation takes on a disturbingly
psychological and class-shaped colouring when seen
against the background of the theme of 'crowded
humanity' in his writing. The presentation of caste
in Brave new world is also thrown into relief.

Although reluctant to endorse analyses of society
in terms of the interaction of groups, there are
occasions when Huxley slips into such a procedure. In
'Notes on Liberty and the Boundaries of the Promised
Land', having posited that even the right not to be
murdered or enslaved is a right held at the expense
of potential murderers and slavers, he proceeds to
contemplate the situation of slaves and potential
murder-victims:

> Many murderees and slaves, however feeble, are
> stronger, in the last resort, than a few slav-
> ers and murderers. From time to time the slaves
> and murderees have actually demonstrated this
> in sanguinary fashion. These revolts, though
> rare, though astonishingly rare (the abject
> patience of the oppressed is perhaps the most

inexplicable as it is also the most important
fact in all history), have been enough to scare
the oppressors into making considerable
concessions, not only in theory, but even in
practice.(6)

This passage is striking both for its recogition of
the 'abject patience of the oppressed' as the most
important fact in history, and also for the note of
puzzlement which Huxley voices. Elsewhere in his
writing Huxley shows considerable awareness of how
that patience may be created and sustained and even
how, as the matter is phrased in Brave new world,
people may come to 'love their servitude'. The case
of murderers and murderees is an extreme one which,
as something of a debating exemplum, distances both
Huxley and his readers from more commonplace social
realities, but the outline of Huxley's thought here,
and his own personal position within the
relationships he sketches, is discernible in more
concrete terms elsewhere in his writing. In India,
for example, as Orwell found in Burma, it was
impossible for the white middle class to claim
complete dissociation from imperialism. If Orwell's
response was to move in sympathy towards the Burmese
and eventually towards the British working class as
victims of similar kinds of injustice, Huxley's
response involved little analogous movement, though
certainly a new awareness of his own complicity and
consequent vulnerability, at home as well as abroad.
The secret of continued British domination in
India is, for Huxley, that 'our credit holds ...
among the masses'.(7) 'Our credit' and 'the abject
patience of the oppressed' are, however, opposite
sides of the same coin. Huxley, moreover, recognizes
that writing has a role to play in the creation of
such credit within structures of domination – or at
least that propaganda has such a role:

You can do anything with bayonets except sit on
them. Even a despot cannot govern for any
length of time without the consent of his
subjects. Dictatorial propaganda aims first of
all at the legitimizing in popular estimation
of the dictator's government.(8)

As far as the provision of 'certificates of
legitimacy' is concerned, however, Huxley maintains a
clear division in his own mind between 'propaganda'
and 'imaginative literature'. There is a deep
resistance on his part to committing himself to the

end his logic seems to demand - to some version, that is, of George Orwell's statement that 'all art is propaganda' (whether or not qualified by Orwell's rider that not all propaganda is art). At times in his writing such an equation may seem implicitly conceded, but at the level of explicit statement the concession is avoided. Certainly, Huxley is willing to acknowledge that dominant cultures may appropriate imaginative literature and subject it to ideological domestication. Huxley observed such a process at work in Mussolini's Italy, for instance, Dante being remade into 'the Italianissimous poet ... the irredentist ... the prophet of Greater Italy ... the scourge of the Jugo-Slavs and Serbs ... a brother Fascist'.(9) But for Huxley the security against such attempted appropriation was the sensibility of the non-attached reader who must inevitably see through such misrepresenation and hence rescue imaginative literature from its prostitution as propaganda.

Huxley's attempts to distinguish between propaganda and imaginative literature, however, show him at his least persuasive. His desire to retain the idea of a body of free, imaginative literature, value-laden within a scheme of universal values, written by individuals transcending class, time and place - a literature ultimately relatable to 'Life' and self-evidently distinct from any category of writing capable of being termed 'propaganda' - is entirely evident. The topic is prominent in the essays collected in The olive tree. Yet the sharpest distinction he is able to muster at the beginning of the essay 'Writers and Readers' is that imaginative literature 'does not set out to be deliberately propagandist'. This cloudy point is further clouded when the reader finds that 'imaginative literature may nonetheless profoundly affect its readers' habits of thought, feeling and action'. The sceptic might observe that at the level of theory Huxley manages to denigrate propaganda for being ineffective as propaganda and simultaneously to praise imaginative literature for being effective as propaganda, while having the decency not to present itself as such.

While conceding the existence of an ideological dimension to the circulation of Stendhal in the Soviet Union, and Shakespeare in Nazi Germany, the point can also be suppressed when Huxley endorses the positive role of imaginative literature as a bond of union within societies and between nations. Here he contemplates the cutting of an essential ligament in Western society through the erosion of high literary culture:

> In the past the minds of cultured Europeans were shaped and shored up by the Bible and the Greek and Latin classics. Today ... even the Bible is rapidly becoming ... a very rarely opened book. The common ground of all the Western cultures has slipped away from under our feet.(10)

The fact that Huxley opposes seminal political utterances by Hitler, Mussolini and Lenin against his own sacred texts emphasizes the particular ideological weight of those sacred texts – which Huxley simultaneously celebrates as 'non-attached'. The claim on absolute values is made, and is made in terms of aesthetics – 'what props the mind, what shores up its impending ruin, is contact with the superior reality of ordered beauty and significance'. The echo of the argument and mood of The waste land is corroborated in the echo of the poem's language. 'Culture', Huxley writes elsewhere, quoting Emmanuel Berl, 'is like the sum of special knowledge that accumulates in any large united family and is the common property of all its members'. The Culture Family thus defined takes a delight in rehearsing its 'tribal gossip', achieving a glow of 'satisfied superiority' over 'those wretched outsiders' who are, thereby, kept 'constantly reminded of their outsideness'.(11) However, humour disappears when his own social and cultural identity is involved and is being challenged from the ranks of 'wretched outsiders'. At that point the dominant culture in which he shares becomes inviolable, transcendent, set apart by virtue of its irreducible aesthetic values – the kinds of authoritative value which can arm his critical demolition of the Taj Mahal and Indian music in Jesting Pilate. Ideology is only something associated with the propaganda of opposing and insurgent cultures, not something inscribed in the texts of traditionally dominant imaginative literature.

At home in Britain, the threat which Huxley principally saw to his cultural values lay not in the competition of Hitler and Marx, but in the 'ready-made distractions that are the same for every one over the face of the whole Western world'. Huxley sketches a golden age of entertainment when the distractions of the people involved a degree of intellectual effort. Erudite sermons and disputes on fine points of theology or metaphysics entertained the seventeenth-century courtier, and in Elizabethan times the competence to participate in a madrigal or a motet was the possession of 'every lady and gentleman of ordinary culture'. Indeed, his Golden Age of entertainment extends beyond royalty and the courtier to take in an entire organic community in which leisure and pleasure are expressions of civilization:

> Even the uneducated vulgar delighted in pleasures requiring the exercise of a certain intelligence, individuality and personal initiative. They listened, for example, to Othello, King Lear, and Hamlet – apparently with enjoyment and comprehension. They sang and made much music. And far away, in the remote country, the peasants, year by year, went through the traditional rites – the dances of spring and summer, the winter mummings, the ceremonies of harvest home – appropriate to each successive season.(12)

Here Huxley plays the 'retrospective Utopist' and sets his lost ideal against a present in which a million cinemas bring 'the same stale balderdash' to the 'interminable democracies of the world' where audiences, required by the medium to make no mental effort whatsoever, 'soak passively in the tepid bath of nonsense'. This is the dominant note of Huxley's attitude towards the cinema in the 1920s and 1930s. On closer inspection, however, it is not without some ambivalence. By the Second World War, of course, Huxley, removed to California, was preparing treatments for Hollywood films. Very soon after his arrival, indeed, he and his wife were dining with Charlie Chaplin and Paulette Goddard. In October 1940 Huxley reported visiting Chaplin's studio for a private showing of The great dictator 'which is really a major contribution to the cause of decency and sanity'.(13) Among Huxley's commitments by then had been a treatment of Pride and prejudice for MGM; soon there would be Jane Eyre for Twentieth Century Fox.

Film, observed Huxley in 1925, can create a 'super-realism' where miracles can occur on the screen. The compliment is certainly somewhat double-edged. Huxley's explanation of the writer's inability to achieve such effects highlights the way words are 'impregnated by centuries of use with definite meanings and aureoled with certain specific associations', and, in consequence, he argues, do not lend themselves to the generation of free and

fantastic associations of the kind characterizing the
Felix the cat cartoons.(14) To some extent, then,
Huxley could pose as not being afraid to be seen
coming out of a cinema. Yet the very stance he takes
is one which in the 1920s was recognizably
'highbrow'. Such enthusiasm as Huxley professed,
moreover, was for the silent movie; the absence of
colour and of mimetic sound (accentuated by the
distinctive super-imposition of the cinema-organ or
piano accompaniment) constituted a stylization which
healthily separated the world of the audience from
that of the screen. Four years after his praise of
super-realism, however, technological advance had
brought the talkie and with it something of a
pinnacle in Huxley's virulent condemnation of cinema
in its broadest form. In 'Silence is Golden'; Huxley
recorded his first encounter with The jazz singer:

There was a horrible tang of putrefaction in
all that music. Those yearnings for Mammy of
Mine and My Baby, for Dixie and the Land where
Skies are Blue and Dreams come True, for Granny
and Tennessee and You - they were all a
necrophily.(15)

This is not film criticism but an attack on the whole
medium. The jazz singer is represented as sheer
corruption. The source of that corruption is baldly
identified as the age of 'urbanization, democracy,
and the apotheosis of the Average Man'. Clearly,
Huxley's recoil from what he understood as the
ideology of popular film outweighed any sympathy he
had for the artistic potential of the medium. Felix
the cat, Chaplin and Fairbanks could only be admired
at too high a price.
    Elsewhere Huxley's specifically political unease
about cinema emerges - or appears to emerge - more
explicitly. In common with many observers, Huxley
quickly recognized the capacity of film to construct
and project nations and national identity.(16) What
worried Huxley was that the projection of Western
Civilization on offer from Hollywood to the world in
the 1920s was only a grossly selective and
exaggerated image. It followed that cinema might well
work to construct a debased image of national
identity and, in particular, undermine the cultural
domination and political power of the western Great
Nations over non-advanced countries. In the context
of his observation that 'the abject patience of the
oppressed is perhaps the most inexplicable, as it is
also the most important fact in all history',

Huxley's 1925 article 'Our Debt to Hollywood: What the Inferior Races Learn of White Civilization from Motion Pictures' explores precisely how film might work to destroy that patience. The body of the article offers no invitation to the reader to question the use of such descriptions of peoples as 'superior', 'inferior', or 'subject' – although these are terms which elsewhere Huxley will occasionally place in inverted commas. Speculating on how the peoples of colonial, mandated, protected or otherwise dominated overseas territories must respond to 'realistic' Hollywood films repeatedly peddling plots of love, jealousy and crime, Huxley emerges with grim warnings. From Hollywood the untutored foreigner receives images of criminality and moral pettiness in which philosophical, artistic and scientific achievement is unrepresented, 'a world, in brief, from which all that gives the modern West its power, its political and, I like patriotically to think, its spiritual superiority to the East ... has been left out'. The danger perceived is specifically political, the consequences for Empire of this subversion by mass culture acutely threatening:

> White men complain that the attitude of many of the coloured races is not so respectful as it was. Can one be astonished? ... I was astonished that they did not all rush in a body through the town crying 'Why should we be ruled any longer by imbeciles?' A few more years of Hollywood propaganda, and perhaps we shall not get out of an oriental crowd so easily.(17)

Huxley's identity and interests are almost zealously identified with the superior, dominant, imperial culture which was being so ill-served politically and culturally by the cinema. But the sketch of a foreign cinema audience in 'Our Debt to Hollywood' is worth contrasting with Huxley's usual picture of the domestic cinema audience. In the former Huxley shows audiences reading 'realistic' films as windows on western civilization and in consequence experiencing an escalation of response in terms of scorn, hostility and violence, through to demands for liberation from a cultural authority now understood as bogus, and from the political domination erected on and through it. At home, however, the audience is usually delineated as uncritical passive consumer. The same experience which has been represented as prompting independent critical judgement and reaction

in the non-advanced countries is presented as
inducing intellectual stultification in the West.
Huxley might argue that the shortcomings of the
Hollywood film are less visible to an audience
submerged in an environment where press and radio
confirm its priorities and standards than to an
audience in an exotic and contrastive setting where
the cultural enveloping of the audience is by no
means as seamless. Yet the absence in this article of
any fear on Huxley's part for the seduction of the
subject-peoples by the visions and values of
Hollywood is revealing. In each instance his account
of audience response would appear to be dictated by a
crude stereotype of each audience and not by any
consistent assessment of the psychology of reading
film. The foreigner is assumed to be secretly
scornful and hostile, likely to become excited and
vengeful - and prone to act violently in a mob. The
domestic audience is assumed to be dull, inert,
unresponsive, tractable. It is in terms of these
stereotypes that the descriptions of each response
are generated. All that unites the accounts is the
audience's rejection of the dominant culture in each
case - on the one hand through the audience scorning
a film received as a version of the imposed dominant
culture, and on the other through the audience
passively absorbing an alternative to traditional
high culture. In his stereotype of the domestic
audience, moreover, Huxley was using a mythic version
of cinema-going frequently deployed by elitist
observers. Huxley's ventures into characterization of
the cinema audience and its response need to be
recognized less as documents than as products of his
stance in the larger contemporary cultural debate in
which his writings and these reports participate.

Cinema and cinema-going is only the most
persistent aspect of Huxley's general concern with
the perils of new leisure. His novels and essays are
packed with images of people of all classes
frittering away their leisure time, whether in
country houses or in Blackpool. In 'Notes on Liberty
and the Boundaries of the Promised Land', he
elaborates his concern with the topic to provide an
image of leisure in the future. It is an image which
in important ways helps to shift one's perspective on
his treatment of the subject in Brave new world:

Already mass production has made it possible
for the relatively poor to enjoy elaborate
entertainments in surroundings of more than

regal splendour. The theatres in which the egalitarians will enjoy the talkies, tasties, smellies, and feelies, the Corner Houses where they will eat their synthetic poached eggs on toast and drink their surrogates of coffee, will be prodigiously much vaster and more splendid than anything we know today.(18)

The passage is particularly interesting for its relative lack of distancing from Huxley's contemporary world. Contempt for the 'future' he sketches is fuelled by a scorn for Lyons' Corner Houses or the ABC chains which are already in place and, indeed, multiplying. The synthetic poached eggs Huxley has in mind need no future for their existence; they are his value-judgement on the fast food of the interwar period, as Orwell's fish-flavoured frankfurters ('bombs of filth') in Coming up for air are his. And it is in reaction to the emotional telegraphese of the cinema trailer and poster that Huxley's 'tasty, smelly, feely' is generated. The hoarding advertisement for Paramount's Close harmony, for example, promised a 'Musical Extravaganza of the Screen! Eye and ear entertainment de luxe! All-talking comedy-drama with "Buddy" (Rogers) as a jazz band leader; Nancy (Carroll) as a girl hoofer. She sings. Buddy sings and plays. And you'll all join in the chorus. Gorgeous girls. A genuine love story. Startling song spectacle of the screen!' The gap between this and the trailer in brave new world is not so great: 'Three Weeks in a Helicopter. An All-super-singing, synthetic-talking, coloured, stereoscopic feely. With synchronized scent-organ accompaniment.'(19) The technology may be unfamiliar, but the language is not – and it is that continuity in language and value which is far more important in Huxley's stance than any worry over specific technical developments. The crucial question thus becomes, both in this essay and in Brave new world, whether the leisure of the future or the leisure of Huxley's present is the subject of the text. Certainly the text would be unreadable without the reference to Huxley's own time; one could not talk intelligibly about the future without something of the kind. Yet the horrors the artefacts of the present supposedly portend rebound back upon those artefacts in the present, and the interwar Corner House and Gaumont are filled with a new menace. From being, as Richard Aldington put it, 'part of the life of our time', the cinemas are converted into symptoms of the apocalypse which is to come.(20) In making the contemporary references he does, Huxley does not just use the present as a stick with which to beat the future; his project is to use his interested vision of the future as a stick with which to beat the present. The Trocaderos of AF600 may indeed cause him anxiety; but it is the Trocaderos of the present which concern him most.

For Huxley the extension of leisure was undesirable for the simple reason that he doubted the ability of people to use their leisure wisely. The argument is one which is prepared to deny leisure to the peers of Orwell's miners or Greenwood's factory-workers on the grounds that those groups are as likely to misuse it as those already in possession of it. And of course there is no recommendation of the diminution of leisure among those who already possess it. On the contrary, Huxley can defend the exclusive possession of leisure with the vigorous chauvinism of a Clive Bell: 'to extend privileges is generally to destroy their value. Experiences which, enjoyed by a few, were precious, cease automatically to be precious when enjoyed by many'. 'The infinitely precious experience of being in a superior minority' is, for Huxley, the touchstone which should guide a policy for leisure.(21) In 'Work and Leisure', Huxley did at least make some attempt to consider the least-leisured classes directly, rather than judging them on the basis of the behaviour of other groups, but the picture Huxley presents is of a class with no cultural roots on which to build beyond those supplied by mass communications, and constitutionally incapable of profiting from leisure, either under current circumstances or under any imaginable in the future.(22)

Consideration of the use of the future in Huxley's essays leads to the possibility of a re-orientation towards Brave new world. Something of a re-orientation is required because of the way this text has existed within British culture and indeed western society at large. Part of that distinctive mode of existence is evident in the way the very title exists in the language of topical debate; 'brave new world' has become a convenient shorthand for radical technological development and for the soulless totalitarian society (most often imaged in terms of Soviet Russia) to which it allegedly points. Huxley himself, in Brave new world revisited for example, was to co-operate in this later distortion of the novel into a prophecy. Brave new world revisited served to re-present the original Brave new world retrospectively as a quasi-scientific book of forecasts whose essence lies in the accuracy and tellingness of those forecasts, a text to be revisited precisely in order to check on how far its prophecies have come true, or been made more likely in the continuing passage of time.(23) This later Huxley was in sharp contrast to the attitudes he showed in the period before Brave new world, when more useful instructions about the reading of writing about the future were given:

Our notions of the future have something of that significance which Freud attributes to our dreams ... Prophecy is an expression of our contemporary fears and wishes.(24)

The past and the future are functions of the present. Each generation has its private history, its own peculiar brand of prophecy. What it shall think about past and future is determined by its own immediate problems ...(25)

In fact, the threat that Huxley was most concerned with was the threat of mass culture, and its primary source was not Russia but America. In turn, the victim of the threat was European civilization - and, naturally enough for Huxley, England in particular.

The 'Englishness' of Brave new world is an extremely important element of the text. If the brave new world is a World-State, Huxley could have set the action anywhere or suppressed location in terms of familiar geography. Instead, however, he focused on England. Huxley's transformation of Eton into a co-educational establishment supervised by a headmistress - and in which the pupils watch films - is designed to indicate to a reader the outrageous degree of perversion of the British hierarchy in his new world - the extent to which new cultural challenge threatens the heartland of the existing configuration. The use, probably learned from H.G. Wells, of familiar landmarks and locations in a radically-changed world - Charing Cross, Westminster Abbey, Stoke Poges, Farnham - created a special disturbance for the British reader - as also would have done the juxtaposition of such names with those of Mombasa and Tokyo. Cultural reference in Brave new world is anything but marginal.

Brave new world essentially models a view of extant cultural relations, accentuated to intensify the author's sense of cultural threat and to recruit

his audience into resistance. In retrospect Huxley
presented the book as less a critique of science than
a critique of the application of science, of 'the
advancement of science as it affects human
individuals'.(26) But it is even more a book about
the danger of control of science - and culture -
lying in the wrong hands. The significant designation
of Mustapha Mond is not 'Chief Scientist' but 'World
Controller'; it is not his devotion to science which
Huxley sees as dangerous, but his desire to control
science in the interests of inimical cultural values.
It is not science itself which is dangerous, but
science in the service of certain masters. Power,
rather than any inherent anti-human bias of science,
was his subject. It is not surprising that writers on
Huxley have frequently had problems in reconciling
the author's attitude to particular scientific
developments and social uses of them as they appear
inside and outside the pages of Brave new world. If
one assumes that soma is inherently evil, how
successfully can one rationalize Huxley's interest in
an analogous drug in Island? If one assumes from
Brave new world that genetic engineering is viewed
inherently as an evil, how can Huxley contemplate
with such equanimity a genetically engineered society
in his essays? The problem of inconsistency only
arises in focusing on the particular scientific
development; once the social and political
implications of the use of science in each case are
considered, a new consistency emerges.

The case of the genetically-engineered caste
system demonstrates that Huxley was not hostile to
every product of science. Huxley was no egalitarian,
and hierarchical structures within societies only met
with his favour. In much of Huxley's interwar writing
the word 'democracy' often carried pejorative
overtones. In Jesting Pilate Huxley confessed that
his own natural prejudices leaned towards democracy
and self-determination, and he could even present
himself without conscious irony as a friend of the
Labour Party. But in the course of that very book the
endorsement of democracy is questioned (as a value
absorbed uncritically from his early environment)
and, eventually, seriously undermined. In Huxley's
texts of the 1920s and 1930s 'democracy' usually
means a misguided belief that all men are born equal
and that all have the capacity to participate in
government. Huxley disagreed with both premises and
deplored political and social systems making both
concessions. In consequence, while he had
reservations about its exclusion of social mobility,

the hierarchical dimension of the caste system in Brave new world cannot be construed as one of Huxley's personal horrors, even though that system has played an influential role in determining readers' attitudes towards the brave new world.

Huxley's presentation of the caste system in Brave new world is further complicated by its interaction with the British class system. Upper caste members are educated at Eton, are elected to the Aphriditaeum and dine at the Savoy. While Alphas read the Hourly Radio (The Times or Daily Telegraph), the lower castes are provided with the Harmondsworth-esque Delta Mirror. Throughout Huxley's new world there are imaginative transformations of interwar class-based behaviour which are simultaneously exotic and familiar. The Blue Pacific Rocket ferries upper castes to distant holidays as did the Blue Train in the 1920s and 1930s. The murmuring of innumerable personal helicopters echoes the spread of the family car; even the soma distribution may find its source in the use of aspirin as consolation. Again, such transformations help to make the future legible (and to some extent credible as a state evolving out of known culture), but the combined weight of such connections makes the reader as aware of his present (the present of the 1930s) as of the future and encourages the impression that the brave new world is now. What results, despite the humour, is not a satire of the British class system as Huxley knew it, but a satire of its trivialization and of its penetration by materialistic mass culture.

Interesting in this connection is Huxley's imaging of the upper and lower castes. The upper castes are relatively 'normal', recognizable human beings who show nothing of the grotesque in their physical appearance, even though they are as much the products of the scientifically bred caste system as the deltas and epsilons and, in their own way, are just as freakishly specialized. Of course Huxley wishes to show their limitations as human beings, but no reader would be shocked to encounter the physical form of a Bernard Marx or a Helmholtz Watson in the street. Fanny and Lenina, chatting in the locker-rooms about relationships, fashion and birth control, are recognizably versions of a stereotype of the 1920s flapper. But Huxley's images of the lower castes and their lives certainly involve the grotesque and, moreover, are controlled by the distinctive perceptions of class rooted in Huxley's own period and social vantage-point. One minor touch which reverberates strongly, for example, is the use

117

of a lift-man to illustrate the extreme limitations
of the representative conditioned lower-caste member.
('"Oh, roof!", he repeated in a voice of
rapture'.)(27) Few people in the 1980s would
immediately think of a lift-man as a representative
working-class figure - a miner, perhaps, a factory
worker, a building labourer, but not a lift-man. The
lift-man, in fact, is a curiously Bloomsburyesque
emblem of the working class as perceived from outside
that class rather than generated from within it.
Virginia Woolf similarly had Mr Ramsay brood on 'why
he wanted to disparage Shakespeare and come to the
rescue of the man who stands eternally in the door of
the lift'; Alec Waugh invented a picture entitled
'Liftman at Piccadilly Circus' as an example of
proletarian painting.(28) The lift-man, particularly
when associated with the London Underground, could
take on this broader function as emblem of the
working-class principally for the metropolitan
middle-class deeply conscious of the lift and the
Tube as sites where one was unavoidably vulnerable to
mingling with lower castes. T.S Eliot, linking a
similar awareness with propositions about mass
culture and its consuming classes was to see the Tube
as the place 'where the world moves/ in appetency, on
its metalled ways', the commuters of the mass society
displaying 'the strained time-ridden faces/
Distracted from distraction by distraction/ Filled
with fancies and empty of meaning', the epitome of
'tumid apathy with no concentration'. Huxley's
lift-man steps onto the pages of Brave new world from
an existing repository of images, from an existing
class-based discourse which Huxley can use to present
a society in which Shakespeare has already been
sacrificed to the lift-man's perceived brutishness
and sterile imaginative life. The lift-man is no
product of any threatening future; he is a product of
Huxley's own social conditioning rather than that of
the brave new world.

The lift-man is one of the few lower caste
individuals Huxley attempts to approach in any
detail. Within the text of Brave new world the lower
castes, ostensibly manufactured as sub-standard by
means of oxygen-deprivation at the foetal stage, are
recognizable as elitist images of dehumanized masses,
from whom Huxley shrinks and whom he can only
contemplate at a distance, with a horror he reserved
for the Cup Final crowds:

Like aphids and ants, the leaf-green Gamma
girls, the black semi-morons swarmed round the

entrances or stood in queues to take their
places in the monorail tram-cars.
Mulberry-coloured Beta-Minuses came and went
among the crowd. The roof of the main building
was alive with the alighting and departing of
helicopters.(29)

The text invites the reader's horror at Lenina's
conditioning; she observes these other castes with
distaste. But at the same time the images of
lower-caste life which Huxley presents are themselves
repulsive - and indeed more repulsive to Huxley than
to Lenina, who has no reason to object to
technologized sport or to community singing or
television or monorails. A form of conditioned
colour-prejudice controls Lenina's response. Huxley's
response stems both from his cultural criticism and
his class uneasiness. Ghosting through his pictures
are images of lower middle-class suburban life and
commuting. The legibility of the images presented
depend upon a reader recognizing a version of the
daily movement of London office-workers in their own
society. These images teeter on the edge of horror,
as one comes to expect as soon as Huxley talks in
terms of crowds. The typical 1930s technique of the
aerial view, as used by Auden and Waugh, here invites
and plays upon a generalized distaste for, and lack
of sympathy with, London's lower-middle class
commuters at rush-hour. Intellectually the distaste
may be directed at genetically engineered and
conditioned humanoids of the 25th century, but it is
generated by an existing fear of, and sense of
separateness from fellow English citizens of his own
society whose lives he is unable or unwilling to
enter into in the way George Orwell entered George
Bowling's. Huxley's fear of the crowd, the mob, the
undifferentiated mass - which is how he habitually
sees the lower classes in any case - overpowers any
potential interest in their situation.

Ultimately what disturbs Huxley most about his
brave new world is that power has shifted away from
the exponents of traditional high culture. Or perhaps
- and this is rather worse - the traditional
guardians have surrendered their public allegiance to
the sacred texts, experiences and institutions for
short-term social ends. Huxley's creation of Mustapha
Mond concretizes his perception of that surrender.
Mond is a very recognizable culture-villain within
Huxley's analysis. He is the man - like Leavis'
rhetorical version of Arnold Bennett - sensitive
enough to know better, but who has nevertheless sold

out to the blandishments of mass culture. He appreciates, and indeed physically possesses, the sacred texts of traditional religion and high culture, but locks them away from the society he controls. Mond is perfectly conscious of his own duplicity. The special importance of Mond is that he is no simple antagonist. He is not in the book simply to give voice to every opinion and argument with which Huxley disagrees. On the contrary, he and Huxley share many insights and opinions, just as they share admiration for the same sacred texts. The insidiousness of the threat of the high-culture traitor lies in his very reasonableness. Reflecting on early opposition towards the brave new world, Mond remarks: 'or the caste system. Constantly proposed, constantly rejected. There was something called democracy. As though men were more than physico-chemically equal'. It is easy for the liberal reader to assume that the text here makes an invitation to side with undervalued 'democracy' against Mond's cynicism, an invitation to wince both at the easy endorsement of the caste system and at the reductive view of humanity implicit in the term 'physico-chemically equal'. But in fact the remark is perfectly consonant with Huxley's own position in Proper studies: just as Huxley was not horrified by the hierarchical structure of the caste system, so too he regarded men as no more than 'physico-chemically' equal and regarded the idea of democracy as a philosophical absurdity.(30) The dismissive rejection of democracy is as much Huxley's as Mond's, and indeed the remark may be read as Huxley attempting to establish Mond's reasonableness for a reader sharing Huxley's views, and not as any attempt to hold him up to the reader's scorn. Indeed many of Mond's reflections and insights find echoes in Huxley's essays; Mond operates from similar insights into the world, but diverges sharply in the ends he wishes to achieve.

Mond's view of the impossibility of an egalitarian society is happily shared by Huxley - along with the view that Alphas would go mad if required to do 'Epsilon semi-moronwork'. 'You cannot pour upper-caste champagne surrogate into lower-caste bottles'.(31) The very degree of shared views disguised by the divergence of allegiance on the parts of Huxley and Mond is an index of the danger that the plausible traitor represents. Mond is Huxley's projection of the British middle-class intellectual disaffiliating from class solidarity, an intellectual who, like Auden and Orwell, Greene or

the moles in the secret service, may still carry with
him his class-training, gestures and residual values,
but who (in Huxley's eyes) may be construed as
ultimately working to destroy that formation and its
continuance. It is significant that, despite his
name, a stereotype of the peculiarly British is
recognizable in Mond's unruffled and understated
personal style which shows no trace of any model in
the interwar dictators, no pre-figuring of Big
Brother. Mond is no alien to British cultural style;
rather he is the viper in the bosom. And from
Huxley's point of view, the real making of cultural
concessions is an absolutely dangerous tactic; it has
led to brave new world in his book; it is leading to
a radical challenge to traditional values in the
society around him. The monumentality of the state at
the end of Brave new world and the ultimate
ineffectiveness of Bernard, Helmholtz and Savage,
emphasizes the irreversible nature of cultural
surrender in Huxley's mind. While Mond may be a
version of such a phenomenon as the interwar
public-school socialist, Huxley held the making of
any real concession to be surrender, and anticipates
no sign of the traitor ultimately reverting to his
deepest allegiances. While Huxley might not have
objected to sharing Helmholtz's exile in the Falkland
Islands, provided that the state 'guaranteed my
safety and left me in peace to work', he would rather
not be forced along that road by peers who fail to
place the same value on their class and its cultural
identity as Huxley himself.

NOTES

1. G. Smith (ed.), The letters of Aldous
Huxley, 1969, pp. 304, 318.
2. A. Huxley, 'Democratic Art', in On the
margin, 1923, repr. 1928, p. 69.
3. F.J. Hoffmann, 'Aldous Huxley and the
Novel of Ideas', repr. in W.V. O'Connor (ed.), Forms
of modern fiction, 1959, pp 189–200.
4. A. Huxley, 'Notes on Liberty and the
Boundaries of the Promised Land', in Music at night,
1931, repr. 1932, pp. 119–32.
5. A. Huxley, Jesting Pilate, 1926, repr.
1930, p. 42.
6. 'Notes on Liberty', p. 121.
7. Jesting Pilate, pp 10–12.
8. A. Huxley, 'Writers and Readers', in The
olive tree, 1936, pp. 23–4.
9. A. Huxley, 'Centenaries', in On the

margin, p. 7.

10. 'Writers and Readers', p. 41.

11. A. Huxley, 'On the Charms of History and the Future of the Past', in Music at night, pp. 134-5.

12. A. Huxley, 'Pleasures', in On the margin, p. 45.

13. The letters of Aldous Huxley, p. 459.

14. A. Huxley, 'Where are the Movies Moving?', Vanity Fair, July 1925, pp. 39, 78.

15. A. Huxley, 'Silence is Golden', in Do what you will, 1929, repr. 1936, p. 44.

16. See, e.g. Commission on Educational and Cultural Films, The film in national life, 1932.

17. A. Huxley, 'Our Debt to Hollywood', Vanity Fair, August 1926, pp. 34, 88.

18. 'Notes on Liberty', pp. 123-4.

19. A. Huxley, Brave new world, 1932, repr. 1955, p. 134.

20. R. Aldington, review of Do what you will, repr. in D. Watt (ed.), Aldous Huxley, the critical heritage, 1975, p. 179.

21. 'Notes on Liberty', pp. 131-2.

22. A. Huxley, 'Work and Leisure', in Along the road, 1925, repr. 1928, p. 238.

23. A. Huxley, Brave new world revisited, 1959.

24. A. Huxley, 'Crebillon the Younger', in The olive tree, p. 135.

25. 'On the Charms of History ...', pp. 139-40.

26. A. Huxley, 'Foreword', Brave new world, p. 9.

27. Brave new world, p. 56.

28. V. Woolf, To the lighthouse, 1928, repr. 1964, p. 50.

29. Brave new world, p. 59.

30. A. Huxley, Proper studies, 1927.

31. Brave new world, p. 175.

3. WRITING, READING AND WORKING-CLASS CULTURE

The term 'working-class novel' does not so much
circumscribe an agreed body of texts with uniform
characteristics as identify an issue. The
ramifications of that issue are such as to make the
working-class novel an inevitable topic for the
cultural historian. In the first place the issue was
consciously seen as an issue within the interwar
period itself. There was a debate in books,
journals, newspapers and in some of the texts
themselves which centred upon the working-class
novel, operating propositions about the relationships
between class, history, power and writing - and
particularly about the case of the novel as a
historical form in society. The perception of the
pre-eminent position of the novel as an art-form lent
this debate urgency and significance. More than this,
and related to some of the stances taken in the
debate, there existed in some quarters a desire to
promote, recognize and support examples of
working-class novels as a vanguard in the cultural
politics of the period. At this point the issue of
the working-class novel became elided with the issue
of the 'proletarian novel', the 'socialist novel' or
the 'new literature'. The profusion of terminology,
suggesting subtly different interests and angles of
perception among observers as well as distinctive
qualities in the texts themselves, created its own
problems and continues to do so. Although
distinctions may be possible between such categories,
one need never assume that such distinctions are
always in operation when the terms are used. Further,
and still within the period, the working-class novel
lent itself to a perspective concerned with
reportage, documentary and social investigation.
Inasmuch as working-class novels depicted
working-class life in certain specific areas (defined

by the history of industrialization), they might be read, more or less designedly in each case, within a spectrum of texts reporting in various modes the condition of the distressed areas to the more prosperous parts of Britain. Love on the dole, for example, may be read within a matrix partially characterized by such texts as The ragged trousered philanthropists, We live and A Scots quair or, alternatively, by such texts as The road to Wigan pier, The problem of the distressed areas, English journey, Housing problems. Both kinds of contextualization in reading are recorded within the period and to some extent those readings mirror broad tendencies in the reception of such fiction as either contributing to a distinctive and self-defined working-class culture, or as messages in bottles from the suffering, documents for the conscience of the dominant class.(1)

More recent discussion of the working-class novel in the interwar period has partly evolved out of the recognition of paradoxical situations in English studies. For a long time the fact of the existence of a working-class novel in the period was more often acknowledged than tested, more usually seen as part of the background to study of such politicized public-school writers as Auden than as a subject in its own right. Some rather obvious texts with some relation to the phenomenon, whatever their assessment by the left, repelled scrutiny on the strength of their status as best-sellers - notably one thinks of The stars look down and How green was my valley. While the qualities of those texts indicated the existence of a dark planet of working-class fiction, viewing the phenomenon directly was difficult as a consequence of publishing history. As a result, it is now accepted, Love on the dole long survived alone on the margins of English studies as not just a working-class novel but, for all intents and purposes, the working-class novel of the period. Remeasurement and reinvestigation of this phenomenon was partially fuelled by the recognition and discussion of contemporary working-class writers such as Sillitoe and Storey, which in turn encouraged an attention to their prewar precursors, some of them explicitly acknowledged by the new writers. Moreover, the broader movement within English studies to resist concepts of canon, and particularly class-based canon, has been crucial. The adjustments required of English studies, however, has worked to highlight other kinds of guardianship of working-class novels. Issues of national identity within Britain have brought their own terms of examination. Dai Smith has recently read Welsh working-class novels as constituting 'A novel history' of Wales, and Raymond Williams has pointed to those texts as offering the heart of a distinctively Welsh writing in the twentieth century.(2) Lewis Grassic Gibbon similarly lives simultaneously in a context of working-class writing and one of distinctively Scottish writing.(3) It should also be emphasized that some stances towards the working-class novel discernible in the interwar period continue into the present: debate about the nature of the proletarian novel and the implications of discussion can remain similar. The issue is not a dead one: discussion of the texts of the period may aim primarily at the elucidation of the cultural politics of the period, but it also inevitably interacts with the cultural politics of the present.

Through discussion of the working-class novel there accumulates an imagined ideal. As the limitations, faults and compromises of particular examples are identified, the proletarian norm is constructed. This might be postulated as a novel written by a working-class writer still in touch with his or her working-class identity and community, written about working-class subjects and for a working-class audience — even if necessarily disseminated by publishing institutions operating the standards of dominant culture and requiring to be supported by a novel-buying audience predominantly middle class in composition. The novel will display working-class standards and values in its attitude towards language, dialect and swearing, eschewing the polite filters of middle-class decorum.(4) (Evelyn Waugh made exposure to swearing the chief culture shock encountered by an upper-class soldier in Put out more flags, but represented the stimulus by the comic formula 'blankety well blanked about all the blanking day'; Bert Coombes, commenting on swearing in the pit in his Left Book Club autobiography These poor hands made use, for one reason or another, of initial letters and dashes; even Lewis Grassic Gibbon was forced back upon the stilted artifice of using such expressions as 'the Bulgar' and 'Bulgary').(5) Cultural reference-points, particularly in matters of literary allusion, will show the same standards and values. The writing will also seek to subvert the model of the bourgeois novel, perhaps by undermining the role of the subjective consciousness within the fiction (the liberal-individualist hero) and substituting representations of a real collective consciousness, as is discernible in certain features of May day, A Scots quair and the novels of Lewis Jones.(6) The novel will assume the movement of history towards a socialist future in its mood and plotting.

The problem is that few examples of texts laying reasonable claim to the description 'working-class novel' wholly conform to the canons of proletarian purity. The committed observer will see the value of persisting in the search and the process of evaluating individual examples in such terms, and of damning the most errant for their embourgeoisement. The outcome of such processes suggests a league-table of individual writers and their works in degrees of proletarian orthodoxy. While not disputing the validity of such judgements, there remains the question of whether the texts under examination all aspired to the same ideal - whether they were playing the same game - and whether the meaning of such texts in working-class history is adequately displayed in the label 'failure' attached to them. Love on the dole, for example, may remain a historically legitimate construction of working-class identity within the society as a whole, even if it is adjudged a bastard ideologically. Rather than the league-table, the cultural historian must work with an idea of a constellation of versions of the working-class novel; through that comes an understanding of the limited nature of the threat to hegemony posed by working-class culture in the period.

To talk about the working-class novel at all is to talk about class and skills of writing and reading. Raymond Williams has observed that although Britain has a literary culture extending back something over seven hundred years, she has a history of relatively widespread literacy extending back in excess of only one hundred years. Clearly there can hardly be any greater de facto exclusion from literary culture than the condition of illiteracy. But there can also operate subtler forms of exclusion, such as failure to identify with the existing dominant literary culture. George Gissing, for example, despaired of the lower orders attaining en masse a higher level of civilization; in The nether world (1889), he perceived this as stemming from the hostility he sees among them to the culture of the book. Although his more energetic characters, who aspire to escape their class, may read a great deal and see their reading as equipping them for life in a higher sphere, they may experience exclusion, a disjunction between the text and the reader. Clara Hewett is such a character; reading a novel she finds herself unable to become the subject of the text:

> It took a hold upon her; she read all day long. But when she returned to herself, it was to find that she had been exasperating her heart's malady. The book dealt with people of wealth and refinement, with the world to which she had all her life been aspiring, and to which she might have attained. The meanness of her surroundings became in comparison more mean, the bitterness of her fate more bitter.(7)

It could hardly be expected of Gissing that he would have developed such an experience of exclusion into an argument about a text's failure to embody the working-class values of the reader, but the experience is recognizable. Beyond questions about the working-class reader and literacy, there are important questions about the individual's ability to recognize and utilize the forms of cultural expression privileged by a particular society – and about the possibility of construction of the self through such forms.

An awareness of the effective exclusion of the working class from dominant literary culture – or inclusion at the price of hegemonic accommodation – is not new. In the great nineteenth-century expansion of publication which stemmed from cheap paper and steam-mechanization of printing processes, there inevitably emerged recognition of ways in which the available traditions of writing and the new and potential markets did not always complement each other. In 1850 The Working Man's Friend declared that 'the men and women that did the work, cultivated the fields, sunk the mines, drove the factories, manned the ships, made the wealth of nations ... are deemed hardly worth a stroke of the pen', stressing the importance of the working class itself becoming the guardian of an appropriated and reinterpreted literary culture in the widest sense. But the very movement between 'we' and 'us' in this extract dramatizes the hegemonic process in moving the literate man from one set of guardians to another:

> We have either starved the masses, or given them intellectual carrion; and then we stand amazed that they exhibit so little taste, refinement, and morality! The wealthy and learned have long boasted that they are the

only persons fit to preside over literature and schools, and have had matters pretty much their own way for nearly six thousand years, and now they tell us that the people are simpletons, sensualists, or semi-barbarians! ... Never will the matter be mended until our working men and women take it up <u>themselves.</u> Heaven never intended us to eat charity bread, nor to be brought up in charity schools, nor to think by proxy. In the acquirement of knowledge, as in the acquisition of wealth, GOD helps them who help themselves.(8)

The expansion of literacy among the working class, however, did not result in a demand-led imposition of working-class experience, values and priorities on writing. Certainly an accommodation of new audiences is everywhere evident in the patterns of nineteenth-century publishing, but it is an accommodation functioning within the hegemonic process, channelling the literacy of the working class towards the acquisition of values consonant with middle-class respectability. The preference of commentators such as those in <u>The Working Man's Friend</u> was not, anyway, for 'fiction' in the traditional sense - 'the Claras, and Julias and Lotharios and Balbinos, who have never been, and never will be' - but for a literature which actively represented the experience and aspirations of working people from their own viewpoint.(9) The preference was for working-class biography and history above fiction. The concept of an oppositional version of what the writer understands as 'novels' was very distant, perhaps because the enemy was seen less as the ideology of middle-class novels than the distractions of the sensational entertainment provided by popular mass literature.

By way of contrast, the long-running <u>The British Workman</u> of the early twentieth century was indefatigably intent on improving its working-class audience by directing readers to the literature of high culture and of Christian conduct. Modifying the SPCK strategy of providing institutional libraries ready-made, Partridge's 'Shilling Library' was one of many allied projects to manage and contain working-class reading within the home and within the bounds of a particular selection of texts. There was even an associated bookcase available designed to contain the library and to emphasize the canonical status of the contained texts.(10) In fairness, however, it must be said that <u>The British Workman</u> did

give significant attention in articles and reviews to
liberal writers ('friends of the working class') and
to working-class, provincial and dialect writers. Yet
the worker-writers who appeared in these pages were
as a matter of course liable to be presented as
examples of working-class self-help.(11) Meanwhile
Robert Blatchford, one of the foremost socialist
propagandists of the nineteenth century, was to be
found criticizing working-class novelists for failing
to reach standards of great fiction exemplified in a
canon comprising Austen, Charlotte Bronte, Thackeray,
Eliot, Hardy and so on.(12) Such penetration of
middle-class ideology into a voice potentially
equipped to formulate a concept of the cultural
politics of the novel from the viewpoint of socialism
and the working class is indicative of the weakness
of the intellectual base for an oppositional
working-class novel in turn-of-the-century Britain.
Positivism and naturalism turned the attention of
novelists to the environment of the industrial
classes; significant novels were available in the
tradition of Chartist fiction and were augmented in
time by American examples supplied by Norris, London
and Sinclair; working-class candidates were not
invisible as literacy developed through the making of
readers to the making of writers.(13) But until the
interwar period the project of a working-class novel
lacked a degree of definition and consciousness among
working-class and socialist intellectuals, except as
a short-term educational medium. If the nineteenth-
century hegemonization of many manifestations of
working-class culture was in general effective, there
seems little reason to doubt that this was also true
of ways of thinking about the working-class novel.

In 1931 Life as we have known it was published, a
collection of testimonies by working women collected
by Margaret Llewellyn Davies and hyped by means of an
introductory letter by Virginia Woolf. Woolf's
presence in the volume is accounted for by the fact
that her Hogarth Press published the book, and that
she had indeed been involved with the Women's
Co-operative Guild; hence she is found in the
introductory letter musing on 'the contradictory and
complex feelings which beset the middle-class visitor
when forced to sit out a congress of working women in
silence'.(14) Despite her sympathies and the
oppositional front of the female to which her
introductory letter contributes, it is difficult not
to see her presence in the book as a continuation of
the nineteenth-century practice of middle-class
intervention in artisan writing (through the means of

annotation and editorial representation).(15) She provides an entry-point for the middle-class reader. On the other hand, she is not a continual presence, and the testimonies retain their force.

Many of the testimonies contain information about reading-matter and the acquisition of reading habits. For the student looking to propose some emergent pattern of working-class reading of a radically distinctive kind, it is tempting to pounce upon Mrs Axten's list of recently-read books which includes as its first three titles James Welsh's The underworld, Patrick MacGill's Children of the dead end and Robert Tressell's The ragged trousered philanthropists. Here, clearly, are the signs of a distinctive taste and intellect bringing the identity of the working woman and a pattern of personal reading into correlation.(16) Such a consciousness perhaps echoes that of the Jack London who brought to the writing of The people of the abyss such inter-texts as works by Engels, Blatchford, Morrison and Wells (as indeed Tressell was similarly to do in The ragged trousered philanthropists). London himself objectified such a consciousness in mean circumstances in his portrait of the docker Dan Cullen, characterized by London as his own Jude the Obscure:

> The man who had occupied this hole, one Dan Cullen, docker, was dying in hospital. Yet he had impressed his personality on his miserable surroundings sufficiently to give an inkling as to what sort of man he was. On the walls were cheap pictures of Garibaldi, Engels, Dan Burns and other Labour leaders, while on the table lay one of Walter Besant's novels.(17)

Yet one needs to bear in mind Richard Hoggart's discrimination between histories of the working class and 'histories of the activities ... and the valuable consequences for almost every member of the working classes ... of a minority'.(18) Mrs Axten's highlighted titles may be a consequence of political consciousness rather than evidence of normal cultural exposure. Besides, her list is longer than just three titles, and not all her titles lend themselves to the same perspective. Moreover, as one must be cautious about viewing the Guildswomen's testimonies as a whole as generally representative of working women, so it is quickly clear that Mrs Axten is not wholly representative even of her fellow-contributors in Life as we have known it. Her co-contributors' testimonies certainly bear witness to the widespread reading of many texts highlighted by the socialist movement towards the end of the nineteenth century – Shelley, Morris, Whitman, Carpenter, Wells, Shaw – but the canon of Victorian middle-class fiction is still noteworthy in its representation, although with a slant towards the 'reformist' Dickens and the Hardy of Tess and Jude. In looking for distinctively working-class reading patterns among adults of the interwar period, Mrs Axten's taste may be what one hopes to find; but other patterns should not be dismissed, for all their degree of overlap with middle-class canons. Working-class traditions of reading show subtle emphases and selection in such areas of overlap, degrees of assent and rejection which makes the wholesale branding of certain middle-class texts and authors as 'bourgeois' less than constructive. Choice is at work, and the presence of a text from the middle-class canon may be evidence of a living tradition of working-class reading rather than just evidence of total hegemonization. This certainly becomes important in considering the textual features of working-class writers' texts in the 1930s.

If it is wrong to over-emphasize Mrs Axten's reading patterns as representative, so it is wrong to assume that working-class readers always digested middle-class or baldly interventionist texts uncritically rather than with scepticism. Even the earnest The British Workman in its formal celebration of 'clean literature' defended its own credibility by including a photograph of one of the London City Mission's colporteurs stolidly having to confront expressions of doubt and gales of laughter from his potential working-class converts ('A Somewhat Critical Reception').(19) Even Arthur Waugh, in talking about the emergence of George Gissing and George Moore as novelists could deploy a sceptical metaphor in remarking that 'art, if it is to represent life with any claim to fidelity, must abandon the Sunday-school prize system and face the real facts of failure and success'.(20) The experience of the First World War, the first major conflict to be fought by largely literate armies, threw into relief for many participants precisely 'the real facts of failure and success', and the Sunday-school prize system of representing experience. The measure of this is not so much the movement between Rupert Brooke and Wilfred Owen as the upsurge of parody and pastiche of establishment views – the rejection of ready-made ideology – among serving private soldiers. This was represented both

in written forms and in soldiers' songs. As early as
1915 Patrick MacGill recorded the existence side by
side of the jingoistic marching song ('but the foe
may look for trouble when we charge them at the
double') and songs which maintain other priorities
than fighting:

> We have escaped from the tyranny of
> 'Tipperary', none of us sing it now, but that
> doggerel is replaced by other music-hall
> abominations which are at present in the full
> glory of their rocket-reign. A parody of a
> hymn, 'Toiling On', is also popular, and my
> Jersey mate gave it full vent on the left:

> Lager beer! Lager beer!
> There's a lager beer saloon across the way.
> Lager bee-ee-eer!
> Is there any lager beer to give away?(21)

This particular song can still exude a jaunty
confidence (the 'saloon', after all, is Germany), but
the transformation of a hymn called 'Toiling On' into
a celebration of German beer hardly needs recondite
interpretation to stand as a riposte to the
paternalisms of Christian Temperance and
officially-phrased war aims. The accelerated
undermining of the authority of privileged discourse
was obviously one significant effect of the Great War
on working-class culture. The flood of war novels and
memoirs which followed the conflict testify to the
felt need that existed for accounts of the war
validated in other ways than by the language of
traditional authority. After the war
'prize-book' interventionist publishing ceased to be
anything like as feasible; besides, the terms of
cultural tension were changing, particularly with the
growth of the mass-circulation newspaper and the
coming of cinema. The issue of the guidance of
literacy in relation to the book now appeared only
part of a larger challenge involving burgeoning forms
of expression which threatened to side-step the
traditional and policed categories. Mass culture,
making its overtures to the bourgeois consumer as
well as to the working class, swung more prominently
into view as the challenge to social control. It may
even be ironic that in the moment of the emergence of
cinema the development of working-class literacy had
reached a point of flowering which coincided with the
adaptation and emergence of a conscious justificative
framework for the role of a working-class literary

culture within processes of social and political change. However, if the intellectual of the 1930s possessed a nagging awareness of the possibilities of cinema, the problems of economics and access to the medium were not easily solved.

The 1930s brought a proliferation of novels by and about the working class. Klaus' influential listing of over seventy novels provides a recent estimate of the scale of the phenomenon.(22) His list could be extended, and may even continue to be extended as unpublished texts of the period find a new audience: Gwyn Thomas's <u>Sorrow for thy sons</u> was written for Victor Gollancz' competition 'for the best genuinely proletarian novel by a British writer', but, unsuccessful with the publishers first time around, was first published fifty years later in 1986.(23) Those novels which were published at the time interacted with a degree of focused debate, particularly in the <u>Left Review</u>, about working-class and socialist writing. The novel, which had previously appeared to lack serious and extended discussion as an ideological battleground, from the British working-class and socialist viewpoint, now enjoyed that attention. And, among the broader politicization of all forms of writing, there were particular reasons being recognized for foregrounding the novel. In <u>The novel and the people</u>, Ralph Fox gave a version of those reasons:

> The novel is the epic art form of our modern, bourgeois society; it reached its full stature in the youth of that society, and it appears to be affected with bourgeois society's decay in our own time .. We can even say that not only is the novel the most typical creation of bourgeois literature, it is also its greatest creation. It is a new art form. It did not exist, except in a very rudimentary form, before that modern civilization which began with the Renaissance, and like every new art form it has served its purpose of extending and deepening human consciousness. Will it die with the death of our civilization, as the epic died with the death of ancient society?(24)

The perception of the novel as the peculiarly bourgeois art-form gave it the status of being one of the most sensitive indicators of the health of bourgeois society. Fox, for example, found Huxley's novels primarily concerned with 'the <u>Encyclopaedia Britannica</u> and the idiosyncrasies of one's personal friends', while Lawrence's merely presented 'highly coloured descriptions of the author's own moods'. The epic function had gone. Such perceived decadence in the potential of the novel to capture man's control of his environment (as Defoe had triumphantly portrayed the establishment of Robinson Crusoe as middle-class hero) not only reinforced other kinds of analysis of the crisis in capitalist society - and lent conviction to such analyses - but invited the determined effort to appropriate the form for the purposes of socialism and working-class culture. Against the possible objection that such a project could only be of marginal importance, Fox emphasized that Marxism allowed art a shaping role in historical change. Even while working within the Marxism of the 1930s Fox found that although he had to reserve 'the final and decisive factor in any change for economic causes', he could maintain that '"ideal" factors can also influence the course of history and may even preponderate in determining the form which changes will take'.(25) George Orwell, by contrast, saw a less dynamic role for working-class writing, arguing that the proletariat could only produce 'bourgeois literature with a slightly different slant' until the proletariat and its culture themselves achieved dominance.(26) Fox's stance indicates a far more combative cultural politics for the novel, as indeed his biography as literary activist underlines.(27) The displacement of the bourgeois novel would in itself be part of the process of displacement of bourgeois society, an appropriation of the jewel in the crown of bourgeois art forms. Within this perspective the novel was not just one underexploited arena for the construction of working-class consciousness, but an unavoidable area of struggle. But, at this level of debate, other views about this targeting of the novel were possible. Was not the act of clinging to the novel itself a symptom of the workings of cultural domination? Orwell suggested that working-class culture might already be more thoroughly enacted in completely different forms - in the performance of a music-hall comedian or in the postcards of Donald MacGill - and certainly so when he considered the instance of self-conscious writings overpowered by 'proletarian cant'. Movements in socialist theatre in the 1930s similarly suggested other ways forward. And Fox himself was clearly sensitive to the idea of film:

But may not the new cinema, equipped with sound and colour, able to use music (it already has a music of its own, the creation of modern technique, differing in quality from music as such), may not this vital, youthful art create the epic of the new age?

It is impossible to deny that it may succeed in doing this to a great extent, but hardly, I think, altogether. For the novel will always have the advantage of being able to give a completer picture of man, of being able to show that important inner life, as distinct from the purely dramatic man, the acting man, which is beyond the scope of the cinema.(28)

These measured reservations can also give way to an indictment of the mindlessness of mass culture in practice, a mindlessness complicit with 'enslavement in the factory'. He almost outdoes Leavis in concluding that 'most of the mass-produced, intellectual life of our age is the product of raving madmen, suffering from every form of moral and mental perversion'. In short, while acknowledging the possibility of the cinema providing the epic of a post-capitalist society, and though he is well aware of the role of Russian cinema, film represents no really practical challenge to his investment of interest in the novel. Moreover, a further advantage to the appropriation of such a long-established form as the novel lay in the opportunity to reinterpret the history of writing, to present the history lying behind the novel not just as a broken monument to the bourgeois past, but as a series of partial precursors of the socialist present and future:

A writer more than any other artist expresses his country. ... The novelist, therefore, has a special responsibility both to the present and the past of his country. What he inherits from the past is important, because it shows what are the sections of his country's cultural heritage which have meaning today.(29)

The greatest weakness of Fox's book is that the theory is not carried forward on a wave of British writing highlighted within its pages. Sholokov, Malraux, Dos Passos and Erskine Caldwell all receive mention, but only Fox's friend Ralph Bates is mentioned among British writers. 'Proletarian literature is still very young, less than ten years old outside of the Soviet Union', notes Fox in mitigation, but also revealing some distance on his part from the movement in British history informing the generation of working-class writers. Indeed, Fox's concern - like that of Christopher Caudwell - is altogether with socialist writing rather than working-class writing, and his project for the novel is as much aimed at the political conscience of the middle-class writer as at a working-class potential (hence the reassurances about tradition and country). Recruitment of writers from the middle class, as poetry had recruited Auden and Spender, was by no means an objectionable prospect:

> Much has yet to be done before the new literature is able to fulfil its tasks and it will always remain true that you must have great novelists before you get great novels. On the other hand, the sceptic would do well to remember that in the grim battle of ideas in the world today, the majority of the best of the writers of the bourgeoisie have begun to move sharply to the left and that this movement has brought them into contact with the declaredly revolutionary writers. From this contact we may be justified in hoping that there will come the fertilization of genius which we are seeking, for it should have been made sufficiently clear in this essay that the revolutionary both accepts all that is vital and hopeful in the heritage of the past and rejects nothing in the present which can be used to build the future.(30)

The new novel may grow out of the Upwards, Isherwoods and Warners as much as from the Lewis Grassic Gibbons and Lewis Joneses, a triumph of cultural popular frontism.

One extraordinary novel of the period which testifies to the moment of conjunction of the history of literacy in Britain and the availability of a framework of thought about writing and culture is Lionel Britton's Hunger and love. Published in 1931, this monumental, indulgent, fascinating and frustrating novel is not mentioned in Klaus' survey, but George Orwell picked it out as a prime example of the proletarian novel.(31) The setting is London during the ten years up to the Great War, and the story is of Arthur Phelps and the development of his consciousness as he struggles to make a living in the lower, menial reaches of the book-trade, and struggles to satisfy his aspirations towards self-fulfilment in the face of meagre opportunities and daunting obstacles. At the point where Arthur, in his mid-twenties, is beginning to find his skills as a publishing writer, he is shipped off to be blown to smithereens on the battlefields - the system disposing of him at the very moment when he has struggled through to offer some challenge to it.

At the centre of Britton's novel is the idea of the book. In Arthur's life it figures as a commodity with a profit-margin in a capitalist market; but also as a gateway to liberating knowledge and to fulfilment of the self. It is also recognized as an instrument of ideological domination preserving the social and political status quo. For much of the novel Arthur is seen struggling against his exclusion from the world of the book, because there is still the yawning gap between Arthur's development of his own literacy and the culturally-reinforced literacy of those attending public schools and the universities. Moreover, it is those institutions which define the nature of culture, the value of culture and the terms of its appreciation for the whole society, leaving Arthur Phelps struggling to catch up and understand:

> He had the Thousand and One Gems in his hand and another old collection of poems in his pocket, got out of a 2-a-1d. dump in Farringdon Road. What its title or compiler was he didn't know, because he had never troubled to look. Here he is, with the sunshine on his neck, and the poor devil would like very much to know something about the wonder and the glory of the human soul. The fortunate ones of the earth, those whose fathers could afford Eton and Oxford, knew a good poem from a bad one; but he did not. They lived perpetually in the pure air and the clear light of culture. They were the Olympians. Man's representatives. Nature - and nurture - they were the lucky ones; they could die and leave a trace; the dust of their bodies formed the roadway of the race. They were the heights he could not tread.(32)

Britton never shifts his focus from this exclusion of Arthur and the network of mutually reinforcing social institutions which function to inhibit his development. His exclusion is further compounded by an absence of middle-class nous which might immediately suggest the opportunities provided by free libraries and evening classes: such opportunities are more visible from above than below. Arthur's situation is brilliantly emblematized in his role as collector for a bookshop. As he travels between the distributors' warehouses and the bookshop, weighed down by the physical burden of his sack of books-as-commodities, he can only snatch the odd moment to dip into Palgrave's Golden treasury, that portable essence of literature, hallowed in turn-of-the-century culture and which Arthur, in conformity, accepts as the route to fulfilment. Meanwhile Arthur carries books for a shopkeeper as he first carried cabbages for a greengrocer. Books are just commodities. When Arthur does betray interest in the contents of books he arouses his employer's suspicions. In the second-hand bookshop in which he works, the books are sold as rarity-objects to purchasers who have not the slightest intention of reading them. Hungry for books, yet paradoxically at the heart of the book-trade, Arthur is literally a ragged-arsed boy whose working conditions prevent him obtaining the contacts with books he most desires:

> It is heavy, this weight of learning; it grows heavier as the day goes on. The shop is an educational bookshop, and the books are bought for London University, mainly for some mysterious purpose known as 'matric' which Arthur did not understand. Evidently it had some connection with being well off and belonging to the upper classes.(33)

When Arthur reads Shakespeare he responds, principally to such a line as 'Why, so can I, or so can any man'; but to his confusion his authorities lead him to understand that he is not responding to the right things. Yet such a line has an obvious resonance for Arthur which it may lack for readers less used to severe constrictions of aspiration:

> You, with your dirty shirt! The leaders of the race, the men who did the thinking for the world, gave you instruction what to admire. ... You with your dirty shirt! You've got your orders. You want culture: we have it! Line up there!
> But it is useless to pretend ... it is impossible to feel or vibrate to any note of greatness in this sort of thing. It IS great. THEY say it is. Damn clod that you are ...(34)

Discovering that critics can disagree over Shakespeare, Arthur is liberated into the possibilities of independent thought, but, swayed by

138

authority, he time and again struggles to respond in the manner laid down for him. Battling with the newspaper reviews of books and concerts Arthur is seen by the narrative voice as being manipulated by Old King Cole's 'Fiddlers Three' - Music, Painting and Words. Artistic form is complicit in the maintenance of the social and political structure. High, bourgeois culture (which Britton opposes to 'Human' culture), demands a shibboleth of style which works to keep the outsider on the outside. In fact, though phrasing the issue from the other side of the fence, the perception is akin to Huxley's account of the workings of culture-snobbery in literary style:

All the difficulty in writing comes from the inability of the human mind to grasp the literary man's demand that you should not be allowed to say what you think as you think it. We poor Arthurs of the earth can't see the need; and simply can't conceive what the difference ought to be. Of course, while this is so, <u>if we respect the demand</u>, it serves the purpose of keeping us from ever writing at all. One can see that it has that use. Can you see any other? D'you think, Arthur, that's really what it's for? Do you get suspicious at all?
... To preserve 'our ancient institutions' - civilization: is that what you call it? - we have to find some way of keeping the fake up. If that way isn't found, our old institutions will go, the conqueror will disappear, a different civilization will come into being, the human will come into its own. It's necessary to keep people blind, and to keep their minds confused. One of the finest blinds in the world is style, the convention that when we write we must be 'different' ... An enormous and laborious process of propaganda throughout all the ages has made it almost impossible for anybody to discover just exactly how he does think, what he is thinking, or to tell anyone else about it.
... The poet may not know he is being used, and may be perfectly sincere about his white sea birds. The reader may not know he is being used, when he mouths the verses.
The harmony rumbles under the earth. The melody twitters up under the skies. Great men. The humble lowly. The State goes on.(35)

For the user, the ideology of language in use becomes

invisible, and 'the right kind' of poetry is
encouraged for the same reasons as are 'sane' labour
leaders. In his chapter 'Romance and Reality',
Britton reinforces the argument by focusing on the
subject of poetic diction and its role in separating
words from their relation to the world and creating a
'dope dream' version of reality in which acceptance
is all:

> A walk through the National Gallery, a nose dip
> into a few yards of poetry, and the mental
> vision is clouded over; the patient is laid out
> on the operating table, and he wakes up
> mentally castrated. His mind will procreate no
> new idea. He lives a little while, he dies;
> it's all one. He is already mentally dead.
> Poetic diction, canon, symbol; life substitute.
> Yes ma'am, yes modom, evey bit as good as the
> real thing. The profits have gone up.
> Plenty of people don't read poetry. But the
> effect of poetry is not confined to those who
> read it; the effect of any bourgeois mechanism
> spreads far and wide through the race. The
> taint of the bourgeoisie is in the very air we
> breathe. There is no way in a bourgeois
> civilization of escaping from the anti-human
> mechanisms which stand between the mind and
> reality and prevent the human from giving to
> the world a naked expression. Naked! ... what
> an indecent word! Watch Committee! (36)

While literature becomes the Newspeak of bourgeois
ideology, history - structured into accounts of Great
Men - offers the working-class reader no version of
the self or the forgotten generations from which he
comes. Britton's bitterness spills over here in a
chilling perception of the erasure of generations
from the book of society which, in the final sentence
of the extract, offers perhaps the most recurrent and
deep-seated motivation of the working-class writer:

> You belong to the underdogs. Time for you
> begins with the beginning of the world. Your
> history begins with the gas-bolt. - ah! and
> before that! You have no robber ancestors. Your
> past is the slave. Nobody writes for you.

At times Britton's development of ideas through
authorial monologue can virtually involve the
abandonment of the illusion of a novel with a central
character. At the end of Chapter 40, after a section

140

in which Britton has allowed himself his head, the narrative voice remarks 'Hi! where's that Arthur Phelps? I've lost the blighter'. Elsewhere the figure of Britton as writer materializes and moves forward: 'I did this lying on my belly in Green Park in shirtsleeves in 1930, revising a manuscript written nearly four years before'. But the plots and illusions of middle-class fiction are part of the mechanisms of writing which Britton refuses to deploy ready-made, and such moments do not read as lapses – or, at least, do read as wittily-rescued waverings on the tightrope. What does emerge through the novel, however, is the priority given to writing – the writing which Britton achieves and Arthur Phelps does not – above any concern to conform to the rules of bourgeois fiction, or even, indeed, Engels's advice to Margaret Harkness. Writing is the end and problem of Britton's novel, the struggle to write for the unwritten despite the shibboleths of style and form erected in existing culture.

NOTES

1.   See C. Snee, 'Working Class Literature or Proletarian Writing?', in J. Clark, et al. (eds), Culture and crisis in Britain in the 30s, 1979, pp 165-92.
2.   D. Smith, 'A Novel History', in T. Curtis (ed.), Wales, the imagined nation, 1986, pp. 129-58; R. Williams, 'Introduction', in G. Thomas, All things betray thee, 1986; R. Williams. 'Working-Class, Proletarian, Socialist: Problems in Some Welsh Novels', in H. Klaus (ed.), The socialist novel in Britain, 1982, pp. 110-21.
3.   See, e.g., R. Johnson, 'Lewis Grassic Gibbon and A Scots Quair', in J. Lucas (ed.), The 1930s, a challenge to orthodoxy, 1978, pp. 42-58; D. Smith, Socialist propaganda in the twentieth-century British novel, 1978, pp. 111-27.
4.   See e.g., R. Johnson, 'The Proletarian Novel', Literature and History, 2, 1975, pp. 84-95; R. Ortega, 'The Language of the Working Class Novel of the 1930s', in The socialist novel in Britain, pp. 122-45.
5.   E. Waugh, Put out more flags, 1942, repr. 1943, pp. 180-1; B. Coombes, These poor hands, 1939, pp. 45-6; L.G. Gibbon, Grey granite, 1934, in A Scots quair, 1946, p. 479.
6.   See, e.g. S. Laing, 'Presenting "Things as They Are"', in F. Gloversmith (ed.), Class culture and social change, 1980, pp. 142-60; T. Davies,

'Unfinished Business: Realism and Working Class Writing', in J. Hawthorn (ed.), The British working class novel in the twentieth century, 1984, pp. 125-38.

7. G. Gissing, The nether world, 1889, repr. 1973, p. 276.

8. 'A Word About Books', The working man's friend, 2, xviii, 4 May 1850, p. 131. 'Books and Reading. Part 2', ibid, 2, xix, 11 May 1850, p. 161.

9. 'Reading and Books. Part 6', ibid, 2, xxiii, 8 June 1850, pp. 289-93.

10. 'Open Letters to British Workmen. 2. Education', The British workman, 58, 1913, p. 17.

11. See, eg, 'Patrick MacGill's "Songs of a Navvy", The British workman, 58, 1914, p.45.

12. R. Blatchford, My favourite books, 1900.

13. See essays by M. Vicinus, J. Rignall and J. Goode in The socialist novel in Britain, pp. 7-66; P. Keating, The working classes in Victorian fiction, 1971.

14. V. Woolf, 'Introductory Letter', in M. Davies (ed.), Life as we have known it, 1931, repr. 1977, xvii-xli, p. xxxi.

15. See B. Maidment, 'Essayists and Artizans – The Making of Nineteenth Century Self-Taught Poets', Literature and History, 9, i, 1983, pp. 74-91.

16. Life as we have known it, p. 118.

17. J. London, The people of the abyss, Nelson, London, nd., p. 187; see P. Miles, 'The Painter's Bible and the British Workman', in The British working class novel in the twentieth century, pp. 1-17.

18. R. Hoggart, The uses of literacy, 1957, repr. 1958, pp. 15-6.

19. The British workman, 58, 1913, p. 40.

20. A. Waugh, Tradition and change, 1919, p. 208.

21. P. MacGill, The amateur army, 1915, p. 74.

22. H. Klaus, 'Socialist Fiction in the 1930s', in The 1930s: a challenge to orthodoxy, pp. 13-41.

23. D. Smith, 'Introduction', in G. Thomas, Sorrow for thy sons, 1986, pp. 5-10.

24. R. Fox, The novel and the people, 1937, p. 34.

25. Ibid, pp. 21-2.

26. G. Orwell and D. Hawkins, 'The Proletarian Writer', in CEJL, Vol. 2, 1968, repr.

1970, p. 54.
27.   See J. Lehmann *et al.* (eds), <u>Ralph Fox: a writer in arms</u>, 1937.
28.   <u>The novel and the people</u>, p. 35.
29.   Ibid, pp. 11-12.
30.   Ibid, pp. 112-13.
31.   'The Proletarian Writer', p. 56.
32.   L. Britton, <u>Hunger and love</u>, 1931, pp. 9-10.
33.   Ibid, p. 24.
34.   Ibid, p. 26.
35.   Ibid, pp. 143-50.
36.   Ibid, p. 448.

4. THE WORKING-CLASS WRITER: DEGREES OF CHALLENGE

Hunger and love possesses the kind of consciousness of Marxist thought about writing and society which would have recommended it to a Fox or a Caudwell; at the same time it pursues its subject in terms of the history of literacy and the British working class. Bearing in mind the place of the book in George Orwell's consciousness of proletarian writing, Orwell's explanation of the phenomenon is not surprising:

> Roughly speaking, before the nineties, when the Education Act began to take effect - very few genuine proletarian writers could write: that is, write with enough facility to produce a book or a story. On the other hand the professional writers knew nothing about proletarian life. It was a big step forward when the facts about working-class life were first got on to paper. I think it has done something to push fiction back towards realities and away from the over-civilised stuff that Galsworthy and so forth used to write. The ragged trousered philanthropists ... recorded things that were everyday experience but which simply had not been noticed before - just as, so it is said, no one before 1800 ever noticed that the sea was blue.(1)

Orwell's account, while salutary, is over-cool. He reduces proletarian writing to the status of a contributory, if beneficial and corrective influence upon the larger body of writing. The influence is not perceived as having autonomous life and value as an insurgent culture, but rather is submerged in the whole and the whole is better for the addition.

Yet it is true that for such as Walter Greenwood, whose novel Love on the dole has at times threatened to occupy the role of the only 1930s working-class novel conceded by modern memory, the novel is indeed not something to be torn away from current practitioners so much as something to be entered into as a long-delayed inheritance, a sharing rather than an appropriation. In his autobiography There was a time (1967) Greenwood particularly stresses the role of his mother (who long outlived his father) in steering her son towards the benefits of traditional culture. It was she who made him a choirboy, and not just for the payments received for singing at weddings; it was she who saved for a piano and communicated to him her love of music, not the music of the halls favoured by his father but grand opera; it was she who gave him a literary background by superintending his learning of Shakespeare and Wordsworth by heart:

> My mother, furthermore, now decided that my education at the council school was wanting in a most important particular – music. She had made a move already to correct this. Playbills from the local theatres were displayed in our shop, and, for this service, Father was given complimentary tickets. Those to do with the music hall were his preserve; drama in any form and, above all, opera, grand or comic, was Mother's. The record of her attendance over many years was kept in a cupboard drawer in the form of programmes jealously preserved.
> ... Already she had had a brush with my headmaster who, meeting Mother and me in the theatre foyer as we came out after a performance of Faust, paused, stopped and said: 'Do you think Faust suitable for a boy of his years, Mrs. Greenwood?' Mother mounted her high horse, answering, 'Where the good things in life are concerned, you cannot begin too young'. As we walked away she said to me huffily: 'Too young indeed'.(2)

Greenwood's portrait of his mother runs to a wry acknowledgement of her sense of respectability which encourages her to see many aspects of working-class life as vulgar. This contrasts with the warmth and humour of his father. But he also presents her, particularly after his father's death, as a woman of courage and resilience with a strong sense of 'the good things in life' which by no means involves disowning her class. She is part of a continuing tradition of working-class consciousness which is

145

emblematized in the glass-fronted bookcase of her
father's. (A young friend of Greenwood's, visiting
the grandfather's house, remarks: 'Coo! All those
books! Are they his?') While a number of commentators
on <u>Love</u> <u>on</u> <u>the</u> <u>dole</u> have been unhappy with
Greenwood's depiction of Larry Meath, Hanky Park's
socialist intellectual, on the grounds of his
received accent, his middle-class tastes and his
apparent lack of family roots in the community,
Greenwood makes clear in the autobiography the
connection he perceives between James Moleyns
(Meath's prototype) and that continuing tradition.
(In the novel Larry is also firmly placed in that
tradition through the episode of the lecture he
gives, with its allusions to <u>The</u> <u>ragged</u> <u>trousered</u>
<u>philanthropists).</u> Moleyns visits the Greenwoods'
house canvassing for the Labour Party:

> Mother invited him in and, to prove that he was
> in the presence of the converted, opened our
> bookcase and showed him her father's treasures.
>   'Yes', she said, pride and defiance in her
> voice, 'thirty years and more ago when I was a
> young woman he'd have us all out at I.L.P.
> meetings selling Blatchford's <u>Merrie</u>
> <u>England.</u>(3)

Greenwood's grandfather and Moleyns meet in spirit,
joined by the act of recognition of his mother. As
the conversation with Moleyns moves on to music, he
insists on lending Greenwood a copy of Shaw's <u>The</u>
<u>perfect</u> <u>Wagnerite</u>: the scene shifts to Moleyn's house
and a tableau which links Moleyns and Greenwood's
mother and grandfather to other pictures – to Dan
Cullen's room in <u>The</u> <u>people</u> <u>of</u> <u>the</u> <u>abyss,</u> to Frank
Owen's home in <u>The</u> <u>ragged</u> <u>trousered</u> <u>philanthropists,</u>
to the spirit of the community activist cultivated by
Blatchford:

> Over the mantel was a framed photograph of him
> and his bride standing in the church porch. It
> was flanked either side by pictures of Robert
> Burns, Bernard Shaw, Wagner, Lenin and Keir
> Hardie. ... from the chimney breast to the
> window wall were crowded bookshelves, the top
> one carrying a row of box-files, parcels of
> political pamphlets and a small stack of
> gramophone records. His collection of Bernard
> Shaw's works was the paperback edition. He
> wrote my name and the date on a slip of paper,
> clipped this to the next volume then, grinning

apologetically, passed The perfect Wagnerite to
me saying: 'I like to keep track. ... We're
starting classes at the Labour Club. We've our
own tutors. We don't favour the Workers
Educational Association - biased the wrong way.
National Council of Labour Colleges. Marxist
slant, that's us. Nothing to stop anybody from
getting a scholarship to Oxford - Ruskin
College.(4)

Greenwood's account of his own development into a
writer is a skein in which the strands of socialism,
literacy and self-improvement are inextricably woven
together in a way which organically connects with the
family's day-to-day life and relationships:

My sister looked up from the library novel she
was reading. 'You'll like this', she said.
'Upton Sinclair's Oil, and', she went on
warningly, 'I'm reading it first. I've had my
name down for it for weeks'.
    Mother took an envelope from the mantel.
'James Moleyns left this. It's for you to type
for the Labour Paper. And he said he wants you
to call at London Road station tomorrow. It's a
Rambling Club he's forming for the Labour
League of Youth. Every Sunday walking all over
Derbyshire'.(5)

    The deliberate reference to Upton Sinclair in
this context shows Greenwood indicating the addition
in his time of Upton Sinclair to what virtually
amounts to a distinctively working-class canon of
reading which has already been shadowed in the
testimonies of the contributors to Life as we have
known it. Sinclair joins such as Shakespeare and
Bunyan, Blake and Burns, Shelley and Wordsworth,
Dickens and Hardy, Morris and Whitman, Blatchford,
Shaw, Norris, London, Tressell and Wells. Such a
grouping may be judged as partially eccentric,
double-edged, impure, regressive or otherwise
regrettable in one respect or another, but, as
Greenwood shows elsewhere, it is the way in which
such writers are read which underlines their
appropriateness:

In later years, my head stuffed with omnivorous
reading and, with particular reference to the
works of William Morris and William Blake, I
indulged myself with delights of an imaginary
Salford, a place of clean air, the girls' and

women's shawls of pastel shades and bright and
cheerful colours.(6)

Blake and Morris enter Greenwood's imaginative life
in a very particular way and one which is different,
say, to the way a Huxley would have read Blake or a
Waugh read Morris. The existence of a literary canon
underpinning Greenwood's writing in such a text as
Love on the dole is particularly apparent in his use
of literary allusion. Greenwood's autobiography There
was a time, alludes to Wordsworth's 'Intimations of
Immortality'; Love on the dole makes frequent use of
allusions to Shakespeare. Certainly a number of
Greenwood's techniques, as has frequently been noted,
indicate his willingness to address a polite
middle-class audience, and his use of such literary
allusion may well be taken as a further instance.
Greenwood goes to some lengths to explain certain
common features of domestic and industrial
working-class life, often inserting the explanations
in parentheses and risking a rather patronizing
anthropological precision. When Greenwood explains
the process of clocking-on in a factory or the nature
of a treble in the world of the bookmaker - as when
Bert Coombes in These poor hands explains to his Left
Book Club audience that in a coal mine the
'coal-face' is the place where the coal is actually
mined - one may reasonably deduce an active provision
for an audience very distant from such experiences.
Greenwood's translation of Lancashire dialect and
accent into standard English may be regarded in a
similar way. Indeed, the degree of contrast with,
say, Lewis Grassic Gibbon's A Scots quair, leads to
charges of treachery on Greenwood's part towards the
language of his own class and region, a deference to
standards of authority which are class-based.(7) Yet
the fact is that Greenwood is content to take a
pragmatic stance, to win over readers by easing their
problems in achieving access to an unfamiliar
culture. Meanwhile, Greenwood's use of literary
allusion may constitute not a mimicry of middle-class
literary technique, but an invitation to re-read such
touchstones. It is worth asking whose Shakespeare and
whose Wordsworth is being quoted. Britton's Arthur
Phelps responds to the Shakespeare of 'Why, so can
I'. When Greenwood finds meaning and resonance in 'a
tale told by an idiot' it is in the idea of the
absurd merry-go-round of the twice-weekly visit to
the pawnbroker whereby families never have their cash
and their domestic goods in their possession at one
and the same time.(8) When Ezekiah Grumpole of the

'Good Samaritan Clothing Club' is described as a 'fat and greasy citizen', the allusion works to bring to bear on the alderman Jaques' vision of those who sweep by and abandon the stricken deer, 'that poor and broken bankrupt there'.(9) Moreover, the ironic force of Grumpole's Good Samaritan Clothing Club is doubled by the inheritance it carries from Oliver Twist and Dickens' presentation of Mr. Bumble's emblematic brass buttons. The Wordsworth Greenwood quotes is the one whose 'shades of the prison house' close round the growing boy - shades which are social, urban and industrial as well as broadly neo-Platonic. Harry Hardcastle's 'intimations' are intimations of mortality, the prison house of Marlowe's cheap-labour apprentice-scheme:

> Terrifying intimations tiptoed through the numb silences of his mind; insistent voices whispered through the harsh truth that he was no longer a boy. ... In a flash he saw twelve months each treading on the other's heel in a never-ending suffocating circle, monotonous, constrained, like prisoners exercising mechanically in the confines of the prison yard.(10)

The Shakespeare, Wordsworth and Dickens floating below or on the surface of Greenwood's texts are distinctively-read writers, read for their relevance to working-class conditions and represented to the reader with their elements of radical vision accentuated and redefined in new images. They are also distinctively mediated writers. Greenwood recalls a Christmas Eve in his mother's house when things are tight and Walter is unemployed and broke; his mother sends him out for a little shopping:

> 'Oh, and - er -'. She opened her purse again, gave me three shillings. 'Bit of spending money. Never say die, lad. And - h'm, here'. I was given three slim books. Hamlet, Macbeth and The Tempest in Messrs Dent's Temple Shakespeare edition. 'And get those in your noddle'.(11)

Like his Keats and his Dickens, Greenwood's Shakespeare and Wordsworth are the Shakespeare and Wordsworth of his mother and of his grandfather's bookcase in which Blatchford and the classical dictionary stand side by side. In short, the fact of Greenwood's using literary allusion to texts

domesticated within a middle-class canon need not be
regarded as cultural appeasement when those texts
also have a separate mode of existence within
literate working-class consciousness and when
Greenwood's particular use of them in context invites
a rereading and reaccenting of the authors cited by
the middle-class reader. To demand that a
working-class writer eschew all use of literary
allusion because the practice and referents are
necessarily tainted would be to strip the writer of a
resource in the creation of meaning – and to deny the
historical conditions in which the writing is made,
conditions involving both those texts and
working-class experience. To parallel the experience
in 'Ode to a Nightingale' to Harry's recognition
during his brief holiday that he and Helen must
return from the 'magic casements' to perhaps a
lifetime of imprisonment in Salford is neither to
debase Keats nor to inflate the experience of the
characters. Greenwood's is a recognition of the
parameters of the human feeling in Keats' poem within
other conditions of living; he has found a meaning
for Keats in the grammar of the lives around him. To
discover that the sod beneath one's feet is actually
the pavement of Hanky Park only looks like burlesque
if one fails to intuit the human capacity for
aspiration and desolation, for the investment of hope
in slight opportunities, that exist in such
lives.(12) The language of Love on the dole does make
concessions to a middle-class audience as part of
Greenwood's project, but his allusions also testify
to a distinctively working-class tradition of reading
out of which his writing is made.

Greenwood's autobiography is constructed around
his making as a writer. The book takes his life up
through the acceptance of his first story to the
acceptance of the manuscript of his novel. Love on
the dole is Greenwood's world minus the making of the
writer. Minus that element, defeatism is apparent.
Young lives are absorbed into old roles, and images
of repetition, circularity and futility pervade the
book, most notably in the parallelism of the book's
beginning and ending where everything is the same as
it was – only worse. Such temporary respite as comes
to the Hardcastle family is won at the cost of the
prostitution of love: the jobs Harry and his father
obtain are arranged by Sam Grundy once Sally has
become his mistress. Defeatism is compounded by
Greenwood's depiction of the suffocating economic and
social relationships which oppress Hanky Park and
which infect the relationships one to another of the

working-class inhabitants. These forces are presented as interlocking and mutually reinforcing: chapel, pub, council, police, pawnshop, bookmaker, clothing-club, money-lenders, employers. Larry Meath partially fulfils the role of Tressell's Frank Owen in attempting to educate those around him into socialism, but the possibilities of political action from inside the community, as depicted within the bounds of the text, do not seem strong: Larry Meath dies in the breaking-up of a demonstration by the police.

These features often result in commentators doubting the radicalism of the text. If there are doubts that Greenwood seriously challenges the form of the bourgeois novel, there are also doubts about Greenwood's faith in a socialist future being indicated by his plotting. But the defeatism of the text does not communicate itself to the reader as a stimulus to defeatism, though it is a warning of the persistence of deterioration if political action continues to fail. The epigraphs with which Greenwood prefaced his text sound a far more revolutionary note than any contained within it and orientate the reader towards a positive response. Moreover, Love on the dole is informed by a very local and short-term set of political frustrations. The scale on which Greenwood works is not that of Gibbon's epic history from feudalism through capitalism to the socialist future. Greenwood voices a particular frustration with the election of the National Government, and traces responsibility for the marginalization of the Labour Party to working-class voters. Greenwood has his mother recall working for the ILP with the words: 'but it was like talking to that wall where some people were concerned', and James Moleyns observes that 'the Tory working man drives me to the limit sometimes'. When Larry Meath tells the demonstrators that the cause 'of their protest was of their own making', it is specifically in the context of recalling 'the scares and the people's response at the general election'.(13)

Love on the dole contains a host of representations of working-class figures who are deeply resistant to socialist argument and who in their own lives mimic the very forces oppressing them. Mrs Jikes and Mrs Dorbell live by cliches and indulge in reminiscences of the times of the true gentry; Ted Munter dreams of being a bookmaker like Sam Grundy while Mrs Nattle operates her little business ventures on the same principles as the Bank of England. Like the man who insistently responds to

Larry's explanations with the observation that you can't do without 'capickle', such figures are seen by Greenwood as contributing significantly to the general inertia of change in Hanky Park – and the particular inertia represented by the National Government. Even Mrs Bull, who sympathizes with Larry's politics, has been affected by the election:

> Ah don't like that there cough of his. An' all that politicianin' he's bin doin lakely in this kind o' weather should ne'er have bin done. ... Luk what's happened wi' all his talk. National Government, an' Labour nowhere. 'Tain't no use talkin' socialism to folk. 'Twon't come in our, time though Ah allus votes Labour an' allus will.(14)

Greenwood believes in the Labour Party and in processes of democratic change, (rejecting, through Larry Meath, Clydeside communism), but he is also the weary Labour canvasser confronted with working-class men and women who can see little sense in voting for the 'bolshies'. Love on the dole works both to account for the election failure and to demonstrate, in its version of an environment lacking the political consciousness he wishes, the circularity of prevailing conditions unless that consciousness is created both within and beyond the community. The creation of the text from inside the community, however, constitutes a political impetus not represented within its pages. The phenomenon of Love on the dole as novel and as play, seen as a set of relationships between author, text and society, is larger than and different in mood to, the images of the text itself. In certain respects Greenwood did surrender the purest status as proletarian novel for his book, particularly given his allegiance to the Labour Party rather than the Communist Party. But he surrenders it not for a mess of pottage, nor in deference – but in a project of communication, and for the act of intervention that his text historically achieved.

As Stephen Constantine has argued, the book shows the North to the South, the working class to the middle class.(15) To that extent it shares the purposes implicit in the title of a volume Greenwood was to write for the Labour Book Service, How the other man lives. in the light of the millions reached through Love on the dole, there must be some latitude in evaluating Greenwood's aesthetic concessions, such as they are. The problem is highlighted by contrasting the success of <u>Love on the dole</u> within the culture and the fate of Gwyn Thomas's <u>Sorrow for thy sons.</u> Thomas' book makes fewer concessions to the potential audience than Greenwood's (although it is no more optimistic politically in its conclusion than <u>Love on the dole</u> or the abridged version of <u>The ragged trousered philanthropists</u>). The Gollancz firm rejected it on the grounds that 'some of the physical descriptions were so realistic as to produce actual nausea', and Thomas was advised that 'as your audience will be 99% tender-stomached, you will frighten them all away if you write in this fashion'. Gollancz had instituted a competition for the 'best genuinely proletarian novel by a British writer', and it is a striking illustration of the tightrope that the working-class writer had to walk that Thomas' book should have been rejected on such grounds.(16) While it may be tempting to embrace a general scenario in which working-class writers were denied a revolutionary audience by conservative publishers fearful of political radicalism, Thomas's problems were with an actively sympathetic publisher, a tender-stomached audience, and hinged perhaps on his descriptions of dirty shirts and trousers and his characterizations of a crowded Labour Exchange as 'congested as a lungful of phlegm'. It is easy to demand in the abstract and with hindsight that 1930s' working-class writers should have subverted bourgeois form and tastes more than they did. While some succeeded, the price that could be paid was non-publication; and there is less than usual solace for a novelist in an unpublished proletarian novel. Certainly the map of working-class fiction in the Thirties would look different for the inclusion of <u>Sorrow for thy sons,</u> but its power found no outlet. This is Hugh, the working-class scholarship boy, writing a letter to his lover on leaving the valleys after years of unemployment: as Steinbeck's hero departs in <u>The grapes of wrath</u> he melts into 'the people'; so Hugh becomes unemployment:

> They should rip out the testicles and the tongue from the body of every unemployed person to complete his abnormality instead of leaving him with the illusion of effective life and robbing him of the substance. Don't consider me as a human being, capable of running luxury buses between the two distinct depots of good and bad. Mark me down as a historical force, a flesh and blood symbol of everything that unemployment is. As such I am denied the

majority of human rights. In return I claim the
abstract right to commit any crime, however
vindictive, needless or brutal, on the head of
any person, and feel no sense of regret or
responsibility for it.(17)

Might it have been worth making certain concessions
to allow that chillingly logical and persuasive voice
to have been heard by the same scale of audience
which encountered Love on the dole?
     Another novel to have suffered the charge of
embourgeoisement is Walter Brierley's Means test man.
Andy Croft reports The Daily Worker's review in 1935
testily asserting that 'the unemployed worker who
sits idly at home waiting for the investigator is not
the rule, but the exception ... A book which brought
out this fighting spirit of the unemployed would have
been of much greater use to the working class'. But,
as Croft argues, Means test man is a brilliant
achievement in communicating the mental and spiritual
experience of mass unemployment to an audience
unfamiliar with it.(18) It records the unrecorded,
the depths of anguish and the deterioration of
relationships caused by unemployment. It is a dour
book, lacking for example the wit and humour of
Thomas' writing. It is also a problematic book in
political terms in the sense that the hero, Jack
Cook, is a figure isolated from his community and
with little contact with, or faith in, working-class
institutions. (There is a suspicion expressed of
trades union officials and of the integrity of the
local Co-Op). Brierley's purposes are most obviously
implied in Jack's words to his wife Jane when she has
collapsed in weariness, grief and frustration after
the visit of the Means test inspector:

He was hating for her sake, visualizing the
majority of women, secure and happy in their
homes. 'If all the women in England could feel
for a minute what you've gone through this
morning, there'd be no more of it, no more
homes upset. Still, no one could understand who
hadn't gone through it; it's like the war, only
worse. The women are in the line as well and
are being tortured and starved instead of being
shot outright'.(19)

Jack's wish is being fulfilled in the availability of
the text to the 1930s book-buying audience; the
tender stomachs of all the women in England are
potentially mustered on his side. Jack and Jane, like

the Hardcastles in Love on the dole, are the respectable working class. Jane has never sworn in her life; Jack's increased swearing is a matter for comment, an index of his deterioration. The family, the home, its privacy and a decent if modest way of life are central values. Jack has been a Sunday-school teacher, and is by no means an extremist:

He was by nature quiet, without strong drive, willing, eager to conform to every moral and social law which the tribe of which he was an ordinary member imposed.(20)

It is perhaps a weakness of Brierley's that he is unsure whether to present Jack as representative or extraordinary in his sensitivity. On the one hand he offers Jack's inner life as the emotional battleground that lurks hidden within every unemployed man; on the other there is a tendency to make a special case for Jack on the grounds of his sensitivity, one of the 'sensitive members of the suffering herd'. Moreover, what Jack and Brierley want in the first instance is work rather than a revolution, work as a condition and definition of humanity and purpose and as a means to personal fulfilment. To that end Brierley communicates the soul-destroying experience of unemployment. The 'means test man' of the title may be the investigator, but he is more properly Jack Cook himself, turned into a new species determined by the fact of unemployment - 'means test man' rather than 'homo sapiens'. While his working colleagues at the pit are identified as 'afternoon men' or 'night men', he is one of the 'means test creatures, the 'sub-humans'.

Time is different for Jack. The book is organized around the days of one week, but Jack's week ends on a Friday because that is the day of the inspector's visit and the rest of the week is a prolonged anticipation. Jack is typically torn between the old rhythms of time in working-life and the new rhythms of unemployment. Saturday should be the day of activity and prosperity in a working-class household, Friday being the pay-day; Sunday should be a highlighted day of relaxation. But the old calendar no longer applies. Jack has too much time in which to work in his garden; the routines of body and mind continue to wake him at the early hour required of working men. The hooters of the workplace seem to indicate to him a real time which is in conflict with the time measured by clocks and watches.

Most poignantly Brierley demonstrates the turning-back of friction into the relationships of the family, exploring in a quasi-Lawrentian rhetoric the wellings-up of hostility. Husband and wife scarify themselves and each other. There is also much that speaks of a condition of clinical depression in Jack: his moods on waking, his conviction of powerlessness, his urges towards self-mutilation. His wife experiences fantasies of violence towards authority figures. Means test man shows no clear way out of the world of the Cooks within its pages; but no other working-class novel of the period explores the psychology of the suffering of the unemployed so effectively. Brierley makes a place for that experience within the concerns of culture.

Other novels also take on this act of testimony. F.W. Boden's _Miner_ begins with a poem which concludes:

> Days thou thought'st dead shall be at thee –
>   old pit-days and drear figures scrambling
> Fetid, low galleries – the rumble of
>   down-sliding shale
> Darkness and silence; then voices – thick,
>   pain-stricken voices rambling:
> 'What hast thou done for us, comrade? Hast
>   spoken? Hast told thou our tale?'(21)

Boden's account of the miners' solidarity during a lockout in the Derbyshire pits is sympathetic and in fact leans towards the heroic:

> 'Men, what is it to be?'
> 'Go on', comes the deep-throated roar, 'We will go on'.
> 'Men', cries their brave, tight-lipped leader, who is soon to go overboard himself, be it as you say. We will go on'.
> Ay, this square-jawed, tight-lipped little man is soon to go overboard himself, worn out with the toil and heartbreak of it all, and now his hard, fearless eyes moisten as he speaks of the cause for which he is to die.
> 'Be brave, men', he ends, 'be brave. We will go on'.(22)

Yet this episode does not control the entire shape of the book which is rather dictated by the following of the early years of Danny, his entering the pit as a boy, his experiences there and the community in which he moves. The telling of the tale of the lives of comrades who could not or cannot speak for themselves in such a manner takes priority. The same note is heard elsewhere, in Boden's poetry, where the duty of his writing to his fellows is made apparent:

Beauty never visits mining places,
For the yellow smoke taints the summer air.
Despair graves lines on the dwellers' faces,
My fellows' faces, for my fellows live there.

There by the wayside dusty weed drowses,
The darnel and dock and starwort run rife;
Gaunt folk stare from the doors of the houses,
Folk with no share in the beauty of life.

There on slag-heaps, where no bird poises,
My fellows' wan children tumble and climb,
Playing in the dust, making shrill noises,
Sweet human flowers that will fade ere their
                                            time.

Playing in the slag with thin white faces,
Where headstocks loom by the railway lines –
Round-eyed children cheated of life's graces –
My fellows' children, born for the mines.(23)

The 1930s certainly did produce works which more closely approached the ideals of the proletarian novel, although mere conformity to the genre did not always guarantee subtlety. Frank Griffin's October day fictionalizes the events of 4 October 1936 when the British Union of Fascists attempted to march through East London but were resisted by socialist organizations and local people. The title-page describes October day as 'a novel', the dust-jacket describes it as 'a novel of the people'. The experiences through the day of a group of diverse people are displayed: Slesser, an unemployed working man; Elsie, an exploited domestic and ex-convict; Bert, a bus conductor; Claire and Calvin, committed communists, and Harold Thurgood, a public school educated policeman carrying on an affair with a fading society widow, Lady Stroud. The novel interprets the events on the streets of London in terms of the spirit of Spain and works to show the reader that England is no less vulnerable than Spain or Germany or Italy: fascism threatens from within, is protected by the police and government, and must be opposed by an anti-fascist front. Griffin entertains the reader with his exciting descriptions of bustling street-fighting, and the general tone, far from being dour, is cheery and optimistic. The characters, however, are rather two-dimensional and their fates predictable. Elsie's past, involving prison and a still-born illegitimate child, is difficult to relate to the character the reader encounters; Bert starts off the day musing on his inability to find a nice girl and ends it engaged to Elsie, having known her for one day. Slesser begins the day at odds with his wife and with a grudge against trades unions and Labour councils; by the end of the day harmony has been restored and Slesser is convinced of the value of unions. Harold's affair with Lady Stroud culminates in his rushing away from her flat in loathing and being killed by a taxi. Lady Stroud (who during the day has expressed the view that what England needs is a strong man like Hitler) is left abandoned, ageing and hollow. The human relationships presented here are marred by sentiment and melodrama and while there is a degree of titillation in the treatment of sex, the reader is also positioned to value different characters according to a somewhat prissy sexual morality.

Nevertheless, the novel communicates confidence through the inevitability of its shape and achieves a satisfying unity through the centrality of the fascist march to the fates of the various characters. Slesser, Elsie and Bert have little by way of political consciousness at the beginning of the day, but drawn into the anti-fascist resistance on the streets, their attitudes develop. They experience the reality and credibility of mass action, the actual possibility of controlling their world in the face of force and institutional power. The day is a political education for them, to some degree in principles and to some degree in techniques. The point of the novel in this respect can hardly be lost upon a reader: the novel is full of positive and relatively well-informed political voices (in contrast, say, to Means test man). Bert's politicized friend Ginger exemplifies that function:

'But doesn't it show what could be done if everybody pulls together? Think what a difference it would make in the Government's attitude to Spain, if only the working class would demonstrate as solidly as they've done today! Think what else could be accomplished!' His eyes glowed with a vision of socialism and a free and happy people.(24)

Moreover, the diffusion of Griffin's attention over a range of characters emphasizes his modification of the concern of the novel as a form with the individual; his eye is rather on a cross-section of the populace. Griffin's novel was not well-timed to win it a prominent position in the history of the proletarian novel; it appeared in 1939 when the issue of Spain was becoming a less clear-cut one for middle-class intellectuals and when the prospect of an anti-fascist struggle was being reconstructed as a national struggle. Nevertheless, October day stands out as a clearly-drawn and clearly-intended model of the proletarian novel.

Lewis Jones' Cwmardy and Lewis Grassic Gibbon's A Scots quair (particularly the conclusion of the trilogy, Grey granite) have proved subtler and more enduring monuments of the proletarian novel, each offering not just novels but readings of history. Gibbon's trilogy reaches back in its allusions to the feudal past, to the Romans, the Celts and prehistory, to a point where the land and its inhabitants merge. That sense of history is reinforced by the intuitive, quasi-mystical links which run between those earliest inhabitants of the land and Chris, Gibbon's central character in the trilogy. Ancient monuments and relics, some of the latter formed into a collection by Chris's intellectual son, Ewan, further reinforce the existence of a history which lies outside the usual textbooks and outside the institutions of dominant culture. In the Museum and Art Gallery Ewan finds Greek civilization represented by casts of statues of the gods, but not by any more representative image such as a slave being tortured before he could legally act as a witness, or weakling children being exposed to the elements to die. Rome is represented by a cast of Trajan while Ewan looks in vain for Spartacus or the executions by crucifixion of his fellows in revolt. Medieval Italy is represented by paintings of cardinals and angels, while Ewan looks for one of a man being broken on a wheel. Ewan is torn by the pain of the commitment he knows he must make to a history to which he belongs - and into which he is personally initiated when he is beaten in the police cells:

> The same everywhere, as though suddenly unblinded, picture on picture limned in dried blood, never painted or hung in any gallery - pictures of the poor folk since history began, bedevilled and murdered, trodden underfoot, trodden down in the bree, a human slime,

hungered, unfed, with their darkened brains,
their silly revenges, their infantile hopes –
the men who built Munster's City of God and
were hanged and burned in scores by the Church,
the Spartacists, the blacks of Toussaint
L'Ouverture, Parker's sailors who were hanged
at the Nore, the Broo men man-handled in Royal
Mile, pictures unceasing of the men of your
kin, peasants and slaves and common folk and
their ghastly lives through six thousand years
– oh, hell, what had it to do with you?(25)

Ewan moves further to the left through the novel,
abandoning the genteel socialism of his girlfriend
Ellen Johns to become a communist worker. But even
with that movement in the novel, Jenny Wolmark has
been able to argue that in its determination to
endorse the experiences of both the politically-
committed Ewan and the Chris who nostalgically
returns at the end of the novel to her rural roots
and a symbolic assimilation by the land, even Grey
granite does not transcend the ideological crisis
which it reveals in its society but also embodies in
itself. For Wolmark the novel attempts to yoke
together distinct and contradictory personal
resolutions. In the context of this study such a
finding can not be regarded as surprising; complete
proletarian orthodoxy remains to be found.(26)
    The plight of the contemporary left, attempting
to win attention to writing about the ideology of
which it must constantly express reservations,
highlights the nature of the cultural significance of
the working-class novel in the 1930s. The phenomenon,
for all its importance, lacks the uniformity that is
suggested in the very phrase 'the working-class
novel'. The novels that were written were the product
of a long history of working-class literacy with its
own dynamic, colliding both with the particular
conditions of the depression and with the crystal-
lization of an overt cultural politics on the left
which assigned them a function with which, however,
they were by no means always wholly in tune. Together
those novels certainly stated the claim of a class to
writing within the culture. Together, in a
culmination of a long-standing theme, they demanded
space within the culture for unconsidered histories
and unconsidered experiences – both with immediate
effect (as in the case of Love on the dole) and with
effects which will continue to be felt (including,
although not only, the special case of Sorrow for thy
sons). Together they laid down precedents and

foundations for an extension of working-class writing
in the novel and for television in the postwar
period. They were, however, divided by degrees and
shades of politicization, sometimes in no small part
as a function of region: a Nottingham miner's novel
was almost inevitably a very different thing to a
Mardy miner's, as was a Labour Party supporter's to a
Communist Party worker's. They were divided by the
priorities of seeking work and seeking revolution.
Confronted by the existing structures of publishing
and the composition of the novel-buying public, they
were divided by attitudes to audience. They enacted
different degrees of awareness (including the
highest) of the class basis of literary technique and
of the relationship of writing to cultural dominance.
Understanding the significance of working-class
novels in interwar culture requires more of an
attention to their positive diversity and to their
part in an extended history of literacy rather than
their merely being judged individually as greater or
lesser - but always partial - fulfilments of the one
constructed ideal. When Gustav Klaus cuts the Gordian
knot of what to call these novels - 'working-class
novels' or 'proletarian novels' - by declaring that
he will simply choose to call them socialist novels,
the problem is not simplified but risks being
obscured.(27) The divisions of the novels are
divisions of the class: that the form offered a
unified challenge to dominant culture only in
potential reflects that the challenge of the class
remained more in potential than actual. But their
status as records of history remains.

NOTES

1.   G. Orwell & D. Hawkins, 'The Proletarian
Writer', CEJL, vol. 2, 1968, repr. 1970, p. 55.
2.   W. Greenwood, There was a time, 1967. p.
59.
3.   Ibid, p. 172.
4.   Ibid, pp. 173-5.
5.   Ibid, p. 228.
6.   Ibid, p. 33.
7.   R. Johnson, 'The Proletarian Novel',
Literature and history, 1975, pp. 84-95.
8.   W. Greenwood, Love on the dole, 1933,
repr. 1969, p. 32.
9.   Ibid, p. 57.
10.   Ibid, pp. 74-5.
11.   There was a time, p. 201.

12.   Love on the dole, Ch. 8.
13.   There was a time, p. 172; Love on the dole, p. 198.
14.   Love on the dole, p. 164.
15.   S. Constantine, 'Love on the dole and its Reception in the 1930s', Literature and history, 1982, pp. 232–47.
16.   D. Smith, 'Introduction', in G. Thomas, Sorrow for thy sons, 1986, pp. 7–8.
17.   Sorrow for thy sons, p. 269.
18.   A. Croft, 'Introduction', in W. Brierley, Means test man, 1935, repr. 1983, vii–xvi.
19.   Means test man, pp. 266–7.
20.   Ibid, p. 98.
21.   F. Boden, Miner, 1932, p. 8.
22.   Ibid, p. 105.
23.   F. Boden, Out of the coalfields, 1929, p. 11.
24.   F. Griffin, October day, 1939, pp. 152–3.
25.   L.G. Gibbon, Grey granite, 1934, in A Scots quair, 1946, p. 407.
26.   J. Wolmark, 'Problems of tone in A Scots Quair', Red letters, 1981, pp. 15–23.
27.   H. Klaus, 'Socialist Fiction in the 1930s', in J. Lucas (ed.), The 1930s: a challenge to orthodoxy, 1978, p. 14.

5. THE BRITISH FILM INDUSTRY AND THE HOLLYWOOD INVASION

The great age of cinema in Britain lasted only about twenty-five years, from the coming of sound at the end of the 1920s to the coming of television in the 1950s. Though going to the cinema in the period after the coming of television tends to be an expensive special occasion, in the 1930s and 1940s it was as integral a part of life as watching television has since become. The cinema generation - those who lived through the 1930s and 1940s - had a unique experience of mass entertainment, the context of which is permanently lost to those who have come after. Only part of the atmosphere of going to the cinema in this period can be recaptured by simply watching the films that they watched then. The stories and the narrative techniques of the films have been altered out of recognition by the different cultural context in which we now encounter them. To deal with the development of the contemporary British film industry, therefore, and to assess the threat posed by the so-called 'Hollywood invasion' it is necessary, insofar as it is possible at least, to reconstruct first the experience of cinema-going, the context in which the films were first encountered.

Cinema was the biggest and the fastest-growing form of popular entertainment in the period. The number of picture houses opened in the period was itself dramatic enough: there were already 3,000 cinemas in Britain in 1926, and by 1938 there were 4,800 with a combined seating capacity estimated at four and a quarter million, roughly one seat for every ten people in the population.(1) The cinemas ranged from the prestigious 'picture palaces' of the big cinema chains to the local 'fleapit'. The Regent cinema in Brighton cost nearly half a million pounds to build, at 1920s prices, and featured a restaurant, a roof garden, allegorical pictures painted over the

walls of the auditorium and huge white candelabra
hung from the ceiling. This type of prestige
institution sold itself as a people's palace, a
fabulous dream world in which contemporary
difficulties could be temporarily forgotten in the
atmosphere of Carnival. Though the more typical
context of film-watching, for the large majority of
the population who did not live in the prosperous
urban areas of the South, was a much smaller and
cheaper establishment, cinema-going even at this
level probably still contrasted favourably in terms
of comfort and warmth with the typical home
environment.

In 1938, 987 million cinema tickets were sold to
cinema-goers, twenty-five times the number of tickets
sold to football fans in the same year. On average,
half of the population over the age of 14 went to the
cinema once every week. Other evidence makes it clear
the many went even more often than that, and that the
lower down the social scale the more important
cinema-going became as a form of leisure. It was, in
fact, in the depressed areas of Scotland, the North
and Wales that the highest concentration of cinemas
was to be found: North Wales had more cinemas per
head of the population than did London.(2) Clearly,
this was because the population was more sparse in
these areas, but it also means that these cinemas
were much smaller and that the experience of watching
these films, in community, must have been very
different from watching them in the large showpiece
theatres of the West End. The reason for cinema's
popularity is clear enough, even leaving aside the
entertainment on offer. Not only were cinemas warm
and comfortable, they were also very cheap. Almost
50 per cent of cinema tickets were on sale for less
than 6d: four out of every five tickets were on sale
for less than 1/-.(3) The unemployed could afford to
go regularly. There was nothing much else to do in
the unemployment areas and, with a change of
programme normally twice a week, they probably formed
the mainstay of the mid-week audiences in the
depressed areas. It is small wonder, therefore, that
cinema-going became such a central feature of
working-class life, or that cinema was the biggest
and most rapidly expanding form of mass entertainment
in the 1930s. With movie magazines, popcorn and
ice-cream, cinema-going took off as a self-
perpetuating sub-culture within the British way of
life for the next two decades.

The importance of cinema-going in this period
gave it a crucial ideological function. In a period

in which political protest was marginalized by the
defeat of the General Strike, by the split between
the Labour Party and the communists on both the
strategy and the tactics of dealing with the
depression, and by the split within the Labour Party
in the crisis of 1931, it is possible to read the
period as one in which class dominance was imposed
relatively easily. Yet it would be simplistic to see
the political significance of interwar cinema in
crude reductionist terms. British cinema, for
example, constantly reiterated in this period the
theme of national unity, mobilizing insistently an
ideology of a national family; a priori, the fact
that this theme was so constantly reiterated is more
likely to signify an attempt to produce such unity
rather than signify its existence in reality.
Alternative cinematic forms, such as the workers'
film movement or the documentary film movemement,
were pushed to the periphery by a combination of
commercial pressure and the social ambience of
cinema-going and film-watching. The contemporary
debate over the significance of the development of
cinematic culture was not a directly political one,
in that cinema's appeal to conservative values could
hardly be doubted. The doubts were, rather,
ideological in a wider sense, on the impact of the
development of what was seen to be a cultural form to
which the audience reacted purely passively, a form
which therefore required no discrimination on the
part of the audience. Cultural elitists, bar very
few, categorized the development of cinema in terms
which reproduced the classic distinction between
'culture' and the 'intelligentsia' on the one hand
and, on the other, 'entertainment' and 'mass market'.
This specific positioning of commercial cinema low
down on the rungs of the cultural hierarchy may have
helped to maintain pride of place for the traditional
high cultural forms but, in the medium term, it was
to have rather more damaging effects on high cultural
interests. The widespread spurning of cinema as a
cultural form which was beyond the pale denied a
hegemonic role for the British elite, actually
opening the way for a more thorough Americanization
of British popular culture than anything which had
yet occurred. This new American challenge was to
prove every bit as serious to the dominance of
British cultural elitists as the revolt within the
ranks that had resulted from the Great War.

The fact that the movies' potential for influence
was immense was undeniable, and the fact that for a
large part of this period British cinema-going was

dominated by the Americans lent a double-edge to the problem; not only would the new mass culture place in jeopardy the high cultural tradition, but the whole basis of the new mass culture would be dominated by an alien and highly materialist world view. Hollywood dominated for a variety of different reasons, but among the most significant was the fact that it was better organized financially. The economic problems that beset the British film industry faced with American competition were analogous to those which Britain had been facing on a much broader front in other sectors of the economy for a very long period. First, Hollywood had a huge domestic market on which to base its expansion. During the Great War, as films from Europe had dried up and as most belligerent nations declared film a strategic item and subject to stringent controls, the American film industry had been able not simply to dominate the huge home market but to begin to expand overseas as well. The domestic market gave Hollywood the capitalization to dwarf the European film industries as they emerged from the Great War. With outside competition in America virtually frozen out by the Hollywood monopoly, European cinema industries could hardly hope to make the kind of profit that would allow them to compete even in their own countries with Hollywood exports. In Britain, by 1926, British films had been reduced to a mere 5 per cent of all films shown in the country. It was symptomatic of the concern felt by government that, in spite of its hard-headed attitude towards other areas of the economy equally blighted by competition, it decided to intervene directly. Under the terms of the Cinematographic Films Act of 1927, the decline in the showings of British films was stabilized. Over the next eight years, cinemas were to be obliged to show an increasing proportion of British films, rising to 20 per cent by 1935. The effect of this legislation on the British film industry is debatable. On the one hand, it certainly kept the industry alive in Britain at a moment when it seemed on the point of complete collapse. But a severe effect in the medium term, at least, was the effect of the so-called 'quota quickies' on the reputation of British films. Studios began producing very low-budget movies in Britain in order simply to comply with the letter of the law. For the audiences, the often quite dismal results may well have had an adverse effect on their overall appreciation of the entertainment value of British films as a whole.

Most of the early development of British cinema had been the result of speculation on the part of relatively small entrepreneurs who were traditionally involved in music hall and variety entertainment. In 1926, however, the Ostrer brothers moved out of cotton milling and into film. The Ostrers' experience in the cinema industry was to prove typical of the boom-and-bust conditions that governed the development of the industry in this period. It was they who helped establish the independence of Gaumont-British from its parent company, merged it with Gainsborough Pictures, bought up distribution companies and cinema circuits, in an attempt to compete with the cartelization that was such an important element in the success of Hollywood. Isidore Ostrer urgently expanded Gaumont-British but he proved difficult to work with, with the result that important talent like that of Michael Balcon was lost. The speed of Gaumont-British's development, moreover, soon threatened its cash-flow. Only some elements in the over-large structure proved to be financially viable in the long-term; broadly, Gaumont-British depended on the monopoly position enjoyed by its chain of 300 cinemas for profitability, and by 1937 their main production studios at Shepherd's Bush had to be shut down. Meanwhile, Oscar Deutsch was building up the Odeon chain, concentrating almost entirely on the new suburban areas, where the familiar design of cream tile fascia and red neon lettering created an aggressively modernist image which fitted well with the idea of the new England of the consumer economy. By the late 1930s, however, Deutsch was as overstretched as was Gaumont-British, and both were taken over by J. Arthur Rank's consortium during the war.(4) With the ABC and Granada circuits also vying for the demand for cinema seats, the smaller independents soon found themselves under intense pressure. Internal competition like this, moreover, only made it even more difficult to face the international competition from Hollywood.

Not only was Hollywood better capitalized than the British film industry, the chain-booking system also virtually guaranteed that the British film industry could not fight back on anything like equal terms. Cinema-owning chains like Gaumont, Odeon and Rank arranged with film companies for exclusive showings of new films through their chains before these films reached the smaller independent cinemas. Hollywood was quick to capitalize on the possible benefits of this practice, offering beneficial terms to the chains. 'Quota quickies' quickly became B movies following the main (usually American) feature, and recognized as such by groans of dismay from the audience. The coming of sound at the turn of the decade proved to be another body blow for the weak British industry, involving extremely expensive re-equipping of studios and cinemas, as well as bringing into play that signifier of social class that was to blight British cinema for so long, the accent. In 1933, however, United Artists proved more willing than most American studios to use the quota system to British advantage, hiring Alexander Korda's London Films to make The private life of Henry VIII, a critical and commercial success which seemed to suggest that new life could be breathed into the British film industry by some shrewd capital investment.(5) By 1936, however, the national film-making industry was once again on the verge of the precipice, having borrowed too extravagantly on the basis of the success of Henry VIII. Associated British Pictures cut back on film production, having failed to break into the export market, while Gaumont-British closed Shepherd's Bush. Twickenham Films, reliant on quota quickies, went under; so too did the Capitol Films group. Time and again, financial crisis found the industry concentrating on the profit-making cinema chains and cutting back on film production.

In 1938, the quota was revised, the President of the Board of Trade, Oliver Stanley, arguing in the House of Commons that nothing less than the future of western democracy and the status of European civilization was at stake: 'I do not want our defences to be made in Hollywood', he proclaimed.(6) This time a clause putting a minimum cost on British-made films was inserted. London Films, in spite of their success with Henry VIII, was not to survive: the result of over-financing films like Things to come proved once again that there simply was not the capitalization available in the British film industry to ride a flop on the American market. London Films collapsed in 1939, and Korda returned to Hollywood. The new quota legislation, however, did prompt the Americans to invest more fully in British film. The most notable result was the establishment of MGM British, with Michael Balcon as head of production. From this position of relative security, Balcon was to emerge as the doyen of a specifically British school of film, creating an atmosphere in which directors such as Carol Reed, the Boulting brothers and Michael Powell could begin to flourish. Nevertheless, the power of the purse still had a magnetic appeal, with the disappearance to Hollywood of a range of first-class talent among British actors, technicians and directors. Perhaps the most important desertion of all was that of Alfred Hitchcock, the most genuinely original contributor to the development of the medium Britain ever produced.

British film might have been able to overcome all these admittedly severe financial restraints, however, if the industry had managed to overcome the most damaging of all the criticisms levelled against it by contemporary audiences, namely that it produced boring films. British films, though they might be considered more 'uplifting' than American productions - and probably retained a certain snob-appeal for that reason - simply failed to excite. Certainly, there were further constraints imposed on British cinema by the extraordinarily prudish attitude of the British Board of Film Censors. In practical terms, the BBFC was set up by the industry itself, as protection against the more direct state interference that would undoubtedly have emerged otherwise. Their task was to grade films into U, A and X categories (children under 16 being excluded from the latter), excising offending sequences or banning films altogether. In fact, the BBFC rarely had to ban altogether; film companies tended to submit outline scenarios to the censors before they began shooting, in order to avoid costly re-shooting or re-editing later; in effect, this meant that films likely to cause big problems for the censors were simply not made, because of the financal risk. This covert censorship made the role of the BBFC as a whole look less repressive than it really was.

The reports of the BBFC are noteworthy for their clear and complete lack of interest in cinema as such, for their absorption in those nuances of language and gesture which might suggest the merest hint of moral or political depravity. T.P. O'Connor, President of the BBFC in 1917, had laid down the basic ground rules on which the censors operated throughout the interwar period, the so-called 'O'Connor's 43'. The majority of these 43 rules were to do with moral matters: anything relating to extra-marital sex or likely to undermine the institution of the family was strictly forbidden; but there was also a tendency to condemn anything at all which might be considered unwholesome, such as horror films or realistic hospital scenes. Overt politics were also taboo, not simply the obvious targets such as Eisenstein's Battleship Potemkin but also the short film entitled Peace of Britain, which urged the policy of collective security in foreign affairs (at this time both government and opposition official policy). The ban on Peace of Britain was later rescinded, the publicity surrounding the attempted censorship ensuring that it was probably seen by a larger audience than any other short film of the time. But The relief of Lucknow was also banned because it 'would revive memories of the days of conflict in India'.

It was not so much that censorship privileged a particular political or social position but that it made it its business to avoid controversy, to ban anything likely to give offence on the screen. This hysterically middle-of-the-road approach is evidence enough of the contemporary fear of the power of cinema, and it can only be explained in terms of a worry about the unguided viewing of the largely working-class audience in Britain, and of the 'backward races of the Empire'. 'Incalculable is the damage', warned one committee reviewing the problem of the film in national life, 'that has already been done to the prestige of Europeans in India and the Far East through the widespread exhibition of ultra-sensational and disreputable films'. It is also clear that it was Hollywood, rather than the home-grown industry, that was considered primarily responsible. While in Britain, a combination of the BBFC and the moral probity of British film-makers ensured that nothing too appalling would get made and shown, 'a little group of men of southern European birth, with no Anglo-Saxon standard of morality and culture have seized hold of the Motion Picture industry of the United States, and it is their type of thinking that is going out to the nations', complained one prominent member of the London Public Morality Council in a comment which typified the response of some vociferously disgusted contemporaries.(7)

The result was that Love on the dole was acceptable for a reading public, and for a theatre public, but not for a cinema public until 1940: suggested outline treatments for such a film were turned down three times in the 1930s. While it is fair to say that censorship made it impossible to treat serious contemporary issues on the screen, however, it must also be pointed out that there was no major outcry against censorship by the industry itself. Film-makers in Britain seemed, as a group, perfectly happy to accept a middle-of-the-road position, content that 'entertainment' should neither question nor threaten normative values. In this sense, most of the British cinema stands in sharp contrast to American cinema in this period which, in spite of the Hays' code - in many ways even more proscriptive than O'Connor's 43 - still managed to excite. In the last resort, the Hollywood product was just as normative as the British, but its appeal rested on its ability to transcend the socially-propagandistic tenor of British film. The success of Hollywood, in fact, rested on the successful disguise of its motivating ideology. Any explanation of the relative failure of British cinema in this period, while taking full account of the enormous financial difficulties that faced the industry in competition with Hollywood, must also accept that most audiences clearly and unequivocally preferred American productions. Largely, this was because Hollywood managed to combine rather more sophisticated techniques to interreact with the audience. The development of the star system was an important case in point. It is well-established that in classic Western cinema a viewer 'understands' a film not only on the basis of his/her familiarity with the conventions of camera language or of narrative development, but also through a process of identification with characters on screen. Identification involves a complex psychological paradox, the voyeuristic pleasure of looking combining with the narcissistic pleasure of looking at oneself. Identification involves using another person as an object of sexual stimulation while simultaneously seeing that other person as a reflection of how you would like others to see you. Laura Mulvey has argued that, in mainstream cinema, this process has traditionally been overdetermined by gender, that camera and screen-character invariably invite the viewer to position her/himself comfortably in a male-dominated world.(8) Clearly, in relation to cinema stars, the psychological process of identification does combine with a reading of the sexual characteristics of the star her/himself, as s/he appears over a number of films, to play a very important part in the production of meaning in film. While it is of obvious importance to her popularity that Greta Garbo was physically attractive, the meaning which attached to her over a number of films and a number of roles, that of the sphinx-like mysterious woman unhappily searching for fulfilment, created a number of expectations on the part of the viewer which were inevitably taken into the cinema the next time the viewer went to see a Garbo film. Type-casting, in other words established the 'meaning' of a star, accumulating over a number of screen appearances. The fact that pre-publicity proclaimed that Garbo or Cagney or Gable were to be in a film made it unnecessary to explain what the film was likely to be about. Stars were short-hand in filmic language, in other words, an economy device in the narrative process.(9)

On one level, it was the sheer sexual attractiveness of so many of the Hollywood stars that helped to give the American cinema industry such an edge. But it was also the way in which the Hollywood star system managed to articulate this sexual desirability to a powerfully developed ideology of individualism that made their productions so appealing. Social comedies from Britain and America, for example, make interesting comparison for the way in which the star system operated entirely differently in the two countries. We have already suggested that one of the dominant themes of British cinema, be it in comedy or social drama, was the notion of the community as hero. In comedy this idea recurrently worked out through the narrative in terms of the incompetence of characters such as those played by George Formby, his reliance on the sense of justice and fair play in the community to ensure that things 'turned out nice again'. Gracie Fields, though her star persona was more aggressive and self-assertive than that of George Formby, similarly functioned in the narrative of the films in which she appeared to point up the inherent soundness of the community, one in which social divisions were best left as they were, with everyone happy in her/his own place. In both, sexual coding enmeshed with social coding, an incompetence with members of the other sex unless they were from similar social backgrounds. Moreover, it was social class which signified sexual attractiveness; a middle-class accent easily overrode any physical plainness; by contrast a working-class accent invariably signified a clown or a criminal, however physically attractive the character might appear with the sound turned down.

Thus, in Britain, film comedy was conveyed normatively by an intermeshing and thus an inter-reinforcement of sexual and social codes, with the social coding tending to overdetermine the sexual. Hollywood social comedy worked over similar ideological terrain but often with markedly different coding strategies and implications. Recurrently in the comedies of Frank Capra, for example, honesty, fair play and a sense of justice were enshrined not in the community at all but in the backwoodsman hero in the James Stewart/Henry Fonda mould. American

social comedy had a sharper cutting edge because it
admitted that problems were institutionalized in
urbanized and materialist America. But these problems
could be overcome if Mr Deeds went to Town or Mr
Smith went to Washington, taking with them their
sense of honesty and their integrity.(10) The nature
of the change that could be achieved which was
projected in these films was hardly radical, rather
it was populist in its heroicization of old-fashioned
American values. It was, however, in the acceptance
that there were problems, in the optimism that these
problems could be solved, and in the belief that the
individual could play a most significant role in the
solution of these problems that the essential
difference from British social comedy lay. In
Hollywood social comedy, typically, the hero embodied
the positive values, and brought them to light for
the benefit of a benighted community. Classically,
Hollywood's style rested upon the individualization
of social issues; general problems, once registered
as problems, were resolved at the level of the
central character. In Britain, typically, positive
values lay in the community and were revealed to
social incompetents in the process of the narrative;
comedy lay in bizarre attempts to bridge class
differences, while resolution and closure lay in
acceptance that class differences existed. Hollywood,
conversely, projected a greater formative role for
the individual in ensuring the victory of 'real'
values, thus subtly and precisely articulating
dominant liberal ideology to that process of
identification through which the viewer reads the
classic narrative film. This quite critical
difference between British and American social comedy
was typical of a more general distinction between
Hollywood and British films. The Hollywood star
system worked to mythicize and heroicize the
individual, thus offering a much more involving as
well as optimistic narrative. Hollywood thus
constructed and projected a much more appealing mode
of address for the audience-individual, in place of
the theme of individual incompetence which typified
British film. Hollywood's stress on individualism,
through its mobilization of star coding, may have
been no more 'real' than the dominant ideology of
community of British cinema, but it did at least
offer a resolution which stressed that fatalism was
neither a sufficient nor a necessary way out of
current troubles. Fatalism made boring social
propaganda, whereas the Hollywood star system made
conservatism dynamic.

Hollywood, what is more, dared to criticize the American status quo in a way that was quite impossible in British film. In I am a fugitive from a chain gang, for example, the penal system of the South was extensively criticized.(11) Warner Brothers had thus invented a commentative edge for cinematic social drama in America which was simply missing from The proud valley or The stars look down, which offered resolution at the mythic level of morality rather than offering institutional targets. Certainly, the institutional target in I am a fugitive was the clear anomaly of the Georgia chain gangs, but the indictment of authority was still a general one; the clear injustice sets up a relationship between state and individual which is basically oppositional. This was developed further into the most succesful genre of the period, the gangster movie. The appeal of the gangster movie was complex, a combination of, on the one hand, the anarchic implications of identification with a criminal character who is an attractive personality in some measure and, on the other hand, the normative implications of that criminal's eventual and inevitable demise. In fact, in the development of the gangster genre, the individualist implications of the star system were explored in imaginative and potentially radical ways. While the early gangster characters, such as Edward G. Robinson's Rizzo in Little Caesar (12), were fairly obvious villains whose overthrow could be seen as a cause of relief, the career of James Cagney in particular created problems of positioning the audience for the narrative resolution. From the beginning, Cagney had a magnetism which threatened to overthrow the normative purpose of the narrative. A small-time tough guy from a deprived background and an ethnic minority, the Cagney character succeeded in crime through a gutsy determination to crawl out of the pit: the typical Cagney plot was simply a roughed-up version of the individualist ethic. Indeed a major aspect of the appeal of the Cagney archetypal character was that his personality and determination were so strong that only a whole team of G-men armed with machine-guns could stop him. Yet, clearly, individualism of this particular type was anti-social. Cagney's appeal to the viewer was the double-sided appeal of rebellion; there is the thrill of identification with the anti-normative hero, but there is also complicity involved in the thrill of violent death which resolves the narrative norma- tively. In the gangster movies' development, it is in

174

fact in the tension between individualism and
normative values that the pleasure of the text
fundamentally resides. In exploring the basic
contradictions here, albeit unwittingly, American
movies were dealing with a quite basic issue in the
structure of Western society, not simply offering a
glorification of violence in fantasy form, as the
British critics of the genre complained. But the
gangster movie did also respond to the pressures of
social propaganda in time. In the development of his
career, Cagney and his studio responded to the
criticism that he was glorifying violence by
modifying his star-image, for example by playing
policeman roles, or by playing good-bad guys who
pretended to collapse weakly as they went to the
electric chair (on the appeal of a priest) so that
youngsters should not hero-worship him. (13)

Hollywood may not have been offering very
edifying values, then, as far as cultural elitists in
Britain were concerned, but it was certainly not
offering mere pap. Hollywood dealt with involving and
serious issues which British cinema simply
side-stepped. Even at the level of what might seem to
be mere fantasy, there was still a valid and relevant
discussion to be deployed. The vision of America that
was so appealing to the interwar generation of
British cinema-goers was of a violent but vibrant
society, in which things went wrong but could be
changed and were being changed, an apparently
classless society which could be contrasted with the
patronizing formal hierarchy of the British
community. In other ways, too, American cinema
offered discussion which British cinema simply
avoided. In its treatment of the 'new woman', for
example, Hollywood offered the 'new man'. Clearly,
some at least of the appeal of a Cagney or a Humphrey
Bogart to the male audience lay in the way they
talked to and treated women. The shock registered
when Cagney pushed a grapefruit into his girlfriend's
face in Public enemy was a natural reaction to the
opening-up of an element in male chauvinist culture
which had simply been disguised in texts before this
time.(14) In response to the emergence on film of the
newly independent or sexually aggressive female, in
star-characters such as Jean Harlow or Joan Crawford,
there emerged the even more aggressive male to
confirm the old gender balance. Yet, even though the
traditional gender roles were eventually confirmed in
the narrative process of these films, stars such as
Bette Davis, Joan Crawford and Greta Garbo did at
least register a recognition of the 'new woman',

talented as actresses and appealing in their independence as well as in their glamour, again in sharp contrast to the middle-class 'niceness' of their British contemporaries. This recognition of the arrival of the 'new woman' was significant even though it is also true that the Cagneys, the Bogarts and the Gables adopted a brasher macho role in response to this more overtly threatening woman.

The reactionary stance of Hollywood's gender politics should not disguise the significance of the fact that it did at least deal with the issues in a relevant way, rather than simply ignoring them, as was overwhelmingly true in the British case. The development of the musical, Busby Berkeley's emphasis on pretty girls with wide-mouthed smiles forming kitsch patterns across the screen, for example, froze the starlet as sex object. The 'new woman' portrayed by Bette Davis and her ilk rarely found real fulfilment except in relation to men; narrative development in these films depended on audience recognition of the ideological disorder signified by the woman's independence and the necessity of the closure offered by her final succumbing to her true role - in a relationship with a man. All this is obvious, and became part of the stock-in-trade of mainstream cinema for the next forty years, but its bravado appeal to a British audience brought up on sexual puritanism can not be underestimated. The strength of plot of the typical Hollywood import, and the economy of the narrative, combined with the promise of the male-dominant individualist ethic to provide a perspective on the 'real' world outside the cinema profoundly at variance with the faint-hearted circumspection of British cinema.

Hollywood did, moreover, develop a notion of Britishness, or at least Englishness, which was innately generous to British audiences. On the one hand, the British colony of actors in Hollywood, from Ronald Colman through C. Aubrey Smith to David Niven, were used as cinematic shorthand to establish the honourable, the gentlemanly, the self-abnegating and the debonair as the prime characteristics of the Englishman, implicitly contrasted with the brash and the vulgar characteristics of American culture even by Hollywood itself. In partnership with the British film industry in the 1930s, Hollywood also developed a new genre of films on the British Empire, in which these specifically British manly virtues were equated with the development of civilization itself, contrasted with the barbaric anarchy of the dark-skinned races. The success of Hollywood's Lives of a

Bengal lancer in 1935 and Prisoner of Zenda in 1937 gave the British cinema industry enough confidence to respond with Sanders of the river in 1935, Sixty glorious years in 1938 and The four feathers in 1939. These, and other films such as Clive of India and Gunga Din, articulated the typically Hollywood treatment of themes of male dominance and individualism to the reinforcing themes of the gentlemanly code and white supremacism, rewriting the history of Britain's fading international position in a way which emphasized the continued relevance of those themes in the contemporary world.(15) Given the undoubted inadequacies of contemporary education, many in America as well as Britain probably learned most of their history from the screen. Though it would be simplistic in the extreme to make any direct causal link between cinematic text and contemporary politics, the role of a mass leisure activity like cinema in constructing a perspective on the world, along with all the other institutional pressures at work in a highly-developed society such as that of interwar Britain, may well have been formidable. Clearly, it may well have been important in determining responses that so many in Britain saw those problems from within a perspective provided by a leisure context which offered a highly selective view of both the trans-Atlantic future and the Anglo-Saxon past.

In other words, it is not just, or even primarily, those films that specifically dealt with contemporary problems in Britain that should be emphasized, which was a small minority anyway, but the wider context of film-watching into which these more 'relevant' films fitted, as well as the even wider economic and cultural significance of cinema-going as a whole. The Hollywood way of telling a story, with all its ideological apparatus, became the only way of telling a story on film in the Western world. Cinema did not exist as pure fantasy; no cultural form ever can; it formed part of contemporary reality if only because it was something that so many people enjoyed so regularly. Neither was cinema speaking to its audience in purely escapist terms; it was using language and ideology which clearly made sense to contemporary audiences. In the process of encoding and decoding, an active ideological relationship was established between film-maker and film-goer. Clearly, the ideological fit with Hollywood was much stronger than that with the home-grown cinema among contemporary audiences. This was a blow not only to the British cinema industry but also to those cultural mandarins who viewed with distaste the onslaught of trans-Atlantic popular culture. The entrancing culture of Hollywood both advertized and was itself part of the new consumer economy, which was changing quite fundamentally the social balance in Britain, and which was forging trans-Atlantic links. This new consumer economy had its own ideological requirements; clearly, they would be difficult to accommodate with those of the high cultural tradition. One significant group did, however, attempt to reform the trend in popular culture by trying to force into alignment the high cultural tradition and the technology of the mass media. This was the Documentary Film Movement. Their history reveals once again the complex interplay of basic economics and ideology, always at work in culture. Eventually, the Movement was to become one of the moving fronts which helped to negotiate a new hegemonic compromise by the beginning of the Second World War.

NOTES

1.   S. Rowson, 'A Statistical Survey of the Cinema Industry in Great Britain', Journal of the Royal Statistical Society, 1936.
2.   A.H. Halsey (ed.), Trends in British society since 1900, 1974, pp. 558-60.
3.   'A Statistical Survey of the Cinema Industry in Great Britain'; see also P. Stead, 'The People and the Pictures', in N. Pronay and D.W. Spring (eds.), Propaganda, politics and film, 1982, pp. 77-97.
4.   J. Richards, The age of the dream palace, 1984, Ch.1.
5.   Private life of Henry VIII, dir. A. Korda, 1936 (London Films).
6.   See P. Stead, 'Hollywood's Message to the World: Britain's Response in the 1930s', Historical journal of film, radio and television, vol. 1, No. 1, 1981, pp. 19-32.
7.   On censorship, see Stead, 'Hollywood's Message'; J. Richards, Dream palace, Pt. 2; 'The BBFC and Content Control in the 1930s', Historical journal of film, radio and television, 1981, pp 95-116, 1982, pp. 39-48; N. Pronay, 'The First Reality', in K. Short (ed.), Feature film as history, 1983; J. Trevelyan, What the censor saw, 1973.
8.   L. Mulvey, 'Visual Pleasure and Narrative Cinema', Screen, 15, 2, 1974.

9.   See R. Dyer, Stars, 1982.
10.   Mr Deeds goes to town, dir. F. Capra,
1936, (Columbia); Mr Smith goes to Washington, dir.
F. Capra, 1939, (Columbia).
11.   I am a fugitive from a chain gang, dir.
M. Leroy, 1932, (Film Distributors Associated); see
N. Roddick, A new deal in entertainment: Warner
Brothers in the 1930s, BFI, 1983.
12.   Little Caesar, dir. M. Leroy, 1930, (Film
Distributors Associated).
13.   See S.L. Karpf, The gangster movie:
emergence, variation and decline of a genre, 1930 –
1940, 1970; P. McGilligan, Cagney: the actor as
auteur, 1980.
14.   Public enemy, dir. W. Wellman, 1931,
(Film Distributors Associated).
15.   J. Richards, Visions of yesterday, 1973.

and so did the equipment necessary to film with such
stock and project the finished product.

Finance, therefore, was a central concern for the
film-maker where, for artists working in traditional
forms, it was essentially peripheral. In the
commercial film world, finance was provided by the
movie moguls who were in the business of making
profits, and the danger of loss of freedom by artists
working in film was acute. Since finance is so
significant in the very process of making a film it
is clear that, unlike any of the traditional art
forms, it was likely to be dominated by the norms of
the economically dominant group in society. Beyond
the act of creation, film-makers were also reliant on
big money to reach a mass audience; on distributors
with the capital to buy copies of films, and on
cinema owners with the capital invested in equipment
and in buildings to show the films, both of whom
needed to show a return on the capital they invested.
The emphasis on profit at every stage in the process
of making through to showing a film meant that
'artistic standards', as such, were likely to count
for very little in decision-making. This is not to
say that excellent films were not made and did not
receive mass distribution in the period with which we
are dealing. But those films got made and got a
showing because it was considered that the financial
risk was worth taking, that they could make a profit;
the fact that they were also good films was just a
lucky spin-off for film-makers who had managed to
sell their ideas.

It is often argued, and certainly was by the
elite theorists, that the merit or otherwise of
cinema ultimately depends on the audience. Audiences,
the argument runs, get the films they deserve; if
they had voted with their feet in the 1930s then they
could have turned Hollywood from a boom town into a
desert again; profit for the film producer ultimately
depends on the audience being prepared to spend money
to see the film. It is along such lines that some
critics of mass society argue that the problems
relating to mass communication and mass culture are
not simply a question of the owners of the means of
mass communication imposing their product on a
passive society, that there is a symbiotic process
involved in the relationship between producer and
consumer. Such an argument is at least implicit in
one of the classic studies of the impact of cinema on
society, Siegfried Kracauer's From Caligari to
Hitler. Kracauer argued that there were pre-echoes of
Nazism in Weimar film, evidence of a state of mind

that would be prepared to accept Nazism when it became a major political force in the late 1920s. The basis on which Kracauer worked was the assumption that cinema could be taken as direct evidence of the mass assumptions of an age, the assumptions not simply of those who made and distributed the films but also of those who went to see them, went on going to see them, paying money at the box-office which allowed more and similar films to be made, presumably because they liked them. Kracauer's was basically the classic economic case that supply and demand work in close harmony, producer and consumer together in effect creating the product. The argument, simplified, is that Germans in the 1920s got proto-Nazi films because they were proto-Nazi themselves.(1) There was, in fact, a confusion in Kracauer's argument based on a simplification, understandably enough in a period when the nature of the relationship between film and audience had barely begun to be explored. Kracauer did not appreciate the extent to which, to continue the analogy with economics, demand could be created by investment, reinforced by the fact that cinema does not and cannot work in isolation, but rather within a whole series of educational and other institutional frameworks which invite conformity with the values of the dominant group in the social formation.

The question of why popular novels and films are popular in the first place is basic to any discussion of mass culture. John Grierson, founder of the so-called British Documentary Movement, was someone who tried to break through the vicious circle of economics which did so much to shape film as a cultural form in Western capitalism. It cannot be said that his attempt was all that successful, because the question of economics in film production is basic, not simply political. Grierson hoped to create, however, an alternative cinema within a capitalist structure, not to undermine it in any way but rather to strengthen those principles of liberal democracy which he held so dear. He worked on the assumption that there were as many potential seats outside the commercial cinema as in them; he hoped to build on the small audience which made up non-theatrical distribution at the time, and thus to reform the whole medium. What he had in mind was the kind of audience who went to see Battleship Potemkin and the other early Russian masterpieces in the film clubs. It was not that he was opposed to the commercial cinemas as such, for he always hoped that they would show an interest in and screen his films;

it was rather that those cinemas were worried about
the commercial potential of the material that the
Movement produced and refused them for that reason.
Only a few of the films of the Movement, such as
Nightmail, achieved the kind of publicity that got
them a commercial showing. Finally, of course, non-
theatrical distribution was never to get anywhere
near the audiences of the cinema chains. At a time
when commercial cinemas were admitting anything up to
17 millions every week, it is unlikely that
non-theatrical distribution was reaching more than
25,000. In short, Grierson was largely preaching to
the converted, those minority 'film buffs' who made
up the audience of the film clubs and who were
interested in film as an art form.

The question of financing the production of the
Movement's films was also one that Grierson never
fully squared. The Documentary Film Movement really
began when Grierson was employed by Sir Stephen
Tallents to create a film unit at the Empire
Marketing Board, not the most obvious sponsor of a
radical new cultural idea, but Tallents was vitally
interested in state agencies organizing the
'Projection of England' largely for commercial
reasons. As a result, the early films of the Movement
were made basically as advertisements for British
imperial products. Drifters, for example, was made as
an advertisement for the British fishing industry,
and Song of Ceylon for the Ceylon Tea Company. The
Empire Marketing Board soon found itself unable to
continue to bear the cost of the films and Grierson
went with Tallents to the General Post Office to form
the GPO film unit, where films like Nightmail were
made, again to specific sponsorship. The material of
these early films was virtually dictated by
sponsorship, in fact. Grierson, through his
formidable personality, was able to maintain a large
degree of freedom of action, and he was undoubtedly
helped in this by Sir Stephen Tallents. As the
Movement developed, many of those who grouped round
Grierson found alternative sponsorship; Shell Oil
formed their own film unit, for instance, and
film-makers like Paul Rotha, in an attempt to win
complete freedom, set up his own production company,
picking and choosing his contracts from industry.

In a real sense, however, sponsorship by the
state or by industry was no real problem for
Grierson, though it may have been for those of a more
radical political bent, such as Rotha. Indeed, this
kind of sponsorship may have been the whole rationale
for the Movement, as far as Grierson was concerned.

For Grierson, cinema was the poetry of the industrial age. Cinema in itself was an invention of sophisticated technology, and he believed that it should be used to create a specifically new art form for the technological age, celebrating technology just as pre-industrial art had celebrated pastoralism. Why, he asked, should 'art' stop at the beginning of industrialization, as so many of the contemporary images of England seemed to imply? Why should artists continue to hark back to the pre-industrial age when the hard facts of the present demanded their poets even more? Grierson argued for a new type of artist, and for his integration into the industrial establishment, sponsored by industry and considering himself to be part of industry, just as the older pastoral tradition had been sponsored by an economy based on the land and of which the artist had then felt himself to be part:

> Our culture is divorced from the actual: it is practised almost exclusively in the rarefied atmosphere of country colleges and country retreats. The hunger for English reality is satisfied briefly and sentimentally over a country hedge. We might make an English cinema, as we might make English art again, if we could only send our creators back to fact. Not only to the old fact of the countryside which our poets have already honoured, but to the new fact of industry and commerce and plenty and poverty which no poet has honoured at all.(2)

To make such a new art form work required a new attitude on the part both of the artist and the industrialist or technologist. Thus, the kind of sponsorship which kept the Movement going was not something to be despised or worried about, as long as it was seen both by film-maker and sponsor as part of the process of re-integrating art and reality, which had become divorced by the Industrial Revolution. In its purest form, this idea could be seen most clearly at work in Arthur Elton's film <u>Aero-engine</u>, a detailed cinematic description of one of the most sophisticated examples of contemporary technology, the camera lovingly handling the machines and the polished steel as aesthetic objects.(3)

Grierson only made one film, <u>Drifters</u>, but he produced and edited many more. As the prime fixer and the prime theorist of documentary film in this

185

period, he influenced, encouraged and oversaw the
development of the whole Movement. His thinking was
based on the central precept that it was possible to
build a new relationship between art and society with
cinema, itself a product of technology, as its
natural form. Grierson therefore concentrated on
building up film as a medium in its own right,
reliant neither on literature nor theatre and taking
its stories from actuality, from the present. Using
real people rather than actors, using real stories
rather than fictions, using real places rather than
sets, Grierson hoped to construct nothing less than a
new culture to articulate advanced industrial
society. In these views, he was undoubtedly
influenced by the Russian theorists, and particularly
by the best known of these in the West, Sergei
Eisenstein. For the Russians, cinema was similarly a
materialist art form, celebrating both the
industrialization of Russia and the victory of the
proletariat in 1917. More than that, however,
film-makers like Eisenstein virtually invented the
'language' of cinema in their editing techniques.
Montage, the juxtaposition of clips of film to make
up a meaning greater than the two parts, and
super-imposition, produced for cinema an entirely new
form of communication which was entirely visual.
Russian editing, indeed, could almost create sound
before synchronized sound was even invented for the
cinema, as in the case of the screams and the
marching boots in the Odessa Steps sequence in
Potemkin, or the surging crowd in October. At its
best, Russian silent cinema could virtually dispense
with story-cards, titles often being incorporated
into the montage as intrinsic elements, rather than
as extrinsic explanation. In this way they learned to
rely simply on visual images to construct an
irreversible and rapid flow of meaning. Grierson used
radical techniques suggested by the Russian films,
rarely seen in Britain. Like the Russians, he hoped
to educate for industrialization, but in liberal
democratic rather than in communistic terms.

The need for the documentarist to involve himself
fully in his subject, to understand it before filming
it, was another important element in Grierson's view
of the new integration of art and reality. His views
on this matter owed a great deal to the work of the
pioneering American documentarist, Robert Flaherty,
who made Nanook of the North and Moana before coming
across the Atlantic to make Man of Aran.(4) Flaherty
would spend months preparing his subject, much to the
indignation of some of his sponsors, until he knew it

backwards and knew precisely what he wanted to do with it. Flaherty certainly influenced Grierson in other ways, too, notably in the choice of subject matter. In his choice of filmic subjects, it could be said that Flaherty internationalized the American pioneer spirit, the frontier culture. In particular, he concentrated in all his major films on the struggle of man against the natural elements. In some cases, he was prepared even to invent to make his point; it seems clear, for example, that the Aran islanders had given up hunting basking sharks for years before Flaherty decided to make a shark-hunt a high-point of his film.

Grierson's interest in Flaherty-like subject matter tended to cut across his avowed intention of creating an industrial art. Grierson's own film, Drifters, after all, was as much about man against the sea as it was about fishing as an industry, or man in industrial society. Drifters set the tone for so much that was to become typical of the British Documentary Film Movement. It is an important film historically, not only for its emphasis on actuality, but also for the way it combined radical American and Russian concepts of film, and also for its handling of the themes of man as individual and man as social animal, the liberal paradox which so much of the work of the Movement addressed centrally. Drifters, according to Ralph Bond, for the first time in British film 'dared to show in the most graphic detail the skills and the "braveries" (Grierson's favourite word) of ordinary working people in an environment full of hardships and dangers'.(5) Certainly, in its choice of subject, one ordinary trip by one ordinary drifter, Grierson chose to avoid histrionics and the sense of the unique, concentrating instead on the kind of risks that fishermen took every time they put to sea. The film followed the boat and its crew through the voyage out to the fishing grounds, the night drifting, the arduous task of hauling in the nets and the race for harbour to get the highest price for the fish. The film then detailed the market mechanism taking over, th auction of the fish and its transport to the market. Overall, the film succeeded in conveying a sense of the fishing industry in its totality, the story of how the fish ended up on your fishmonger's slab, from beginning to end.

Ralph Bond suggests that there was a social critique subtly implied at the end of the film, the fact that the dangers the fishermen faced was reduced to a straightforward cash nexus in the market place.

Clearly, the way in which the film superimposes images of the auctioneer's bell over shots of the raging sea which the men have fought through might be interpreted in this light, but it could just as easily be interpreted as a concluding cinematic remark emphasizing the connections between various phases in the whole operation of dealing with the catch. If it were intended as a critical social comment, it was so anodyne as to be virtually unnoticeable. More significant is the way in which Grierson emphasized both the individuality of members of the crew, but also the teamwork and co-operation necessary to bring in the catch. There are recurrent images of fishermen, bearded and wearing oilskins, caught in silhouetted profile against the horizon and scudding clouds, in a style reminiscent of Soviet heroic socialist realism. At the same time, the critical moments of the whole operation require the most meticulous co-operation between the various skills involved; each has his role to play and there is no room for slipshod work, which would endanger the whole boat and her crew. Grierson thus constructed a message of heroic working men, of the dignity of labour, and of the significance of teamwork in a common cause, using the language of silent cinema — the choice, juxtaposition, and mixing of images in superimposition or in montage — to articulate these concepts together.(6)

Grierson it was who first coined the word 'documentary', which he defined as 'the creative treatment of actuality'. Actuality was important, indeed it was basic to the idea of documentary, but creativity was equally important. Grierson was, after all, talking about a new art form, not simply a new method of reportage like the newspaper story or the cinema newsreel. What mattered to him was the creation of a 'super-fact' by an image of actuality, normally but not necessarily filmed on the spot. The herring, dogfish and conger eels filmed in the nets in Drifters were not in fact filmed under a North Sea drifter but in a tank in Portsmouth. The shots of the interior of the mail coach in Nightmail were not filmed on a moving train — the lighting was too bad — but in a studio. This kind of tinkering with reality was permissible, as long as the image of actuality created was still 'true'. Geoge Orwell dramatized reality in a similar way for Wigan pier; the sequence of events in the 'Wigan Pier Diary' is different in a number of ways, in particular it is less persuasively inter-connected, than that which appears in the published book. It is, of course, in this tinkering with actuality that the specifically political implications of the phrase 'treatment of actuality' become most apparent.(7) A major problem which Grierson set for himself in his high claims for documentary, was the difficulty of moving away from the idea of art as beautification. In his attempt to make the everyday life of the industrial nation into art, there was the inherent problem that such attempts might degenerate into what he would have seen as the merely political. Experiments with sound, such as the specifically written poetry or music for Coalface or Nightmail were a long way from what we would now expect to classify as 'documentary'.. Alberto Cavalcanti, who worked on both of these films, was already well-established as a documentary film-maker on the Continent before Grierson introduced him to the British Movement. After Cavalcanti's arrival, the Movement split, broadly speaking, into two wings, one concentrating on the aesthetics of documentary and the other on the politics of realism. On the one hand, Cavalcanti developed the cinematic techniques of 'poetic realism' in extravagantly experimental films like Coalface or Nightmail, which were soon elevated into cinematic high culture. It would certainly be difficult to call Coalface in any sense radical from the political point of view, however, even though it was made about the coal industry in a period in which that industry was in serious trouble and might have been an obvious vehicle for any radical intentions.

Coalface, the direction of which was credited to Grierson even though most of the directorial work seems to have been undertaken by Cavalcanti, combines a matter-of-fact commentary on the workings of the coal industry with the music of Benjamin Britten in a narrative which, like that of Drifters, sets out to describe the industry in its totality, from beginning to end of the process. 'There is the mine. There are the miners', sings the musical chorus at the beginning of the film, followed by the opening commentary: 'coal is the basic industry of Britain'. These three sentences are repeated in reverse order at the end of the film by chorus and commentator, reinforcing that symmetry which is the principal ideological purport of the film. The first part of the film deals largely with the production of the coal, set around one night shift, images of pit-head gear and miners working underground used as establishing shots for a welter of facts and figures about coal production. Male bodies stripped to the waist in the underground heat signify the macho heroism of the miner, but also his vulnerability: emphasis is as much on the threat of death and injury in the mines as on average daily production. The chorus provides counter-point both for the down-beat commentary and for the visuals. While throughout the film the emphasis, visually, is on the teamwork of man and man, and of man and machine, when the commentator specifically mentions the fact that machine supplements labour, the chorus counterpoints with 'cost of cutting reduced ... men per shift'. Similarly, when the bald facts of mining accidents are recited, the chorus counterpoints with 'trapped underground...rescue efforts abandoned ... cannot account for 200 lads'. In this way, the chorus provides almost an oppositional narrative partly inaudible in the background of the film, apparently that of the miners themselves. This much is confirmed at the end of the first section when, as the shift finishes, the chorus identifies more explicitly with the miners; 'how much did we do?' and, as the miners head for the shaft, 'we're going up!'

In the second part of the film, referring briefly to the life of the miners outside the pit, the emphasis is on the all-embracing nature of the industry in which they work; 'the miner's life is bound up with the pit. His home is often owned by the pit. The life of the village depends on the pit'. The accompaniment is now a female choir, gendering the family side of life. Two pans of the camera from industrial chimney-stacks to wind-blown trees establish the relationship between townscape and a struggling pastoralism, reinforced by shots of a miner walking through lines of washing, and the ruins of a building, before the film develops into its third part, the transport and distribution of the coal. The film, in the juxtaposition of visual image with commentary and sung chorus, thus celebrates the working-class miner both as hero and as victim. The potential tension here is resolved by inflecting the issue in gender terms with a mobilization of male narcissism, in the shots of half-naked miners underground, and its implicit distinction between male work-time and female family-time. The class issue is registered for the typical non-mining viewer constructed as the audience of the film, but the class issue is overdetermined by gender. Taken together with the over-arching celebration of male team-work and the team-work of man and machine, and the importance of coal mining to society as a whole, the film stands as an aggressive tribute to the inter-dependence rather than the contradictions of a male-dominated industrial society.The film constructs a myth of male steadfastness and solidarity in a tough world. Aggressively modernist in its form, too, the film reworks pastoralism (here referred to in the form of a tree bravely hunched against the wind - the pastoralism of a 'real man's world') in naturalizing a discourse on the awesome struggle with nature for coal, for the benefit of society as a whole.(8)

Coalface thus reworked many of the ideological themes already apparent in Drifters and Man of Aran, though here they are more clearly industrialized in their setting and in their content. Nightmail, made by Basil Wright, Harry Watt and Cavalcanti, with words and music by W.H. Auden and Britten, similarly reworked the well-trodden theme of social inter-dependence in its 'national-collectivist' mythic-ization of the contemporary industrial society. Once again, gender coding played an important role in displacing the class issue: work is a male world in both Coalface and Nightmail. The film presents the mail-run from London to Aberdeen as the complex inter-meshing of men, machines, administration and procedure in the train, and alongside the line, co-operating with feeding mail-runs, and ever-changing seas of faces (even the locomotive changes at Crewe, and the commentator as the train approaches Scotland), brought together to perform a necessary service for the community while that community sleeps on in blissful ignorance. And yet, 'all Scotland waits for her'. As the narrative develops, the train itself becomes a condensation of the national-collectivist myth. Not only is the mail-run reliant on no single person and on no single machine, but rather on the accumulating input of every man and every machine involved, its very role in scooping up, sorting and distributing the national mail becomes mediatory. Only the train provides coherence for the varied countryside, the clash of rural and urban, the different accents at stations as the train moves further north. As the train leaves Crewe, it picks up the mail of 'the mines of Wigan', 'the steelworks of Warrington' and 'the machine-shops of Preston', relevant industrial noises mixing with the sound of the steam train on the sound-track, all over the same long shot of the racing train, with no visual reference to these passing towns at all. The noisy clash and visual violence of the netted postal-bag collectors on the side of the train as the Carnforth mail is picked up ends with a quiet and comfortable shot of the three bags safe and sound on the floor of the carriage and on their way. The contrasts and the frictions of the nation outside the train are resolved in the train's passage through the national family as it sleeps. Inside the train, the postal workers work quietly and efficiently, subsuming into their routine the 'new man' with friendly and encouraging tips. Outside, the nation is aware of the passage of the train, if at all, merely as a low rattle of a wash-basin.Thus, what appears to be a 'merely' factual report on how the mail trains work becomes an ideological map of the national-collective myth.(9)

It is fair to say that the 'creative treatment of actuality' was an inherently political concept. Around Grierson grouped many of those from the radical ferment of the 1930s universities, Cambridge in particular, drawn by Grierson's ideas on the need for a new relationship between art and environment. Edgar Anstey and Arthur Elton, for instance, were willing to use industrial sponsorship to make direct comments on contemporary housing conditions. Housing problems was made as an advertisement for the Gas, Light and Coke Company, which stood to gain a great deal from any substantial rebuilding programmes. Anstey proved to be much less interested in cinematic techniques as such, though his style was to prove much more influential in the later development of documentary than the 'poetic realism' of the Cavalcanti camp. He was much more interested in the use of cinema as direct social comment and critique. He decided to leave the obtrusive camera simply square-on in front of the slum-dwellers and let them talk because, as he put it, 'it was their film'. The result was a striking early example of the kind of campaigning style that was to be associated with television documentary in the 1960s. There was no ostentatious editing or camera work. At one point, indeed, the hand of the cameraman's assistant appeared in frame as he steadied himself against a doorframe. The film sold itself as 'the unvarnished truth' about slum housing conditions. Grierson was said to be a trifle miffed by the film; it was certainly actuality, but where was the creativity? To this extent, it appears on the surface of things to be a more 'radical' film than, say, Coalface or Nightmail. Yet closer analysis reveals that it is still based on a rock-hard expectation of consensual values triumphing, a 'revelation' of contemporary social conditions that the 'typical' social democratic Briton will not allow to continue and which, the narrative makes clear, is not being allowed to continue.

Colin McCabe has rightly pointed out the reactionary practice of classic realism in film, which involves 'the petrification of the spectator in a position of pseudo-dominance offered by the metalanguage' of realist conventions, a metalanguage which resolves all contradictions and thus places the viewer outside the realm of contradiction. First of all, Housing problems clearly is not the slum-dwellers' film, in spite of Anstey's later comments. The commentary at the beginning of the film informs the viewer that the film will 'introduce you to some of the people really concerned'. (Who is 'you'?) The film is constructed like one of those journeys into Darkest England which became such a regular feature of social investigation at the end of the nineteenth century, designed to introduce one England to the other in terms which appealed to the charitable instincts and national pride of the audience, which is explicitly constructed as not being slum-dwelling. Certainly, we do see and hear a number of the slum-dwellers, but the constant reference is to experts, either in the shape of Councillor Lauder, chairman of the Stepney housing committee and our guide for most of the film, or in the guise of the architects and engineers whose model flats and estates form the fulcrum between the squalid past and the enlightened future in the structure of the film. Apart from a general assertion that the inner-city problem is a result of a century of neglect, no attempt is made to explain the nature of deprivation in economic terms. The role of the slum-dwellers' appearances is simply anecdotal, to confirm the need for the changes already taking place, without actually challenging either the scope of those changes or the form they are taking. The nearest anyone comes to taking the bit between their teeth is a man who hopes 'the local council will buck their ideas up so that every working man can have decent, hygienic conditions'. This is the cue for Councillor Lauder's assertion that more enlightened authorities have been applying themselves with vigour, but that there has been a problem of where to put people while their new homes are being built and their old ones pulled down. The detailed problem disguises the more fundamental one of basic inequities in the division of wealth, and even the detailed problem, once registered, is marginalized as the film switches immediately to the thought that 'architects, engineers and other experts' have been putting into the design of new estates. The emphasis, in fact, is on the social engineering role that the

193

intelligent elite is already performing in contemporary society. Councillor Lauder predicts that within the next ten years considerable strides will have been made in clearing the worst of the slums.

It is in ways such as these that the documentary realist film, like contemporary feature film, removes the viewer from the realm of contradiction. There is more than just a hint in the film that the enlightened elite knows best; Housing problems makes ironic viewing in the 1980s when the estates which featured in the film as models have in turn been overtaken as the new slums. There is more than a self-conscious hint, too, of educating the middle class, reminiscent of Orwell at his most embarrassing, such as in the assertion that slum-dwellers are not inherently dirty, that if they are housed in decent conditions they will respond. Moreover, one questionable symbol of the experts' brave new world of housing is a caretaker whose job specification seems to include making sure that the working class do not in fact behave like pigs in their new surroundings, by parading the courtyards, keeping the children in order and preventing noise after midnight. The film is full of such little ironies which expose the depth of the class gulf while at the same time congratulating the nation on its enlightenment.(10) The role of the expert social engineer in films such as Housing problems or Enough to eat, which had the eminent zoologist Julian Huxley expounding on the dangers and the waste of the contemporary working-class diet (11), found many echoes in the contemporary written social surveys. Generically, they fit with the Pilgrim Trust's Men without work and with Seebohm Rowntree's Progress and poverty. As such, they provide evidence of the continuing tradition of faith in a socially-conscious intelligentsia and an enlightened bureaucracy in Britain, inherited from the age of Jeremy Bentham, Edwin Chadwick and the Victorian social reformers. This tradition was also to find political impetus in the so-called middle way in politics in the 1930s, those on the right of the Labour Party and the left of the Conservative Party, who were to seize on the ideas of John Maynard Keynes and, eventually, the Beveridge Report, as the unifying principles of a reconstructed hegemony.

It would clearly be wrong, then, simply to dismiss the work of the British Documentary Film Movement as the interest of yet another self-appointed elite who preached to the converted. Though it may certainly be true that the films they made reached very small audiences compared with those of contemporary feature film, yet they were representative of a very influential faction within British society which operated at the core of the hegemonic process, registering social differences yet mediating them in the very act of registration. They had links, moreover, with many of the more avant-garde cultural movements of the day. Grierson's ideas on the need for an industrial art found echoes in contemporary advertising ideas such as those of Ted McKnight Kaufer; 'taking art to the masses' through advertising may have helped to naturalize high culture in a way that the high cultural elite, however much they may have despised the approach of a Grierson or a McKnight Kaufer, had no hope of achieving themselves. Film-makers like Humphrey Jennings, brought on by Grierson in the 1930s, combined interest in film with interest in Surrealism and Mass Observation, the organization founded by Tom Harrisson with the express intention of bridging the gap between governors and governed. During the Second World War Jennings, together with others of the founding fathers of British documentary as well as younger film makers, was to articulate most powerfully on film one of the most sophisticated and enduring of recent British national myths, that of the 'People's War'.

Jennings and the other war-time documentarists were in fact to bring together what had tended to develop separately and fissiparously within the 'Movement' (and it is this which makes the term 'Movement' so problematical), the 'poetic realism' of Cavalcanti and the more educational realism of Anstey, Basil Wright or Paul Rotha. But even before the flowering of the documentary idea began to have a major impact on the commercial film industry there were to be many points of infiltration in terms of techniques and personnel. One only has to compare superficially a film from the early 1930s like Cavalcade with a film from 1939 or 1940 like The stars look down or Love on the dole to notice the change. The insistence on the part of the documentarists that the working-class experience should be included in the national culture - however refracted their own view of the experience of working-class life-styles may have been in fact - and their insistence on realist techniques to gear national consciousness to the industrial age was to be much more influential than a mere counting of the viewers of their films would suggest. Grierson's was a serious and well-focused attempt to come to terms with the role of the artist in mass industrialized society. If he failed to establish for documentary film at that time the large claims he had made for it, his ideas nevertheless stand out as those of one of the most clear-sighted liberals of his generation. He laid down the ground-rules for that revitalization of British commercial cinema, and of television, which were to make them the dominant hegemonic cultural forms of the ensuing decades.

NOTES

1. S. Kracauer, From Caligari to Hitler, 1947.
2. F. Hardy (ed.), Grierson on documentary, revised ed., 1966, p.32.
3. Aero-engine is unfortunately not available for hire. One copy is held by the National Film Archive.
4. Nanook, dir. R. Flaherty, 1922 (Harris Films); Moana, 1923/4, dir R. Flaherty (BFI); Man of Aran, 1934, dir. R. Flaherty (Rank Film Library).
5. See E. Sussex, The rise and fall of British documentary, 1975.
6. Drifters, 1929, dir. J. Grierson, (Central Film Library).
7. 'Road to Wigan Pier Diary', CEJL, vol. 1, 1970, pp. 194-242; see also C. Pawling, 'Orwell and Documentary', Literature and history, 1976, 4, pp. 81-93.
8. Coalface, 1935, dir. A. Cavalcanti (BFI).
9. Nightmail, 1936, dir. H. Watt (Central Film Library); see P. Colls and R. Dodd, 'Representing the Nation, British Documentary Film, 1930 - 1945', Screen, 26, 1985, pp. 21-33.
10. C. McCabe, 'Realism and the Cinema: Notes on Some Brechtian Theses', Screen, 15, 2, 1974.
11. Housing problems, 1935, dir. E. Anstey and A. Elton (BFI).

1. 'TODAY THE STRUGGLE': LITERARY POLITICS AND THE
SPANISH CIVIL WAR

It is clear that no study of British culture in the
interwar period can rest solely on an analysis of the
internal divisions, cohesions and cross-
fertilizations at work within British society alone.
The British way of life depended upon, and
inter-related with, both an international economy and
an international culture. The famous insularity of
British culture had never been by any means total,
and simply could not be in a period when
international trade and international methods of mass
communication were breaking down, at the edges at
least, the possibility of wholly separate national
identities. The increasing dominance of American
culture within the popular culture of Great Britain
was clearly related to the imposing economic strength
of the United States, though cultural theorists might
argue about the precise nature of that relationship.
Moreover, the problems caused by the Great Depression
were problems which affected, to a greater or lesser
extent, the whole of the Western world; other
solutions to these problems, and other analyses of
their causes and impact, could hardly fail to
penetrate. Clearly, dominant culture would have to
adapt substantially if it were to survive the
implications of that penetration. Particularly
difficult was the fact that such an adaptation had to
take place within an international political context
which offered two opposed, holist explanations both
of the international economic situation and of the
role of culture in contemporary society. The
revolution in Russia in 1917, the rise of Stalin to
pre-eminence in the 1920s, the example of what a
planned economy could do in the 1930s, provided the
basis of an alternative-in-being to Liberalism. On
the other hand, the seizure of power by the Fascists
in Italy and, ten years later, by the Nazis in

Germany provided the basis for a polarization of European politics in which Liberalism might soon appear to be irrelevant.

The appeal of the Soviet Union and of Marxism to the middle-class intellectuals in Britain has been well-documented, so much so that the 1930s has become, in one construction, the 'Red Decade'. The notion that the British intellectual establishment turned markedly to the left in the period, however, is at least as much an instance of the remarkable power of self-advertisement of certain individuals within that establishment as an accurate reflection of the numbers that actually turned to Marxism for more than the most temporary solace. Clearly, as R.H. Tawney argued, it was essential that the impact both of contemporary domestic social problems and of the international political polarization be taken into account in any analysis of the cultural future of Britain. For Tawney, 'culture' could only be saved by social revolution, and intellectuals would have to drop their elitist pretensions and jump into socialism with the working-class movement. Even Tawney's appeal, however, was somewhat compromised by his conception of what constituted 'culture'; he was arguing, implicitly at least, for a mere shift of the social parameters within which high culture was enjoyed, rather than admitting the possibility that the shape of culture itself would be redefined by the newly-powerful.(1) The shift to socialism would involve, in other words, much more than a shift in the ownership of culture; it would involve a shift in its very conceptualization. Orwell, somewhat similarly to Tawney, believed in 1936 that in the alliance with the working class, the radical intelligentsia would have 'nothing to lose but its aitches'.(2) In proposing radical shifts in the cultural hierarchy in Britain, however, the middle-class socialists were soon to find that much more was involved than that.

The Russian revolution, of course, provided a model. For one section of the left-wing intelligentsia, an idolatry of the Soviet Union rested on an assumption that the role of the intellectual in Soviet society was assured in a way that it no longer was in Britain, where the intellectual had been forced out of the centre of direct political power by the development of party organizations more populist in their decision-making processes than their predecessors. The dominant Conservative Party of Stanley Baldwin would not think of publicly boasting, as had the dominant Liberal

Party of the mid-nineteenth century, of the host of intellectual talent in its ranks. The Labour Party was dominated by trade unionists who often looked askance at the theorizing pretensions of Tawney, the Coles and the Webbs. In the Soviet Union, by contrast, it appeared that intellectuals like Maxim Gorky still inspired the respect of the whole population. There was also a fascination among the Webbs and their ilk for the intellectual elegance of the Soviet system on paper, in particular with the theoretical sophistication of the idea of democratic centralism, an apparently perfect symbiosis between leaders and led. Among this most directly political section of the middle-class intelligentsia in Britain, support for the Soviet Union was unswerving through most of the 1930s, dismissing evidence of the excesses of the Stalinist programme either as propaganda or as unfortunate necessity in the name of ultimate progress.(3) The fellow-travellers set about arguing the case hoping to use the very methods of mass communications which so worried their liberal elitist contemporaries. Harold Laski, John Strachey and Victor Gollancz formed the Left Book Club, for example, hoping to reach a mass audience. One third of the publications of the LBC were written by Communist Party members. They also carefully avoided any anti-communist material, publishing Orwell's appeal for a cross-class alliance, The road to Wigan pier, but refusing his critique of the tactics of the Communists in Spain, Homage to Catalonia.

The LBC may have ensured that Marxist opinion reached a wider audience than ever before in Britain but it would be easy to overstate its influence. LBC sales have to be seen in the context of the very large rise generally in mass-produced publishing, especially in the context of the beginning of the paperback revolution in the late 1930s. LBC publications were not on sale directly to the public but only through club membership - some 57,000 at its height in 1939 - and even allowing for multiple readership of each copy it seems highly unlikely that readership of any of their publications (let alone the Webbs' dour and lengthy Soviet Russia: a new civilization) reached 150,000.(4) By contrast Penguin Specials offered much the same in terms of coverage of international affairs, though from a much milder and more liberal political perspective; Richard Pares' Russia, for example, sold 273,000 copies. Allen Lane's publishing enterprise was indeed founded on the principle that mass communications, in this case paperback publishing, could go a long way along

the road towards bringing not only liberal politics
but also the liberal concept of culture to the people
as a whole. The mass production of classic literary
texts, in his view, provided cheap culture, not
cheapened culture:

> Plans exist for a whole series of books in
> every field of Art. So that the Pelican books
> bid fair to become the true everyman's library
> of the twentieth century, covering the whole
> range of the Arts and Sciences and bringing the
> finest products of modern thought and art to
> the people ... There are many who despair at
> what they regard as the low level of people's
> intelligence. We, however, believed in the
> existence in this country of a vast reading
> public for <u>intelligent</u> books at a low price,
> and staked everything upon it. The truth of
> this we have proved - and in so doing have
> provided a complete answer to those who despair
> of the state of England.(5)

The success of Penguin and Pelican was, indeed,
evidence of the ability of the literary establishment to adapt to the new conditions of the mass
market, and a slap in the face for the arguments of a
Q.D. Leavis as well as for those of a more radical
bent. Nevertheless, the hard-working entrepreneurs of
British middle-class Marxism pushed energetically not
only for a mass readership but also for the literary
converts from among their own social ranks. In this
they had little, though famous success; the
Auden-Spender group's association with Marxism was to
be short and unhappy, though it may have afforded the
Communist party some useful ammunition. The
Auden-Spender protest, which temporarily allied
itself to the wider Marxist cause, was much more a
struggle within a class than a commitment to
inter-class struggle, much more a generational
dispute brought on by the after-effects of the Great
War. Marxism was for this clique more the solidarity
myth of a group cut off within a class; its villains
were the 'old men' and false values; its heroes were
certainly not the working class but rather
themselves, for being able to see through the
pretensions of the older generation. In this sense,
the stance of the Auden-Spender clique turned out to
be more a manifestation of youth protest than
evidence of cross-class support for the wider social
struggle.
    Many were to toy, some only very temporarily,

with communism but very few from this background were to become committed. It was during the Spanish Civil War, the so-called 'dress rehearsal' for the fuller-scale conflict with the fascists, that major doubts were to be raised about the advisability of commitment to Marxism from within this group. And it was in the threat to traditional concepts of culture and its guardianship that it soon appeared that not even alliance, let alone full commitment, was going to be possible. By the end of the 1930s, Auden, Isherwood and Spender were to move away from any political commitment to neutrality. Of the canonical literary figures who survived the Spanish Civil War, only George Orwell actually moved further to the left as a consequence, though certainly not towards the Russian formulation of Marxism (and, anyway, Orwell had not at this stage joined the literary canon). The rest had either been killed off in Spain or become resigned to political muteness. This switch of allegiances, even if the allegiance to Marxism was never very strong anyway, is significant because it left the former literary radicals with nowhere else to go, ideologically, except to return to the traditionalist fold. Reform of culture was then to continue from within dominant conceptions of culture rather than in the guise of a fundamental attack from without.

The Spanish Civil War raised particularly acute problems for intellectuals brought up in the public-school and Oxbridge tradition. Partly, their view of the war was undoubtedly simplistic, and their early naivete was soon to be heavily dented by the realpolitik they encountered if they actually went to Spain, particularly the impact of the international context in which the war was fought. They were also to find it difficult to adjust to the kind of discipline that successful prosecution of the war demanded. Brought up in the liberal individualist tradition, they found it difficult to subsume their individuality and to accept uncritically the totalitarian tendencies among the Republicans and their sympathizers in Spain and abroad, tendencies which were probably essential if they were to have any chance of winning. In particular, they questioned the role of violence as an agent of political change, however necessary that political change might be in itself. Having rejected the public-school code in face of the hideous slaughter which it had produced on the Western Front, many of them found it difficult, if not revolting, to see socialist ideas becoming as tarnished by bloodshed as

imperial ideas had been by the trenches. Fundamentally, there was an even deeper question involved,
however, and one which articulated together these
others, and that was the problem of the triumph of
mass civilization which seemed to be implied if
either side were to win the conflict in Spain. This
became a central and telling argument in the rapid
retreat from commitment to neutrality.

At this distance in time, the issues of the
Spanish Civil War have again become simplified into a
straightforward struggle between left and right. To
understand the dilemma in which British intellectuals
were placed by the war at the time, it is essential
to reconstruct the context in which the issues were
actually encountered. From the beginning, it should
be pointed out, the political issues were never as
clear-cut in Spain as they seemed at a distance.
Though depicted in so much writing in the earlier
part of the war as a straightforward fight between
fascism and communism, those who went to Spain found
the conflict a great deal more complicated in fact.
Franz Borkenau mentioned in the preface to his
Spanish cockpit: 'I began my studies under the common
delusion that the Spanish revolution was simply an
incident in the fight between Left and Right,
Socialism and Fascism in the European sense of the
words. I have been convinced by observation on the
spot that this is not so'. The comment earned the
immediate suspicions of his reviewer in Left Review
(6), but it was not at all clear that the issue was
simply that of a fascist coup against a properly
elected democratic government. In a sense, Franco's
rebellion was just another coup d'etat in a long
tradition of military intervention in Spanish
politics, and a military coup d'etat was not the same
thing as a fascist takeover. It was in fact the
international context in which this military coup
took place which gave it its apparently central place
in the contemporary European struggle. Spain was
predominantly a rural country in which the landowners
had overwhelming political influence, backed by the
spiritual influence of the all-pervasive Roman
Catholic church. The landowning class provided the
largest number of recruits for the officer corps of
the Army; Roman Catholicism and monarchism were the
guiding principles of the Army as a result. On the
other hand, the fast-developing industrialization of
Spain created an alternative economic and a
juxtaposed political structure to that of rural,
traditionalist Spain. Much of that industrialization,
moreover, was taking place in areas of Spain which

considered themselves to be separate nationally. Catalan as well as Basque nationalism mixed with the development of left-wing thought in the industrialized areas to break Spain effectively into two opposed countries. The Left Review in Britain sought wisdom in Stalin's views on nationalism, the idea that only through participation in the international working-class movement could true national characteristics revive and flourish (7), but the political weakness of the Spanish Left on this issue could not easily be disguised.

In 1923, the Army had seized control under General Primo de Rivera but, as the international economic crisis hit Spain at the end of the decade, King Alfonso felt strong enough to dismiss the generals. The King's intervention came too late, however, to save the monarchy; the Second Republic was formed in 1931. Between 1931 and 1933 a coalition government composed of left and moderate republicans introduced a programme of agricultural and clerical reform designed to break the back of traditionalist support in Spain. As early as 1932, this led to an attempted coup by the Army. At the end of 1933, however, a confederation of right-wing political groups achieved power in the elections and immediately began reversing the legislation of the previous government. A general strike in the Basque region and a separatist rising in Catalonia were put down by the Army, using Foreign Legion and Moorish troops. During these early years of the Second Republic politics had so polarized in Spain that it became clear that electoral victory for either side promised a quite fundamental threat to the other, so that when a left-wing Popular Front government came to power with the elections of February 1936 it was a virtual certainty that the right would move at some point to overthrow the democratic verdict. In June, the frequent calls from the right for the Army to restore conservative values was answered by Franco's rebellion.

At this point, what had occurred was simply a military coup, supported predominantly by rural Spain, a revolt of the landlords and the Roman Catholic church against the godless socialists. The Spanish Fascist Party, the Falange, remained small in number, largely because it was anti-Catholic and anti-monachist in outlook and therefore at odds with mainstream right-wing opinion in Spain. On the Republican side, too, there was as yet no evidence that the war would develop into a confrontation between fascism and communism. The Spanish Communist

Party was small; Spanish left-wing politics, alone in Europe, had developed more strongly in the anarchist than in the Marxist tradition. The right in Spain was divided, certainly, but it was united above all in its Catholicism. The left was more fatally divided: Basque and Catalan nationalists were fighting for autonomy as much as for Republican Spain, while the revolutionary socialists were unwilling to be seen in active collaboration with the reformists who dominated the Republican government. Discipline, both political and military, was consequently difficult to maintain - especially, almost by definition, for the anarchists. Faced with a professional army, the problems of the Republicans were immediate and profound. Nevertheless, after the early days of the coup, and Franco's failure to follow up success, the Republicans began to show real resilience. And as the fighting developed into a stalemate, both Nationalists and Republicans began looking for outside support. It was the arrival of this outside support which changed quite fundamentally the nature of the war in Spain.

In late 1936, the League of Nations accepted the policy of Non-Intervention; the war was a civil conflict and was therefore beyond the purview of collective security. Mussolini and Hitler began supplying the Nationalists almost immediately, however, flying Moorish troops over the Straits of Gibraltar in Ju-52s, for instance, right at the beginning of the rebellion. Throughout the war, German-built and German-piloted air power was to be a most important military asset to Franco. As a result of this support from the fascists, Franco began to adopt the trappings of fascism, and brought the Falange closer to the centre of his entourage than had previously been the case. In response, the Soviet Union began to supply the Republicans, Russia no doubt being fearful of the consequences of a Western Europe wholly dominated by fascism if Franco won. The communists immediately began exerting considerable influence over the development of Republican policy, with disastrous results on the already fissiparous basis of Republican support. Moscow's main target was the Trotskyite and anarchist elements in the Republican ranks. Russian aid was decisive in shaping government policy on this issue. During 1937 the social revolution was halted and, in May, the POUM was put down by the government.(8) Orwell, fighting with the POUM, found himself fleeing Spain not from the Francists but from other Republicans. The politics of the Civil War were, then, a great deal

more complicated than the black-and-white rendition
of events circulated in contemporary newspaper and
pamphlet accounts. The influence of the Russians on
the Republican programme seemed to cast the Soviet
Union in a decidedly reactionary, as well as bullying
vein. As Orwell was to demonstrate, much of the
effect of Russian policy in Spain was to be disguised
by fellow-traveller influence among the left in
Britain.

The mainstream left in Britain was slow to
respond coherently to the situation in Spain. The
Labour Party, led by the pacifist George Lansbury
through the early half of the decade, was still not
entirely clear whether support for the policy of
non-intervention or clear support for the Republicans
was the right course. Only when it became quite clear
that Mussolini and Hitler were breaking the
Non-Intervention agreement did they switch to a more
unequivocal support of the Republicans. Even then,
they were not prepared to contemplate sharing a
platform with other groups on the left to help the
cause. For advocating the establishment of a Popular
Front with the communists and the Independent Labour
Party, Stafford Cripps and Aneurin Bevan were to be
expelled from the party in 1939. The left in Britain
was divided in response to the war then, just as was
the left in Spain. It was agreed that fascism had to
be defeated but there was no firm agreement on a plan
which could accomplish that aim.(9) Given the
complications of the situation which faced
contemporaries looking at Spain from Britain, it is
hardly surprising that the literary reaction to the
war should also be highly convoluted.

From the outset, Left Review was quite
unequivocal in its stand on the issues in Spain. C.
Day Lewis, though not mentioning Spain specifically,
wrote in an issue shortly after the rebellion had
begun that writers must 'act now ... throwing off our
parochialism and political apathy in the interest of
the civilization we have helped to build and can help
to save'. A Popular Front of writers should stir the
imagination of the Labour movement, countering every
tendency in press, fiction, broadcasting and cinema
towards imperialism. 'We must beware of phrases like
"forcing art into the foreground of cultural strife".
Art does not need any such forcing; it is there
already: the question for writers is not "how are we
to disentangle art from cultural strife?" It is "what
direction do we wish this strife to take?"'.(10) The
notion that culture and political action were
inseparable, and that the writer and intellectual had

major roles to play in the shaping of contemporary events, informed every issue of Left Review. Basic to this view was the understanding that the Review had been founded with the intention of making culture safe by rooting it in the life of the people, making it something people knew they could not do without. Yet along with this political commitment went an assumption that the artist and intellectual stood apart from other people, superior in sensitivity and therefore better equipped than most both to judge what was right and to fight for it. Participation in the Spanish struggle was therefore a crucial testing ground of commitment to save culture from fascism, and writing about the issues was as important as fighting:

Here in Catalonia and in Spain the defence of culure is a reality and is achieved with arms in hand ... But behind the lines we are also at the front. We have the same rights and duties here as our brothers who are giving their lives on the battlefield. The artist is a man who lives his life more intensely and vitally than other men – he must therefore take part in the struggle with more means at his disposal than other men.(11)

There can be no doubting, and no room for cynicism in relating the history of Left Review's commitment to the Spanish cause. Not only were the pages of so many issues devoted to the war and its implications, many of its most prominent contributors played a role in the military side of the war as well. Tom Wintringham, co-founder of the Review and a frequent contributor, led the British contingent of the International Brigade. Ralph Fox, John Cornford, Felicia Browne, W. Rowney ('Maro', the cartoonist), Charles Donnelly, Christopher Caudwell, Julian Bell – all frequent contributors to the Review – lost their lives in Spain. Nevertheless, the notion that the Spanish conflict was a 'Poet's War' so urgently pressed by the Review, and which has become such an important entrenched element in the mythology of the 1930s, does not really bear close examination. Certainly, the poetry produced by the war proved enough to fill several anthologies, and there was a flowering of interest in the Spanish romanceros tradition, but it would be an injustice to overplay the role played by artists and intellectuals. Some 2,700 volunteers went from Britain to fight in Spain, technically an illegal act because of the Non-

Intervention legislation. Some 80 per cent of these volunteers were working class in origin, many of them unemployed and politicized by their contact with the National Unemployed Workers Movement or the Minority Movement. Many Welsh miners went to fight alongside the Basque miners in Asturias, a manifest gesture of international solidarity. Of the 2,700, some 540 did not come back, evidence enough both of the commitment of the volunteers and of the ferocity of the fighting.

Nevertheless, if it would be wrong to see the conflict simply as a 'Poet's War', what it did was to provide an opportunity for cross-class solidarity. Apart from the chance to save culture, Spain offered for many middle-class socialists the chance to participate in a way that was not really possible in Britain. Auden and Isherwood, for example, seem to have found it very difficult to translate their politics into social contacts at home. Having themselves rejected the values of the social class into which they were born, they were unable to associate fully with the working class except, perhaps, in a superficial sexual sense; Isherwood was later to re-write his personal history of the 1930s in terms of a frank admission that he and Auden went to Berlin for the boys rather than to see Nazism at first hand.(12) In Spain, however, the difficulties of 'belonging' were to a large extent overcome by the sense of 'communitas', the liminal experience of moving out of the traditions and signifiers of class distinction in Britain. Isherwood and Orwell were apparently in the habit of faking cockney accents in Britain (no doubt to the merriment of real cockneys), while Christopher St John Sprigg liked to be known as Christopher Caudwell. In Spain, however, accent and name had none of the class signification that they had in Britain. While writing The road to Wigan pier, Orwell had been the observer, looking into working-class homes and often being rather revolted in his prudish way by what he saw, yet still longing to belong. He was cut off by being so obviously 'a gentleman'. In Spain, however, he was able to participate. In spite of all his bile when writing about the communists, one has the sense that Orwell in his writings about Spain felt that he 'belonged' for the first and perhaps the only time in his life. This emerges from the very first pages of Homage to Catalonia with his description of his meeting with an Italian militiaman, a cross-class, trans-national contact to which Orwell returned in Looking back on the Spanish Civil War as the central and symbolic experience of the war and the issues involved:

> I hardly know why, but I have seldom seen
> anyone - any man, I mean - to whom I have taken
> such an immediate liking. ... As he went out he
> stepped across the room and gripped my hand
> very hard. Queer, the affection you can feel
> for a stranger! It was as though his spirit and
> mine had momentarily succeeded in bridging the
> gulf of language and tradition and meeting in
> utter intimacy ... One was always making
> contacts of that kind in Spain.(13)

The incident is significant because it stands out so
singly in the work of a man who so rarely mentioned
personal associations in his publications. In the
poem he wrote about the incident two years later,
moreover, the personal liking had sharper political
and social overtones:

> ... the flyblown words that make me spew
> Still in his ears were holy,
> And he was born knowing what I had learned
> Out of books and slowly.(14)

The Spanish Republic was equally willing to help the
intellectuals feel that they belonged. When the
Second Congress of the International Association of
writers met in Valencia and Madrid, they were greeted
with cries of 'Viva la republica! Viva los
intelectuales!', 'that extraordinary, unbelievable
greeting from even the smallest village, the most
isolated group of peasants', Valentine Ackland
recalled.(15) Spender, however, later cringed at the
thought that the Spanish actually believed that this
visitation of intellectuals was going to save them,
and began to acquire an education in the real power
of the poet when villagers asked him to stop the
rebel aircraft machine-gunning them on the roads.(16)
Spender was among those who began to question the
issues at stake in Spain fairly early on in the
conflict, but Valentine Cunningham has argued that
support for the Republicans among writers may not
have been quite so unequivocal as is often supposed
anyway. In his analysis of the Left Review's survey
of writers' opinion on the conflict, Cunningham has
shown quite clearly that the Review fudged the
evidence. The question the Review asked writers was
loaded from the start: 'Are you for or against the
Legal Government and the people of Republican Spain?
Are you for or against Franco and Fascism?' Given the

framing of the question, one would have thought it would take a brave individual to admit to admiring Franco. But when the Review published their findings in a pamphlet entitled Authors take sides, 5 writers were declared as being against the Republic, 127 for and 16 were classed as being neutral. This is highly suspicious, especially the fact that known anti-Republicans like Roy Campbell, Yeats, Wyndham Lewis, Robert Graves and Henry Williamson do not feature on the list at all. Perhaps they were not even asked, or perhaps they opened the questionnaire, saw the Review letterhead and simply chucked the contents in the waste-paper basket. Some of those classed as neutral, moreover, were only questionably so in fact. Eliot, for instance, declared that it was necessary for some authors to stand aside, though his general cultural and political attitudes can leave us in no doubt where the large part of his sympathy lay. Eliot, however, raised an issue in his reply which was to become increasingly the crucial one, namely the exact nature of the relationship between culture and contemporary politics. Though the Left Review assumed that the connection was obvious, Eliot implied that culture should be above politics: this was to become an increasingly credible position to adopt as the war developed for many of the writers here mentioned.(17)

Certainly, the stance of the Left Review was apparently vindicated when Lorca was killed, proving that the Francists were simply barbarians. For Geoffrey Parsons the murder of Lorca symbolized what was involved in Spain if Franco won; the death of great artists but not the death of great art, which would live on because it had become the property of the people left behind:

The   Fascists have   only   one   answer for a
                                        poet
Their stuttering lead syllables prevent
                                  repartee
Putting an end to his stanzas and his
                           fancy speech. ...

But this side of the line, and secretly
                        that side
His friends, the people, the peasants
                    remember his songs
And chant them through Spain. And to them
                    there will be no end.(18)

At the same time, many saw victory for the Republicans just as clearly as a threat to culture. Anti-clericalism on the Republican side was deeply offensive not just to Roman Catholics and Anglo-Catholics such as Waugh, Greene and Eliot but also to other religious men who had a great deal of sympathy with the Republican cause. Ralph Bates carefully pointed out that works of art were saved before a church was burned, and that the companeros always politely asked neighbours to move out of their homes before they applied the torch, but this was hardly the point.(19) Auden returned to Britain after just three months in Spain and refused to talk about his experiences. It seems clear from his later comments that his developing Christian beliefs left him profoundly at odds with Republican anti-clerical sentiment. Christianity, even in its somewhat exotic Spanish Catholic form, appeared to traditionalists to protect the long European Christian cultural inheritance. The same could hardly be said of the uncompromisingly anti-clerical left, ransacking churches and murdering priests. For the revolutionaries in Spain, anti-clericalism was an absolutely essential cleansing operation to break the overweening hegemonic power of the Church, but the results left many of their supporters in the British Left feeling a little queasy.

For this hypothetical 'typical' British intellectual, moreover, both sides in Spain, as mass movements, presented potential threats to culture. Geoffrey Grigson's highly ambiguous reponse to the Left Review questionnaire is a case in point. Grigson declared himself to be 'equivocal enough to be against, politically, and not for, to fear and distrust any mass in its own control'. The Review simply marked him down as 'for the government' but he had clearly entered a very big reservation.(20) The tendency of the war to push intellectual opinion towards the left, in other words, should be offset by the evidence that there was an equally marked ambivalence among many brought up in the Western liberal tradition when faced with alternative forms of totalitarianism and told to choose. Some stalwarts such as Leonard Woolf tried to reconcile liberal culture with Stalinist communism. In Barbarians at the gates, Woolf wrote that the ultimate end of Stalin's policy was not the establishment of a classless society but the widening and enrichment of the individual's existence, the creation of an association in which the free development of each was the condition for the free development of all.(21) On first reading this looks like simple Marxism, but in the context of Left Book Club publishing as a whole it reads more like intellectual sleight of hand designed to appeal to a liberal readership. What was in question was not just what happened to individualism but also what happened to the high cultural tradition. Stephen Spender is perhaps the most obvious example of this ambivalence in action. The book he wrote under the title Approaches to Communism eventually appeared under the title Forwards from Liberalism. A drawing-back from positive commitment was a basic theme of the book, for Spender insisted that there was 'a point where the clerk must insist on an absolute justice', and Marxism appeared to him to refuse to allow this. The Left Review commented that the 'disinterestedness to which Spender attaches so much importance is in fact the intellectual's fear of committing himself finally, a clinging still to the privileges of isolation'. This the reviewer put down to the author's lack of knowledge of the basic works of Marxism.(22)

Spender's drawing-back from commitment did not dissuade the Communist Party from encouraging him to go off to Spain. He later recalled, probably apocryphally, that Harry Pollitt told him the best way he could help was to go off and get himself killed, because the cause needed a martyr. In Spain, Spender soon grew dispirited with the propaganda job he was doing and began to write material which was hardly flattering to the Republican cause. In particular, he began to disassociate culture from politics:

Far too many writers and artists have been driven away from the centre of their real interests towards some outer rim of half-creating, half-agitation. A great deal is said about saving culture but the really important thing is to have a culture to save.(23)

Directly, Spender was now attacking the core of the Left Review position:

However much we admire the actions of a John Cornford or a Rupert Brooke, poetry is not the same as action and a poem is not the same as a political thesis.(24)

Orwell came to a similar kind of conclusion but by a

rather different route, believing that both communism and fascism presented the ultimate threat to culture - not so much in Orwell's case to the culture of high art but to the lived culture of a society as a whole - by the ability of the totalitarians to rewrite history to suit themselves.

Writers from a background such as that of Spender or Orwell also had to cope with the fact that the experience of the Great War had severely undermined the notion that violence was a legitimate means of securing change. We have already discussed the effect of the Great War on those public-school men just too young to have fought. For Isherwood war was the 'test', and for men of his social class and age the conflict in Spain brought much of the old neurosis back to the surface: 'are you really a man?'.(25) Orwell certainly felt that the Great War accounted in part for the mesmeric effect that the Civil War had on him:

> The dead men had their revenge after all. As the (Great) war fell back into the past, my particular generation, those who had been 'just too young', became conscious of the vastness of the experience they had missed. You felt yourself a little less than a man because you had missed it. ... I am convinced that part of the reason for the fascination that the Spanish Civil War had for people of my age was that it was so like the Great War ... I know that what I felt when I first heard artillery fired 'in anger', as they say, was at least partly disappointment. It was so different from the tremendous, unbroken roar that my senses had been waiting for for twenty years.(26)

But the basic problem of writing about violence as an acceptable way of securing change created a real tension in writing about the war. After all, Owen, Sassoon and Blunden had, in the trenches, established anti-war poetry as the norm in place of the jingoistic bombast of the 'Vitae Lampada' kind. Those seeking to confirm the necessity of fighting to stave off fascism had to break through not only the conceptual difficulty the collective memory of the Great War bequeathed but also the form of war poetry that had been established by the trench poets. Jack Lindsay produced an aggressive argument for the form of mass declamation to replace the introverted and individualized style of contemporary bourgeois poetry. Though his 'On Guard for Spain' reads now as

a turgid piece of poetry, it undoubtedly had very
much more impact in the 1930s when read dramatically
to a mass gathering with the war actually in
progress. In Left Review, he argued that:

... the elegists of bourgeois decay, however
witty, must sink with the fading audience
unless they can make the leap which will bring
them to solidarity with the workers.(27)

The need to fuse actively with a proletarian
audience, to help to create a Popular Front of artist
and worker, was a central concern of left-wing
writers of the time. John Cornford was perhaps the
most successful of those who tried the leap to become
the Rupert Brooke of the Spanish Civil War. 'A Letter
from Aragon' is a poem still very much in the Owen
mould, with its somewhat detached description of an
undignified funeral and its ironic repetition of the
theme 'this is a quiet sector of a quiet front'. The
political message, that there is simply no
alternative to fighting to stop Fascism, sits rather
crudely on the end of the poem. Cornford, in other
words, was still stuck with the emotional legacy of
the trench poets.(28) In 'Full Moon at Tierz',
however, he managed to break the mould. In this poem,
it is the historical context and contemporary
politics which justify the conclusion that 'freedom
was never held without a fight'; personal fear and
loneliness disappear, 'fuse in the welded front our
fight preserves'.(29)
    Auden did something similar to Cornford in the
single most famous British poem of the war, 'Spain'.
Again, it is the historical context which makes the
war significant and which provides the poem with its
Marxist framework. But the poem then hares off at an
Audenesque tangent, providing reasons for going to
Spain, as well as visions of the future, which are
hardly Marxist in their tendency. One element which
really disturbed Orwell was the apparent cynicism of
the poem's acceptance of violence (30):

Today the deliberate increases in the
                    chances of death,
The conscious acceptance of guilt in the
                    necessary murder.(31)

Though the poem does evince a sense of the
significance of the war in Spain, and an acceptance
that today's struggle is absolutely necessary, there
is an ambivalence of tone and a detachment of style

in the verse which is typical of Auden's poetry as a
whole, and which makes it difficult to view him as a
political writer in the sense that, say, Cornford
was. Spender, moreover, did not even try to break out
of the Owen mould. Rather he used the authoritative
Audenesque imperative form to underline the
pointlessness of it all:

> Consider his life which was valueless
> In terms of employment, hotel ledgers,
> news files.
> Consider. One bullet in ten thousand kills
> a man.
> Ask. Was so much expenditure justified
> On the death of one so young, and so silly
> Lying under the olive trees, O world,
> O death?(32)

The experience of the Great War, and the influence of
the form of war poetry established by the trench
poets was not something lightly to be cast aside in
the search for new positive commitments. Along with
increasing worries about the cultural future if
either side in Spain won, the increasing violence
helped to accelerate the drift back from commitment.
      Orwell later wrote about Cornford's 'Full Moon at
Tierz' that if you compared the last lines of the
poem ('Raise the red flag triumphantly / For
Communism and for Liberty') with the last lines of
Sir Henry Newbolt's 'Vitae Lampada' ('Play up, play
up and play the game'), you could see that
emotionally they were exactly the same.(33) For
Orwell this proved the possibility of 'building a
socialist on the bones of a blimp', of transmuting
old loyalties into new ones. By the end of the
Spanish Civil War, however, the move to find new
emotional, social and political identities among
writers from the same background as Orwell had been
severely dented. Though it is clear that there could
be no return to the loyalties of the 'old men', the
tendency towards radicalization had been all but
halted. As the Second World War loomed, the emphasis
was to be increasingly on the cultural worries that
such a conflict implied and, consequently, on a
process of consolidation rather than continued
confrontation. The effect of the Spanish Civil War on
the literary establishment, finally, was not to
radicalize but, if anything, to produce a drift back
towards centrist politics. Marxism, as much as
fascism, was seen to be a threat to a tradition
which, thrown into perspective by the conflict in

Spain, appeared worth saving after all. Orwell spent what time was left before the Second World War 'spilling the Spanish beans', railing as much against the Soviet Union as against Nazi Germany or Fascist Italy. Auden retreated into a political muteness. In the vacuum of political commitment among the intellectuals that ensued, made even more pronounced by the infamous Nazi-Soviet pact of August 1939, a new perspective on the British cultural tradition began to emerge, a quiet re-assessment of where Britain had come from and where she was going. With no alternative left on offer, the intellectual establishment prepared itself to defend by adaptation what it had inherited, in order to face the monumental struggle which, the Spanish Civil War had made quite clear, would threaten the most basic and unquestionable tenets of the British cultural tradition.

NOTES

1. R.H. Tawney, Equality, 1931, repr. 1964, p.230.
2. G. Orwell, The road to Wigan pier, 1937, repr. 1980, p.230.
3. D. Caute, The fellow travellers, 1973.
4. S. Samuels, 'The Left Book Club', Journal of contemporary history, 1, 2, 1966.
5. A. Lane, 'Books for the Millions', Left Review, 3, 16, 1938.
6. V. Ackland, 'Review of Borkenau's Spanish Cockpit', Left Review, 3, 8, 1937, pp. 484-6.
7. E. Rickward, 'Stalin on the Nationalist Question', Left Review, 14, 2, 746-9.
8. R. Carr, Spain, 1966; S. de Madariaga, Spain, 1961; G. Brennan, The Spanish labyrinth, 1967; S.G. Payne, The Spanish revolution, 1967; P. Preston, The coming of the Spanish Civil War, 1983; R.A.H. Robinson, The origins of Franco's Spain, 1970; H. Thomas, The Spanish Civil War, 1961.
9. J.F. Naylor, Labour's international policy, 1969; B. Pimlott, Labour and the left in the 1930s, 1977.
10. C. Day Lewis, 'English Writers and a Popular Front', Left Review, 2, 13, 1936, pp. 671-4.
11. Editorial, Left Review, 1937, p.857.
12. C. Isherwood, Christopher and His Kind, 1977, p.10.
13. G. Orwell, Homage to Catalonia, 1938, repr. 1980, pp. 1-2.

14.   G. Orwell, 'Looking Back on the Spanish Civil War', Collected essays, 1961, p. 223.

15.   V. Ackland, Daily Worker, 21 July 1937, p.7.

16.   S. Spender, World within world, 1953, pp. 208-9.

17.   V. Cunningham, 'Neutral? 1930s Writers and Taking Sides', in F. Gloversmith (ed.), Class, culture and social change, 1980, pp. 45-69.

18.   G. Parsons, 'Lorca', repr. in V: Cunningham, (ed.), Spanish Civil War verse, 1980, pp. 206-7.

19.   R. Bates, 'Companero Sagesta Burns A Church', Left Review, 2, 13, 1936, pp. 631-7.

20.   'Neutral? 1930s Writers and Taking Sides'.

21.   L. Woolf, Barbarians at the gates, 1939.

22.   R. Swinger, 'Spender's Approach to Communism', Left Review, 3, 2, 1937, pp. 110-3.

23.   S. Spender, The new realism, 1939, pp. 23-4.

24.   S. Spender, 'Poetry', Fact, 1937, p. 21.

·25.   C. Isherwood, Lions and shadows, (1938. repr. 1968), pp. 46-7.

26.   G. Orwell, 'My Country Right or Left', CEJL, vol. 1, 1968, p. 537-8.

27.   J. Lindsay, 'A Plea for Mass Declamation', Left Review, 3, 9, 1937, pp. 511-7.

28.   J. Cornford, 'A Letter from Aragon', Spanish Civil War verse, pp. 16-7.

29.   J. Cornford, 'Full Moon at Tierz', Spanish Civil War verse, pp. 130-2.

30.   G. Orwell, 'Inside the Whale', CEJL, vol. 1, 1968, p. 516.

31.   W.H. Auden, 'Spain', Spanish Civil War verse, pp. 97-100.

32.   S. Spender, 'Ultima Ratio Regum', Spanish Civil War verse, p. 341.

33.   G. Orwell, 'My Country Right or Left', CEJL, vol. 1, 1968, p. 540.

2. THE APPROACH OF WAR

A sense of doom is perhaps the most pervasive of the
themes that dominate the literature of the interwar
period. Certainly, the reconstruction of the period
by those literary figures who survived it centres
above all on the sense of threat that hung over
contemporary writing. Stephen Spender wrote later of
'a fatality which I felt to be overtaking our
civilization and which influenced our thinking more
explicitly than was generally realized'.(1) John
Lehmann, among many others, also remembered that
'like so many of my contemporaries, I was haunted by
the feeling that time was running out ... '.(2) This
was not just retrospective prophecy: it is difficult
to pick up any book written in the interwar years
without being immediately aware of the sense of
threat, of writers who, in Lehmann's words, 'crouch
paralysed as the hawk descends'.

This sense of threat was an amalgam of many
factors but, analytically, it can be reduced to its
three major component parts. First, there was the
threat of mass culture drowning out the high cultural
tradition, the concern of the cultural theorists like
Richards and Leavis, as well as Eliot, Waugh, Greene
and Lawrence in their various ways. Second, there was
the threat of economic and social crisis in the
aftermath of the Great War, associated particularly
in the literary canon with writers like Lewis Grassic
Gibbon, Walter Greenwood and George Orwell. Indeed
for both these sets of writers it was the threat - in
whatever guise the threat appeared - that became the
primary reason for writing. Orwell explained that:

In a peaceful age, I might have written ornate
or merely descriptive books, and might have
remained almost unaware of my political
loyalties. As it is, I have been forced into

becoming a sort of pamphleteer.(3)

But above all hung the threat of war, a threat which indeed unified all the other threats and gave them concrete form. We have already noted the major contemporary temptation to look back to pre-1914 as the blissful Golden Age of pre-Depression and pre-mass society, to see the Great War as a barrier cutting off the present from the 'real' roots and the 'real' condition of England. Indeed, this was at the same time the most abiding and the most unifying myth of the interwar period, either in direct reference back to pre-1914 - in the case of, for example, Orwell or Lawrence in literature or Anthony Asquith in film - or in the comparison implied by inversion, as in Eliot or Auden. Along with this reaction to the Great War, however, developed an equally significant sense of future-shock, a concern with the appalling prospects of a war fought with a more destructive technology even than the Great War, and against an enemy which seemed to personify the threat of mass culture. It was this concern at the possibility of being trapped between two major European catastrophes that lent a particular frustration and fear to the interwar structure of feeling, adding weight and point to both the cultural and social fears.

With all these complicating inter-reactions, an unequivocal response to fascism among the intellectual elite could not have developed early on in the period. As we have seen, reactions to the use of violence in the Great War made it difficult to absorb the political necessity of renewed violence to cope with the unprecedented political threat of fascism: in the Spanish context writers like Auden and Spender found the conundrum simply too difficult to solve. Neither was it altogether clear that fascism represented a greater ideological threat than any other contemporary mass movement. Many of the assorted strands of fascist theory could, after all, touch a chord among the hegemonic myths of English culture. The fascist concept of the importance of the pre-industrial organic community, for example, was not far removed from the 'real England' of the pastoral tradition with all its ideological implications for interwar Britain. In association with the idea of England as 'one big family' pastoralism echoed the fascist concept of race in some of its aspects. Anti-semitism, too, had strong cultural roots in British culture: T.S. Eliot, most famously, was to pen some verse which was to seem particularly obnoxious once Hitler had finally

218

made anti-semitism unacceptable. It is possible to find at least some associations with fascism in British literary people of most political persuasions: this does not mean at all that they were fascists, merely that fascism cannot be dismissed as a wholly new and superficial growth in European culture; it fed on deep roots.

To argue that there were similarities and even points of direct linkage between so much of British mainstream culture and fascist theory is not to argue, of course, that Britain could have gone the way of the New World Order and the Final Solution; there was an inter-connecting mesh of other strands in British culture to prevent any such possibility. Fascism developed from the same cultural traditions that produced so much of the 'common sense' of interwar Britain but there were important differences. The major difference in the British experience of the interwar years was that the hegemonic crisis that enveloped countries like Germany never reached quite the same proportions in Britain. The British left, divided though it was, never broke up as it did in those countries that went fascist. As an intellectual framework, Marxism never looked like denting the libertarian tradition of British socialism.

The Labour Party continued to develop as the only viable mouthpiece of working-class interests but also continued to develop as a Party which attempted to appeal on cross-class terms. The Party moved further and further to the political centre, picking up votes from the moribund Liberal Party in the process. Though it split disastrously in the 1931 crisis, within four years Labour was producing electoral results that demonstrated that the wounds had been only superficial. There was no left-wing alternative, in the context of interwar Britain, to a policy of attracting non-socialists to the notion of a consensual sea-change in the nature of the state. If revolutionary socialism was only a minor force in Britain, it is also true that no group preaching revolutionary reaction had any real chance of establishing itself either. The Conservative Party continued to build up its support within the lower-middle class, that section of the social formation which proved most likely to move to fascism in other countries. The British lower-middle class did not fare as badly in the Depression as many of their continental counterparts, and the Conservative Party of 'Honest Stan' Baldwin made very conscious efforts to image the lower-middle class family as its own peculiar political property.(4)

Nevertheless, among some writers, the associations with fascism were particularly troublesome. D.H. Lawrence perhaps came closer to a proto-fascism than any other writer of the period. His attitude towards industrialization, his fascination with the idea of the charismatic leader (especially in conjunction with his sexual politics) took him towards a stance which, in retrospect at least, appears highly questionable. If Lawrence had developed further along the line that he seemed to be taking when he wrote The plumed serpent, with its theme of a mystical communion with the past, then it seems unlikely that his place in the literary canon would have been quite so secure as it now appears. Other writers, notably Henry Williamson, G.K. Chesterton, Beverley Nichols and P.G. Wodehouse, did toy more directly with fascism. They were, of course, merely naive in so doing, and many later recanted, but this is not the point; for them, fascism offered a sort of order, authority and stability in an increasingly anarchic world, in the same way that for others of their background (and again sometimes only temporarily) the Roman Catholic church or Karl Marx offered a similar order and stability. The point in short is that the fascist path appeared to some, if only temporarily, to offer an authoritative alternative way forward for traditional values. It seemed to offer, in some of its manifestations at least, an embodiment of those traditional values. Only the passage of events was to prove that there was more to fascism than simply a defence of conservative values or making the trains run on time. Traditionalism was only one aspect of fascism, and this traditionalism was transmuted by the full context of fascist theory.

The conceptualization of fascism as a threat was also overlaid for much of the period by the contemporary economic conditions. It could be argued that the impact of mass unemployment tended to concentrate working-class militancy in the earlier part of the period on the domestic rather than on the possible foreign threat. Middle-class left-wingers, perhaps because they were not so immediately affected by unemployment, may have seen earlier than most on the left the threat being posed abroad. (Orwell's articulation of the domestic and foreign threats in The road to Wigan pier is a typical case in point.) The linkage between the threat posed by economic dislocation at home and the threat posed by fascism abroad, moreover, was to put the left in a real tactical bind. Appeasement was seen as British capitalism turning in its hour of need to fascism for help. The left, though condemning fascism, refused to support the government's rearmament policy on the grounds that the weight of the rearmed state might be turned on the people. Without a thoroughgoing social revolution, the argument went, any decision by the government to resist fascism would only result in Britain herself going fascist. John McGovern, a Glasgow MP of the Independent Labour Party, typified the hard-left line in arguing that there was no need for the British to go abroad to fight fascists when there were many fascists sitting on the government front bench.(5)

Orwell's Spanish experience had brought him to a similar conclusion to that of McGovern and the hard left. Orwell's condemnation of communist policy against the POUM led him to argue that only a socialist state could fight fascism without becoming fascist itself. In 1938 and 1939, Orwell seems to have been preparing to help to sabotage a British war effort with anti-war literary propaganda. The left, however, came near to an outright split on this issue. The attitude of McGovern or Orwell found perhaps its nearest campaigning expression in Stafford Cripps' attempts to form a People's Front to bring down Chamberlain in order to face Hitler. But to the pacifist element in the Labour Party war was wrong on any terms. Though this pacifist element was virtually crushed during the party's debates on how to respond to Mussolini's invasion of Ethiopia, the dominant right in the party would not accept Cripps' alternative plan of sharing a platform with the communists. Their view was that the failure of the concept of collective security through the League of Nations, and the failure of the Republicans in Spain, proved that there was no realistic alternative to fighting for liberal social democracy – even Chamberlain's variety – if the alternative was the risk that fascism might triumph. It was with this attitude that the British left was to go somewhat reluctantly to war. They were eventually shorn of the need to answer embarrassing criticism from the communists when the Soviets signed a pact with Hitler in August 1939.(6)

Quite apart from these cultural and political complications, however, a generation which had been brought up with a view of war very different from that of the pre-1914 generation found it very difficult to make the adjustment necessary to face the fact that only war would stop Hitler. In Spain,

poets like John Cornford had tried to alter the
structural parameters which Wilfred Owen, Siegfried
Sassoon and others had helped to establish as
normative in thinking about war but, as we have seen,
it proved an almost impossible task. Fascism might
well be a threat to culture, but so too was war
itself. Sidney Keyes encapsulated the frustration of
the inevitable, the pressure of basic political
facts, in his poem 'War Poet':

> I am the man who looked for peace and found
> My own eyes barbed.
> I am the man who groped for words and found
> An arrow in my hand.
> I am the builder whose firm walls surround
> A slipping land.
> When I grow sick or mad
> Mock me not nor chain me:
> When I reach for the wind
> Cast me not down:
> Though my face is a burnt book
> And a wasted town.(7)

The Great War had been bad enough, with the appalling
waste and carnage of the trenches, with the massive
extension of state power which had so affected
traditional liberalism and civil liberties in the
mobilization of the population to the demands of
total war. The war of the future, however, would be
even worse. The contemporary revolution in weapons
technology, especially the advent of the long-range
strategic bomber, would bring the war literally into
everyone's home.

Bomber theory in the interwar period rested on
the assumption that, next time round, war would be
decided not so much by uniformed armed forces but
rather by the will to war of the nation as a whole.
Rather than go for long-drawn-out battles of
attrition as in the trenches in the Great War, the
bomber would attack directly the sources of
production, the factories, without whose produce the
armed forces could not operate. More than this, it
was believed that civilians were inherently weak on
morale, that bombing would cause rioting in the
streets, forcing the opposing government to sue for
peace. The next war would consist primarily, in other
words, of an overwhelming knock-out blow from the
air. In essence, bomber theory was yet another
example of that depressed faith in the masses that
coloured so much of the established mode of thinking
in the years after the Great War and the Russian

Revolution. The result was a state of mind not far removed from contemporary fear of the effect of nuclear weaponry, but with the important difference that this state of mind was as common on the right in Britain as on the left. We now know that strategic bombing was incapable of inflicting the kind of moral paralysis that pre-war pundits assumed would occur, though the Blitz and the Air Offensive against Germany proved that air war was capable of inflicting massive damage. To the interwar generation, however, the threat from the air was an ever-present and all-pervasive one. The economic dislocation caused by the Depression, the class friction that sometimes seemed to be just a policeman's baton away from spilling over into open warfare, seemed evidence enough that the modern industrial economic and social structure had become inherently unstable. What indeed would happen if bombers appeared over Jarrow or Merthyr? It was against the background of the General Strike of 1926 that Stanley Baldwin chose to ask the House of Commons rhetorically: 'Who does not know that if another great war comes our civilization will fall with as great a crash as that of Rome?' Neville Chamberlain's final justification in the House of Commons for the Munich settlement of 1938 was the prospect of what the next war would be like, of 'people burrowing underground, trying to escape from poison gas, knowing that at any hour of the day or night death or mutilation was ready to come upon them'.(8)

The next war was a pervasive theme in popular literature, constructing for a mass-reading public an apocalyptic future. I.F. Clarke lists 133 books published in English in the interwar period dealing with the war of the future, either popularizing new military theories or in the form of predictions of what would happen. What stands out even from just a casual reading of some of these books is the extraordinary regularity with which the tie-up is made between the war of the future and social revolution, especially the socialist threat (with titles like The red fury, The red tomorrow, Red ending, Red invader). (9) For the political right and centre air war, as it was perceived at the time, was indeed a frightening prospect. All that they had worked for in terms of blurring the harsh edges of class conflict might be simply ripped apart in a few hours by bombers arriving unannounced out of a clear blue sky.

If popular politics and popular literature helped to project the war of the future in terms of a revolutionary destructive potential, socially and culturally, then cinema also kept the threat at the forefront of the popular imagination. Newsreel featured air war in China, in Abyssinia and in Spain: it made exciting footage from exotic locations, and that was its entertainment value, but it also brought the prospect home as no amount of theorizing could do. Over shots of ruined Guernica the newsreel commentator intoned: 'this was a city. These were homes like yours'.(10) Until the mid-1930s, the government would not even mention publicly that they were considering Air Raids Precautions, for fear that the very phrase would spark off public panic. In the late 1930s, however, newsreel was to play a most important educative role in Air Raids Precautions, supporting the government's attempt to allay public anxiety by demonstrating that simple precautions would offset the worst of the danger. In fact, footage of individuals footling about with stirrup pumps and buckets of sand might well have had the opposite effect. Certainly, there is little evidence that the public either understood or believed government propaganda in this area by the time war broke out. In 1939, the government employed the GPO Film Unit to make a film about ARP to educate the public. They were not, however, prepared for the realist techniques that the documentarists would bring to bear. When it appeared, the film was considered potentially so frightening that the Home Office demanded radical changes. The film was re-edited as If war should come For all its bland assurances that the government had made satisfactory preparations, the pictures of empty suburban streets, abandoned vehicles and the sound of air-raid sirens still proved too much for the government; it was withdrawn soon after issue and never put on public release.(11) By way of contrast Paul Rotha's Peace film, a moving poster designed to show the appalling consequences of another war and calling for a popular outcry to force the government to start disarmament talks, was the subject of censorship by the British Board of Film Censors. The huge publicity surrounding the attempted censorship – disarmament was, after all, official government as well as opposition policy – led to its eventual distribution to an estimated two million people.(12)

Nevertheless, the Conservative Party carefully nurtured its links with the newsreel companies, understanding the significance of the new form of political communication in a way that no other political party of the time was able to do. In no

sphere was this more important than in defence and
foreign policy. Throughout the 1930s, newsreel
consistently and faithfully followed the intricacies
of government rearmament and appeasement policies,
converting Stanley Baldwin and Neville Chamberlain
almost to cinema stars in their own right in the
process. The two leading Conservatives became, in the
hands of the newsreel companies, champions of
honesty, integrity and common sense. The culmination
of this campaign was the extraordinary cinematic
publicity that surrounded the Munich Agreement, with
Chamberlain hailed as the epitome of the sensible
values of the man in the street: 'History will thank
God as we do now, that in our hour of need there
appeared such a man - Neville Chamberlain!'.(13)
Newsreel's bizarre elision of 'entertainment' and
'real' fears prompted C. Day Lewis's famous sneer at
the new mass medium:

Enter the dream house, brothers and sisters,
leaving
Your debts asleep, your history at the door:
This is the home for heroes, and this loving
Darkness a fur you can afford.

Oh, look at the warplanes! Screaming hysteric
treble
In the long power-dive, like gannets they
fall steep.
But what are they to trouble -
These silver shadows to trouble your watery,
womb-deep sleep?

See the big guns, rising, groping, erected
To plant death in your world's soft womb.
Fire-bud, smoke-blossom, iron seed projected
Are these exotics? They will grow nearer
home:

Grow nearer home - and out of the dream-house
stumbling
One night into a strangling air and the flung
Rags of children and thunder of stone
niagaras tumbling,
You'll know you slept too long.(14)

The theme of having 'slept too long' was one
which pervaded William Cameron Menzies' production of
H.G. Wells's Things to come, a film which began with
the destruction of civilization in a future war
(pictured as only four years away from the vantage

225

point of 1936). A surprise attack from the air wipes
out a city centre - a cinema's facade crumples under
the bombs - and the social tissue disintegrates
leaving the war to be kept going by noticeably
Mussolini-like warlords such as the Chief. Wells,
however, as the eternal optimist, saw collective
security providing a way out, in the very year that
the concept of collective security was being
destroyed in the international response to
Mussolini's invasion of Abyssinia. Wells constructed
for his audience an optimistic view of the
consequences in which the airmen appear as saviours
of the world, using their overwhelming technology to
stop the war. The self-destructive possibilities of
contemporary weaponry are ranged argumentatively
against the possibility that technology can be used
beneficially. But these destructive possibilities are
also ranged argumentatively against the notion of the
inevitability of technological progress, given man's
desire to know, whatever the dangers might be. At the
end of the film, as a future trip into space comes up
against popular disapproval, there can be no question
that the audience is invited literally to reach for
the stars rather than to protest at the malevolent
possibilities. The horrors of a possible air war are
thus recontextualized as a soluble side-issue in an
endless and inevitable search for knowledge and
progress.(15)
     For the literary left, however, this
self-destructive aspect of modern weaponry provided a
kind of paradigm of the self-destructive impulse of
contemporary bourgeois society. For John Betjeman,
for instance, it was the irony that it was precisely
the dormitory areas of the new lower-middle class
suburbia that would be the target of the bombers
which provided the black humour of the lines:

   Come, friendly bombs and fall on Slough.
   It isn't fit for humans now.(16)

For Orwell, too, the superficial and the slick in
contemporary Britain, the elements that were sending
the nation to sleep, were in for a dreadful
awakening. But so too was the 'real' England, cut
off from the England of the dole queues. As he
returned from the trauma and the excitement of the
war in Spain, he concluded:

   The industrial towns were far away, a smudge of
   smoke and misery hidden by the curve of the
   earth's surface. Down here it was still the

England I had known in my childhood: ... the
slow-moving streams bordered by willows, the
green bosom of the elms ... ; and then the huge
peaceful wilderness of outer London ... the
posters telling of cricket matches and Royal
weddings, the men in bowler hats, the pigeons
in Trafalgar Square, the red buses, the blue
policemen - all sleeping the deep, deep sleep
of England, from which I sometimes fear that we
shall never wake till we are jerked out of it
by the roar of the bombs.(17)

In Keep the aspidistra flying, the bomber appears as
a figment of Gordon Comstock's fantasy, smashing the
most obvious manifestation of the consumer society,
the advertising hoarding across the street from
Gordon's bookshop:

For can you not see, if you know how to look,
that behind that slick self-satisfaction, that
tittering fat-bellied triviality, there is
nothing but a frightful emptiness, a secret
despair? The great death-wish of the modern
world. Suicide pacts. Heads stuck in gas-ovens
in lonely maisonettes. French letters and amen
pills. And the reverberations of future wars.
Enemy aeroplanes flying over London; the deep
threatening hum of the propellers, the
shattering thunder of the bombs.(18)

Noticeably Orwell, at his most desolate, comes up
with yet another of his lists of pet hates in
forecasting Armageddon. But it is the bomber, the
image of the war of the future, that becomes the
engine of destruction of materialist superficiality,
a cure worse than the disease.

Again, it is Orwell's concern with what he sees
as the superficiality, 'the tittering fat-bellied
triviality' of his times, that gives the key to his
frustration at the refusal of the rest of the country
to see things as he does. The underlying arrogance of
his stance is only justified in retrospect by the
fact that he did actually foresee that war was
coming. In Coming up for air, the bomber again plays
a most prominent role, shadowing the train as George
Bowling commutes into town ('Christ, how could they
miss us?', he wonders). It is the bomber which quite
literally smashes Bowling's pre-1914 fantasy when the
RAF drops a bomb on Lower Binfield by mistake. The
accident leaves him pondering a frightening future of
fascists fighting fascists, armed with all the modern

weapons available to the totalitarian state:

> It's all going to happen. All the things you've
> got at the back of your mind, the things you
> tell yourself are just a nightmare or only
> happen in foreign countries. The bombs, the
> food queues, the rubber truncheons, the barbed
> wire, the coloured shirts, the slogans, the
> enormous faces, the machine-guns squirting out
> of bedroom windows. It's all going to
> happen.(19)

By 1939, Orwell appears to have been convinced not
only that the dreaded war was indeed going to happen
but that he, on the basis of his experience both in
the depressed areas and in Spain, was going to have
none of it: Britain was on the road to becoming a
fascist state. What resolved the issue for Orwell,
however, between 1939 and 1940, was his fundamental
patriotism. The Nazi-Soviet pact of August 1939 was
the excuse for his change of heart. In 'My Country
Right or Left' one can almost sense his glee that
everything that he had been saying about both the
communists and the fascists since the Spanish Civil
War was true: in the last resort there was nothing to
choose between them. In The road to Wigan pier,
Orwell had mentioned that the road from Mandalay to
Wigan, the process of his switch to socialism, had
been a long and arduous one. It could also be said
that the road back to patriotism after the Spanish
Civil War had been equally difficult. But now it was
English 'decency' against totalitarianism and, in
such circumstances, he was unable to let his country
down:

> But let no one mistake the meaning of this.
> Pariotism has nothing to do with conservatism.
> ... Only revolution can save England, that has
> been obvious for years, but now the revolution
> has started, and it may proceed quite quickly
> if only we can keep Hitler out. Within two
> years, maybe a year, if only we can hang on, we
> shall see changes that will surprise the idiots
> who have no foresight. I dare say the London
> gutters will have to run with blood. All right,
> let them, if it is necessary. But when the red
> militias are billeted in the Ritz I shall still
> feel that the England I was taught to love so
> long ago and for such different reasons is
> somehow persisting.(20)

Orwell then began his campaign for a specifically English revolution, articulating his particular definition of traditional English 'decency' to the socialist principles that he had espoused in the 1930s, loyal neither to Chamberlain's nor Churchill's England but to the mythical 'decent' England of the past and of the future.

The situation produced by the onset of war helped Orwell to piece together a compromise between his upbringing and his more recent experience and theorizing. He was himself to become 'a socialist built on the bones of a Blimp', as he had described John Cornford, espousing what Alex Comfort sarcastically dubbed 'the doctrine of Physical Courage as an Asset to the Left Wing Intellectual'. Others from the intellectual elite, however, were by no means so sure. Already disheartened and confused politically by the Spanish experience, Auden and Isherwood departed for the States, writing off the 1930s famously as the 'low dishonest decade'. For most of those who remained, too, it was by no means clear that the road through the woods lay in a defence of Britain as she stood against the international threat. Answering the question so often put by the press in the early months of the war, 'Where Are the War Poets?', the writers who had sprung so spontaneously to the nation's defence in 1914, C. Day Lewis explained the reasons for his muteness:

They who in panic or mere greed
Enslaved religion, markets, laws,
Borrow our language now and bid
Us to speak up in freedom's cause.

It is the logic of our times,
No subject for immortal verse,
That we who lived by honest dreams
Defend the bad against the worse.(21)

Soon Orwell, the British documentary film makers, J.B. Priestley and others of the alternative cultural canon of the interwar period, were to be drawn into the biggest exercise in mass communications ever undertaken by the British state. The development of the Ministry of Information, the BBC, and those other institutions involved in mass communications, in an exercise absolutely necessary to mobilize Britain for the Second World War, was to take their ideology, adapting as it was in the face of both the domestic effects of the Depression and the international situation, to the core of the idea of the 'People's War'. Defending the bad against the worse was at least a half-hearted commitment to the need to put up the barricades for conservative values. The recontextualization of the cultural protest of the interwar years in the particular circumstances of the Second World War, however, was to place that protest in a position of unaccustomed privilege and influence which was to help to reconstruct the experience of the interwar years, to produce the myth of the 'locust years' and to herald a 'new beginning', a regeneration of 'real' British values.

NOTES

1.   S. Spender, World within world, 1951, p. 249.

2.   J. Lehmann, Whispering gallery, 1955, p. 225.

3.   G. Orwell, 'Why I Write', CEJL, vol. 1, 1968, p. 4.

4.   See, e.g., D. Marquand, Ramsay MacDonald, 1977; K. Middlemas and J. Barnes, Baldwin, a biography, 1969.

5.   House of Commons Debates, vol. 309, 9 March 1936.

6.   See J.F. Naylor, Labour's international policy, 1968; B. Pimlott, Labour and the left in the 1930s, 1977.

7.   S. Keyes, 'War Poet', in R. Blythe (ed.), Components of the scene, 1966, p. 171.

8.   House of Commons Debates, vol. 339, 6 October 1938.

9.   I.F. Clarke, Voices prophesying war, 1966.

10.   Gaumont British, 6 May 1937 (Visnews).

11.   If war should come, GPO Film Unit for the Ministry of Information, 1939 (Imperial War Museum).

12.   The peace film, 1937, dir. P. Rotha (No copies available for hire).

13.   Gaumont British, 'Munich', October 1938 (Visnews).

14.   C. Day Lewis, 'Newsreel', in R. Skelton (ed.), Poetry of the thirties, 1964, pp. 69–70.

15.   Things to come, 1936, dir. W. Cameron Menzies (London Films).

16.   J. Betjeman, 'Slough', Poetry of the thirties, p. 74.

17.   G. Orwell, Homage to Catalonia 1938, repr. 1980, p. 248.

18.   G. Orwell, Keep the aspidistra flying,

1936, repr. 1962, p. 21.

19.   G. Orwell, Coming up for air, 1939, repr. 1971, p. 223.

20.   G. Orwell, 'My Country Right or Left', CEJL, vol. 1, 1968, p. 539.

21.   C. Day Lewis, 'Where Are the War Poets?', Components of the scene, p. 170.

3. 1940

1940 still has an almost talismanic quality for those who lived through it in Britain, a quality which transcends social class or political barriers. To appeal to the spirit of 1940 is to appeal to a set of values assumed not to have existed before 1940 and to have re-emerged only briefly since, based on a selfless devotion to the community, in which social class is irrelevant and political differences mere details to the 'national family'. Charles Loch Mowat, at the end of his very detailed and apparently detached academic work on Britain between the wars, published in 1955, allowed himself to slip into purple prose in the last few sentences:

> In the summer of 1940, as they awaited the Battle of Britain, [the people of Britain] found themselves again, after twenty years of indecision. They turned away from past regrets and faced the future unafraid.(1)

Thus, in the traditional periodicization of British twentieth century history, 'interwar' gave way to 'contemporary', the 'bad times' gave way to 'the good times'.

Even for those who did not live through it 1940 is part of the collective conscience, shaping and conditioning reactions to contemporary events and problems. Three events inter-relate centrally in the mythology of 1940, events which occurred in quick succession after May 1940, and which combined to underpin a powerful cultural coalescent. First, the formation of the Churchill government as the epitome of national unity brought together groups as disparate as the right wing of the Conservative Party, the Liberal and Labour Parties, and even

elements from outside parliament altogether, from
press barons like Beaverbrook to labour barons like
Ernest Bevin. Second, the end of the Battle of
France, the Dunkirk evacuation, was treated at the
time and since as 'a victory snatched from the jaws
of defeat'. The third element in the cult of 1940 is
the Battle of Britain and the ensuing Blitz, perhaps
the most powerful of all the totemic elements
conjured up by merely mentioning the date 1940. Power
cuts in London, with darkened streets and tube-trains
suddenly stopping, still bring back a folk memory of
the Blitz, melting the urban reserve of middle-aged
Londoners. Combined, these elements have a lasting
impact.

Mythology is the stuff of which cultural studies
is made, and myths created in war are particularly
potent. In war, or other periods of acute national
danger, propaganda machinery is likely to simplify,
to make black and white, issues which in fact may
have been much more complex. In later years,
moreover, there grows up a folk memory of an episode,
coloured perhaps by the contemporary propaganda,
which forms part of the intellectual and emotional
apparatus with which every problem is viewed. In
1976, Tom Harrisson published Living through the
Blitz. In the Introduction, Harrisson wrote of the
problems of going back to the Mass Observation
archive, the source that he himself had done so much
to accumulate thirty years before:

> One of the difficulties which became evident as
> the present book developed, was that of
> avoiding the imposition of one's own ideas and
> accepted attitudes as they had been written
> down some thirty years before. The record from
> a third of a century ago can seem improbable
> today because it reads so differently from the
> contemporary established concept of what
> 'really happened' in that war. There has, in
> particular, been a massive, largely unconscious
> cover-up of the disagreeable facts of 1940-41.
> It amounts to a form of intellectual pollution:
> but pollution by perfume.(2)

Harrisson then proceeded to debunk this rosy,
perfumed and comfortable view of the Blitz, producing
evidence of the real tension and near breakdown that
occurred in some cities, for example of Town Clerks
bolting for the countryside and not being on hand to
operate the post-raid services just when they were
needed.

The question that really arises from Harrisson's book is not only 'what did really happen in 1940?' An equally significant question is 'why is it necessary to demythologize 1940?'. Is it in the interests of 'historical objectivity' or for some other purpose? Indeed, is a changing interpretation of historical events in the name of 'historical objectivity' anything more than evidence of changing political assumptions among those who re-write history? To debunk a historical myth is, in a very real sense, a political act in the here and now. Myths provide an explanation of the world as it is, and position each of us in relation to the rest of society within that explanation. Myths function as social and cultural articulators, constructing a shared system of assumptions which make a society click together. It follows that dominant mythology will be socially normative, and to destroy a myth is to undermine a social coalescent constructed in the ideology of the culturally-dominant group, a radical act. The fairy tales of the past are at least as important as what 'actually' happened in the past, because what people think happened in the past can tell us a great deal about the society that shares that historical perspective. While it may well be true, as Harrisson argued, that people were scared by bombing and some of them even ran, this does nothing to touch the real crux of the mythology. It may be true that conditions of life were often appalling in the blitzed areas, and that local and central government was shown up in a very bad light, but such 'revelations' do not deal with the central core of the mythology which is that, in spite of all hardships, 'People's War', 'the unconquerable spirit and courage of the people', won through in the end. The point is that the mythology of 1940 and the Blitz has been, and continues to be, such a potent force that we should learn to see it as a cultural phenomenon in its own right, an event to be explained rather than a lie to be uncovered.

No doubt there was an urgent political need for the construction of such a myth. Governments of the 1930s had dominated the political centre on the basic issue of government at the time, which was the state of the economy; all other issues, including foreign policy, had been subordinated to the overpowering need to combat the depression. But with increasing opposition to the appeasement policy, the right wing of the Conservative Party and the Labour Party could begin to make common cause. As war ensued, and early military disaster, this odd combination began to make sense. Chamberlain's downfall in 1940 provided the opportunity for one of the most bizarre coalitions in modern British history. Churchill, villain of Tonypandy and of the General Strike, joined forces with Labour. There were, however, very serious weaknesses in the combination. In particular, the coalition agreed only on one issue - the need to win the war; that was now as over-riding an issue as saving the economy had been in the 1930s. In these circumstances, the Guilty men thesis began to prosper. Initially launched as Gollancz's Victory Books No. 1, Guilty men was a personal attack on Chamberlain and the 'Men of Munich' for bringing Britain so low. It was from this point that Chamberlain became the great scapegoat for everything that had gone wrong in the 1930s: the weaknesses and the failures had not been the inevitable result of Britain's decline as a power but the result of culpable personal weaknesses of ministers of the time. As 1940 wore on, the Guilty Men thesis was expanded into an attack not simply on the foreign policy of the 1930s but on the domestic policies as well; the dole and the means test were seen as complementary to appeasement as a major attack began on the whole ideology of interwar Conservatism. Wartime Conservatives proved relatively powerless to prevent this slip to the left. The fall of Chamberlain had created a vacuum in Conservative thinking which Churchill was either unwilling or unable to fill, concentrating fully as he did on the war effort at the expense of the Home Front, which was virtually left to Labour and Tory Reform Group ministers. A united front against fascism, it was argued, involved a united front too against the social conditions of the 1930s; the building of the New Jerusalem was an essential precondition for winning the war.

The Ministry of Information argued strongly that the government must publish its 'peace aims', since it was essential to strengthen public morale, to heal the rifts left by the interwar experience, before the bombs began to fall. The extent of the MOI's concern may be realized when it is remembered that as early as 1937, the Air Staff were calculating that the German Air Force would be capable, by 1939, of dropping six hundred tons of bombs a day in a sustained campaign, and might be able to launch an attempted knock-out blow of three thousand, five hundred tons a day for a few days. Probably, all of this would be dropped on London, in an attempt to wipe out the administrative centre of the nation in one blow.(3) The projection was of a possible fifty eight thousand dead and one hundred and sixteen thousand hospital casualties in every twenty-four hours of intense attack, of ten thousand dead and twenty thousand hospital casualties as a typical daily average. By July 1940 the Prime Minister's office was still expecting eighteen thousand deaths a day.(4) In the context of these projections, fears about the fragility of civilian morale were understandable. How long could morale have lasted under such an impact, if the Luftwaffe had been capable of inflicting it?

A sustained campaign by both the Labour Party and elements in the MOI followed to launch a new social commitment that would prove the 1930s dead and buried, both to strengthen home morale and as a new credo for worldwide social democracy to counter the proclamation of the Nazi New Order in Europe. Coupled to this increasingly millenarian projection of the war as a 'People's War' was the extreme nationalism of the right wing of the Conservative Party, epitomized by Churchill himself with his constantly reiterated message centring on the manifest destiny of Britain. The result of this unlikely combination of millenarian socialism and extreme nationalism was a sensationally successful form of populism which could appeal right across the political board. In many ways, the groundwork for this success had been prepared at the cultural level in the previous decades but it was in the organization of the experience of 1940, its elevation into myth, that the final resolution of the interwar hegemonic crisis lay.

One significant element in reinforcing the case for a new attempt to bridge the gap between governors and governed was the Ministry of Information's decision to use Mass Observation and the Home Intelligence survey team to find out what the public was thinking. What was significant about the early months of the war was the way in which Home Intelligence and Mass Observation re-projected the public presentation of policy back to government. It is impossible and, moreover, unnecessary to discover whether the division between governors and governed was 'real' among the population at large, but it is clear that organizations like MO and HI pointed out such a division, real or not, and acted as mediating agencies. By June 1940, over two million people were employed by government or local authorities in ARP and post-raid duties. Their primary function in current government attitudes was to provide a form of

direct social and political control, to be backed up
by the regular armed forces if necessary. The
officiousness of this sizeable community became one
of the grumbles of the early days of the war.(5) It
would require a major change of attitude on the part
of government to convert this slightly sinister
looking organization into the 'People's Army' of the
London can take it image. The division between 'them'
and 'us' was constantly reported in surveys of home
morale by Home Intelligence and Mass Observation. It
became clear, in their view, in public reaction to
the first big poster campaign of the war:

> Your Courage
> Your Determination
> Your Resolution
> Will Bring Us Victory.

Mass Observation found that this poster had
disastrous results. Many people found it patronizing
and supercilious, and many found the apparent
distinction between 'You' and 'Us' especially
distasteful. Moreover, the poster was simply not
understood by many: a resolution was something you
passed at a Union meeting and its contribution to the
war effort seemed at best tangential. This reaction
to what was simply a gaff by the Ministry of
Information was symptomatic of a wider gulf between
governors and governed, in MO's view.(6) Even after
Chamberlain had been replaced by Churchill as Prime
Minister, Home Intelligence found that, though
Churchill's personal capacity was unchallenged, there
was no close identification with the rest of the
government at all.(7) This, as HI pointed out, could
have the most serious implications when the bombing
started. Even before that, in fairly minor matters
like government attempts to communicate basic
information, it had repercussions. Government
instructions were misunderstood, not understood at
all or not even noticed. ARP, for example, issued a
pamphlet on how to deal with an incendiary bomb, the
main gist of which was that it was extremely
dangerous to try to put it out with water. Mass
Observation found that a substantial number, when
asked what the pamphlet said, replied either that
they had not read it or that it suggested that water
was the best way to deal with such a bomb. One
respondent even suggested that the best way to deal
with an incendiary was to lie on it.(8)
    The Ministry of Information, working on this kind
of feedback, urged strongly that people needed more

guidance and less exhortation;the public was fed up with being told to be cheerful. They felt perfectly cheerful but, faced with constant exhortations to keep their chins up, they began to worry that there was something they ought to be feel worried about. Allied to this, and what particularly worried the Ministry of Information, was the apparently radical drift of the country, the feeling according to HI and MO that was beginning to develop in working-class areas, for instance, that they were being made to carry an unequal burden in food rationing and taxation.(9) Then, in May, June and July of 1940, Home Intelligence began to give attention to the feeling of some sections of the middle class, the intelligentsia in particular, that government should publish its peace aims, which must include large measures of social reconstruction after the war, peace aims to pit against the Nazi New Order for Europe.(10)

Whether this radicalization of public opinion in the summer of 1940, the gap between the Battle of France and the Battle of Britain, really did develop is difficult to say. What can be said with a degree of certainty is that the growth in wartime of the information services themselves had brought new people into the propaganda machine, especially the radical intelligentsia. Tom Harrisson's Mass Observation, for instance, had been founded in 1938 on the assumption that there was a gap between governors and governed that needed to be bridged, that government should give people what they wanted, not what was considered good for them.(11) Now MO was being employed by government to tell government what the public thought. The government was also employing radical documentary film-makers in the Crown Film Unit, men like Basil Wright who wrote in the Documentary News Letter in June 1940:

... a nation fighting desperately to defend the present lacks the inspiration which springs from a vision of the future. Now, more than ever, it is necessary to repair past errors and fortify national morale with an articulation of democratic citizenship as a constructive force which can mould the future.(12)

During 1940, Grierson's documentary film makers became part of the machinery of government when the GPO Film Unit was taken over by the Ministry of Information as the Crown Film Unit. By the end of 1940, the film-makers at MOI were beginning to inject into their films an inspirational quality that was not quite politically neutral. The process that George Orwell noted at work in 1943 had already begun: 'almost every writer, however undesirable his political history or opinions, has been sucked into the various Ministries or the BBC'.(13) The answer in part to C. Day Lewis' question 'Where Are The War Poets?' was that many of them were writing propaganda leaflets for the MOI.

Another example of this process was the introduction of J.B. Priestley into a regular evening radio spot to counter Lord Haw Haw. The evolution of Priestley's 'Postscript' series is typical of the drift of opinion in the radical intelligentsia, a section of the community which suddenly found itself in a position of unaccustomed potential power and influence. As a clearly new direction in broadcasting policy compared with Reithian days, Priestley's talks were symptomatic of a new populism that began to operate at the BBC. As the weeks went by and the Blitz began, Priestley began to inject a new political content into his talks, though it was always fairly anodyne, a generalized and romantic, patriotic and classless neo-Socialism. He moved from expressing the sentiment 'we can take it' to the idea of 'people's war':

We have to fight this great battle not only with guns in daylight, but alone in the night, communing with our souls, strengthening our faith that in common men everywhere there is a spring of innocent aspiration and good will that shall not be sealed.(14)

Finally, he moved to the view that Britain was fighting to gain something:

We should mean what we say: be really democratic, for example, while fighting for democracy: we should make some attempt to discover the deeper causes of this war and to try and find a remedy for them, thus making this a colossal battle, not only against something but also for something positive and good. If all this, together with certain obvious elements of social justice and decency seems to you Socialism, Communism or Anarchy, then you are at liberty to call me a socialist, communist or anarchist, but there's a danger that as this high mood passes, apathy will return, and selfishness and stupidity.(15)

Home Intelligence found that Priestley was second only to Churchill as a popular radio speaker, and that up to 80 per cent of those listening approved of the sentiments expressed. The Ministry of Information urged that some of these sentiments should be included in a public statement of peace aims to meet what it described as a growing popular demand. Firstly, it was argued, such a statement would produce an immediate stiffening of home morale, a bringing together of governors and governed before the bombing began in earnest, a proof that the 1930s were dead and gone, not only appeasement but also mass unemployment, poor housing and the means test attitude, all those things which were now being assumed to have affected the stability of prewar society. Secondly, such a statement would stand as a manifesto to the world of a new social democratic credo for which Britain would fight on, if necessary, alone.(16) The implicit appeal was not only to the Home Front but to America, and to some extent to Russia as well. This argument found real echoes in cabinet, among Labour members especially but also paradoxically among the so-called Guilty Men, Halifax, Chamberlain and Kingsley Wood. In Churchill, however, there was a solid block of resistance. Churchill believed that they should not promise for the future what they were not sure that they could provide. On that resistance the whole idea of a statement of peace aims floundered, temporarily at least.(17)

Yet the cultural sea-change was taking place anyway, with or without a government commitment. The mythology of the Blitz presents us with a series of related oppositions which construct a value-system which is self-validating. Destruction-Redemption is its major theme, with the British people caught in the middle of a major turning point in the historical process. The myth is given its epic quality, for instance, by the way in which it incorporates quite elemental oppositions embedded in the whole idea of bombing: air/land in the concept of flight; fire/water in firefighting images, destruction/reconstruction as in the phoenix imagery associated in particular with Coventry. The newsreel, other film and newspaper materials from 1940 incorporate these elemental binary oppositions in a way which projects the Blitz as nothing less than an apocalyptic event. The survival of St Paul's, itself a symbol of the reconstruction of London after the Great Fire, is a most obvious example. After the great fire raid of

December 30, 1940, the <u>Daily Mail</u> printed a large photograph of St Paul's haloed by smoke and fire on the front page, under the caption 'War's Greatest Picture: St Paul's Stands Unharmed in the Midst of the Burning City'. Below the photograph were printed the feelings of the photographer as he witnessed the sight, and the words: 'Here is his picture, one that all Britain will cherish, for it symbolizes the steadiness of London's stand against the enemy: the firmness of Right against Wrong'. On an inside page, the argument constructed on the front page was developed as a reporter commented on his feelings as he walked through the City after the raid:

> Here was a sight at which to marvel. Fire blazed all around, flames dangerously close. The cathedral itself, its cross above the dome calm and aloof above a sea of fire, stood out, an island of God, safe and untouched. On, and deeper into the City. Fires, always fires; to the left, to the right, before and behind. Every now and then a shower of burning rubble would whirl down from a rooftop, caught by the wind, dance along the road and clothe one for a second in a sea of sparks. Everywhere, great armies of firemen, professional and amateur, worked grimly on, too absorbed in their own fierce business to worry about the danger to fools like myself, drawn to this scene of destruction by an instinct too deep to be denied.(18)

This notion of the apocalyptic nature of the Blitz is deeply embedded in the myth as a whole. Between the elemental oppositions, the British people are caught not just as spectators but as the active participants, dignified by the grandeur of events going on around them. It is the epic quality of the struggle between the oppositions that gives the British people, caught in the middle as it were, a spectacular heroism and a particular destiny, the essence of the idea of the 'People's War'. As one Ministry of Information film – <u>London can take it</u>, – had it:

> Many of the people at whom you are looking now are members of the greatest civilian army ever assembled... They are the ones who are really fighting this war. The firemen, the air-raid wardens, the ambulance drivers... Brokers, clerks, pedlars, merchants by day, they are

heroes by night... It is true that the Nazis
will be over again tomorrow night and the night
after that and every night. They will drop
thousands of bombs and they'll destroy hundreds
of buildings and they'll kill thousands of
people. But a bomb has its limitations. It can
only destroy buildings and kill people. It
cannot kill the unconquerable spirit and
courage of the people of London. London can
take it.(19)

It was by no means only at the level of popular
and mass culture that this epic quality was built
around the experience of the Blitz. T.S. Eliot added
the sanction of high culture to the mythology, as did
so many other writers, painters and commentators from
among the cultured elite. In 'Little Gidding', the
apocalyptic symbolism of the Blitz plays a key role.
Sitting in a little country church, in the village
from which his ancestors came, the imagery of the
Blitz dominates his view of the apocalyptic moment in
time:

Water and fire succeed
The town, the pasture and the weed.
Water and fire divide,
The sacrifice that we denied.
Water and fire shall rot
The marred foundations we forgot
Of sanctuary and choir,
This is the death of water and fire.

1940 in turn becomes the still turning-point of
history, Eliot's theory of time — that past and
future are contained in the present – combining with
the historical facts of the period in which he was
writing:

... A people without history
Is not redeemed from time, for history is
                                      a pattern
Of timeless moments. So, while the light
                                      fails
On a winter's afternoon, in a secluded
                                      chapel
History is now and England.

There is even a hint of a veiled reference to the
formation of the new national government!:

We cannot revive old factions

> We cannot restore old policies
> Or follow an antique drum.
> These men, and those who opposed them
> And those whom they opposed
> Accept the constitution of silence
> And are folded in a single party.

At the end of the poem, Eliot's incantation incorporates echoes of the Phoenix myth bringing the actual moment of redemption for the rose of England, atoning for the years of 'The Waste Land' and 'The Hollow Men':

> And all shall be well and
> All manner of things shall be well
> When the tongues of flame are in-folded
> Into the crowned knot of fire
> And the fire and the rose are one.(20)

The war, in a sense, was to put the right-wingers of the 1930s into a very peculiar position. Eliot, one of the cultural conservatives of the interwar years, was to reject Orwell's Animal farm for Faber and Faber, the publishers, on the grounds that it might offend Britain's Russian allies. The circumstances of 1940, however, and particularly the populist combination of nationalism and socialism that those circumstances demanded, produced the conditions in which the younger middle-class intelligentsia could move comfortably. From the time he announced his reconversion to patriotism in 'My Country Right or Left', Orwell became the archetypal mouth-piece of the ideology of the 'People's War', particularly in his argument in 'The Lion and the Unicorn' that England was just one big family with the wrong members in control, that the war would produce a specifically English revolution.(21) The fact, too, that the mobilization of the literati for the war brought so many of the writers and film-makers in from the cold, took them from the periphery of the cultural world in the 1930s to the centre of the biggest informational exercise ever undertaken by the British state, put them in a position of unaccustomed influence. Orwell himself, for instance, twenty years after he had left the Burma police and renounced imperialism and all its works, found himself broadcasting to India and the Far East on the BBC. In the same way that the party political alternative of the late 1930s came to dominate politics in the coalition of 1940, so the cultural alternative that had begun to emerge as a via media between the 'old men' and Marxism also came to dominate.

The Thirties receded into the past with extraordinary speed once the barriers had been broken. Finally, after three rejections in the 1930s, a film script for Love on the dole was accepted by the censors and filmed by John Baxter in 1940. But the film of Love on the dole is infinitely less depressing than the novel precisely because the 1930s figure as 'the past'. The original story is re-contextualized by opening and closing rolling captions which seek to remove the intervening narrative from the here and now, re-siting it as a dire object-lesson. At the beginning of the film, over a bright cloudscape, roll the words:

> This film recalls one of the darker pages of our industrial history. On the outskirts of every city, there is a region of darkness and poverty where men and women for ever strive to live decently in face of overwhelming odds, never doubting that the clouds of depression will one day be lifted. Such a district was Hanky Park in March 1930.

The mediation in this passage in fact takes place at two levels. First, there is the distancing involved in placing the story firmly in the past, in the first sentence. Immediately following the rolling title, the camera descends sharply to an industrial landscape, then into a dark slum street, to the Hardcastles' back door. It will repeat the journey backwards at the end of the film, distancing the 'then' from the 'now'. In the second sentence, however, the present tense is used; the distancing technique here is rather to assume that the cinema audience is not part of this poverty; the poor regions are 'on the outskirts of every city', and they are thus geographically and socially marginalized, and thereby objectified as elements for libertarian concern. There follows very little of the patronising middle-class refraction of working-class accents and experience that typified film of the previous decade; Sally and Larry and Harry have become, in a real sense, the hero-figures of the 'People's War', a repositioning of the experience of the Depression made clear in a statement by A.V. Alexander, a Labour minister in the government, as the camera sails up into the sky at the end of the film to complete the narrative loop begun with the film's opening camera move:

Our working men and women have responded
magnificently to any and every call made upon
them. Their reward must be a New Britain. Never
again must the unemployed become the forgotten
men of the peace.(22)

Love on the dole was in fact cinema's opening
shot in the People's War and, though there were to be
many throwbacks to the style, the themes and the
modes of address of the prewar period, cinema made a
decisive move away from the interpellative strategy
of the 1930s which defined middle class as hero in
the ensuing years. Though the real hero remained the
community, the national family, the values that
typified the community were to be read increasingly
as embodied in recognizably working-class as opposed
to middle-class characters and characteristics. In
Went the day well, made in 1942, the typically heroic
figures of the prewar have, in fact, become either
incompetents or even traitors. Leslie Banks, who had
played the archetypal imperial hero in Sanders of the
river in the 1930s, played a German spy among the
squirearchy in Cavalcanti's film. The symbolic
destruction of the country house, the quixotic fatal
gesture of the local aristocrat to offset her former
stupidity, the positive action of the lower social
rungs of the village hierarchy, all testify to a
cultural reorientation.(23) The England that was
being saved would have been as recognizable to the
generation of the 1930s as it would have been to the
generation of 1910; it is in the people who do the
saving that the change has taken place. By the time
of the Ealing comedies of the late 1940s, the
embodiment of the values of community lie firmly with
the upper working class, with the artisans and the
small shop-keepers who had typically been the comics,
the patronized or the villains of the earlier
generation of cinema.

The official cinematic culture of the war years
showed a similar, perhaps even more marked move
towards focusing the working class as being most
typical in their Englishness, and in their heroism.
After the brief reign of Joseph Ball, former head of
the Conservative Party's film division, at the Films
Division of the Ministry of Information, the GPO Film
Unit was taken over to become the centre-piece of a
huge films programme for the home front. Early MOI
films such as Miss Grant goes to the door or Mr.
Proudfoot shows a light, while being educationally
efficient in terms of explaining the need to
immobilize cars and bicycles and to maintain the

black-out, remained embarrassing because of their
painful class bias and their complete abstention from
reality in the context in which they set their little
English parables. The intervention of the Documentary
Film Movement produced an immediate and dramatic
change in the content and the style of these films.
Films such as <u>Fires were started</u> and <u>Western
approaches</u> featured working-class heroism and
team-work as matters of everyday experience; the
themes of <u>Drifters</u> and <u>Nightmail</u> became nationally
significant propaganda. In a series of elegaic
shorts, too, Humphrey Jennings was to poeticize the
People's War. <u>London can take it</u>, on which Jennings
worked with Harry Watt in 1940, began what was soon
to become the 'Jennings style', relying heavily on a
rapid editing which fused a variety of images into a
multi-faceted unity. His interest in the surreal
allowed a play on images, a toying with the
fantastic, which paradoxically made the ordinary more
endearing. In <u>London can take it</u> well-known electric
trains cross demonstrably unsafe bridges and
commuters travel to work on the back of a horse and
cart, as the result of another night of bombing. The
extraordinary experience of the Blitz allowed
Jennings to idealize the ordinary and the
commonplace; 'Humphrey was the first man to notice
the Louis Quinze properties of a Lyons swiss roll',
Grierson once commented. By the time he made <u>Listen
to Britain</u> in 1943, Jennings was moving effortlessly
between high and popular cultural registers, mapping
both as co-ordinates of a shared and diverse culture,
in a series of snap-shots for the national family
album. Jennings performed a neat cultural bridging
strategy in his films, simultaneously recognizing
differences in the national family but denying their
significance in comparison with what was held in
common, and above all emphasizing the dignity of and
the values of Englishness in a People's war. By 1945,
in <u>Diary for Timothy</u>, Jennings could contrast the
comfortable, safe surroundings of a newly-born
middle-class British baby with the conditions that
would face him 'in wartime Poland, or a Glasgow or
Liverpool slum', as if both were as bad as the other:
'you're one of the lucky ones', and baby Timothy's
role will be to make the most of the fight against
fascism and 'the locust years' to build a new world
of 'decency'.(24)
    It does not really matter that very few saw
Jennings' films at the time, any more than it matters
that many millions saw <u>Love on the dole</u> or heard
Priestley's <u>Postscripts</u>. The point is rather that

these films could be made as official government
issues constructing, though apparently reflecting, a
new national consensus. What is significant is the
fact that the minority culture of Jennings' 'arty'
films had so much in common with the popular culture
of the commercial cinema of the period in their
dominant ideological discourse, which was not an
appeal for a consensus but an assumption that
consensus already existed in comparison with what had
gone before. This was no revolutionary change; it
was not even radical but, rather, hegemonic in its
implications. Jennings and Orwell were to become part
of the new intellectual elite, the educated men who
had grown up in the interwar years alienated, to a
greater or lesser extent, from the social mores with
which they had been inculcated yet unable to break
through into a revolutionary consciousness. They were
given the opportunity in wartime to speak to the rest
of their caste, to tell them that their values had
arrived in power and that it was up to them to spread
the gospel. It was the mythology of 1940 - the notion
that the national family had been reunited by the
crisis - which gave them the confidence to complete
the hegemonic transition. Through radio, commercial
cinema and the network of the mass media their ideas
were to spread widely, thus helping to prepare the
psychological ground which worked itself out
politically in the Labour landslide in the general
election of 1945.

More specifically, there were political binary
oppositions that depended on this elemental
superstructure in the myth: especially the opposition
between 'The Thirties' as against 1940 as a new
beginning, and the many ways in which this
specifically political binary opposition was
articulated: Chamberlain as against Churchill; means
test as against Welfare State; Fascism as against
Social Democracy; 'Two Englands' as against national
unity. It is only by seeing this system of binary
oppositions as a whole, as an inter-related and
self-sufficient structure, that the mythology makes
full sense. 'The Thirties' = 'bad thing' only if it
is understood that '1940' = 'good thing'; the two
ideas did not exist separately, they were linked in a
way that made them appear self-explanatory, and were
given added point and reinforcement by the other
binary oppositions to which they related in the
structure as a whole. This had deep political
significance; it was a self-validating system which
constructed the minutiae of political consciousness
as long as the myth held. To treat 1940 as a myth, as

a construction, is not to deny the significance of
the events which actually did take place, only to
emphasize the importance of the way in which that
experience was organized in the national
consciousness. The myth of 1940 had the effect of
turning a fairly typically evolutionary response of
British government to questions of social
administration into a crusade. Constructing an
opposition to the Thirties both distanced Britain
from the policies of that period, creating scapegoats
in personalities rather than in institutions, and
also focused attention on the future. The Blitz
itself provided the basis for the apocalyptic imagery
and the politics of Revelation that characterized so
much of the media coverage of the bombing. To survive
a Nazi bomb became not just a matter for profound
personal relief but also a vindication of the
soundness of social democracy and an instrument in
the further definition of the future of social
democracy in Britain.

The construction of the mystical doctrine of the
people's war created a climate in which the
technocratic architects of the Welfare State began to
move more freely. In the winter of 1940/1, Keynes
pioneered the first official statistics of national
income and expenditure in the economic offices of the
cabinet, thus paving the way for the most basic shift
that could be made in a capitalist and social
democratic state towards state intervention in
economic affairs. In September 1940, William
Beveridge had become convinced that if the war were
to be won, then the government had to plan production
and consumption as never before. In May 1941, he was
to get his chance to look at the broad field of post-
war social policy when he was made chairman of a
committee to look into the question of health
insurance. The Beveridge Report was to be the final
stage in the campaign for an ideological counter-
offensive for which the propagandists had been
arguing since the summer of 1940. The publication of
the new social democratic credo, accepted broadly
both by the right and the left in Britain, was
welcomed by the BBC among others, as 'the dawning of
a new age'. The switch in the emphasis of social
democracy that became the basis of the post-1945
political consensus began in 1940. It is in this
sense of 1940 as a new beginning, a revolution in
social awareness in the middle of an acute national
danger, that gave the mythology of the Blitz its
particular mystique and its longevity. The belief
that people's war had become a reality made it

possible to believe that, though there may be Heinkel
111s today, there would be Bluebirds over the White
Cliffs of Dover tomorrow, just you wait and see.
There was no hint of a radical reorientation of the
structure of the British economy involved, only a
managerial commitment by government to social
engineering. It was at the level of culture that
these changes were given their dynamic thrust,
articulated to the notion of the national family and
its tradition of 'decency'. If, for left and right
alike, the high ideals of 1940 were to be lost in the
years that came after, that only added a poignancy to
the myth, the sense of a great moment lost and never
to be retrieved. But the belief that something truly
significant had indeed happened proved extremely
tenacious. The re-evaluation of 1940, as well as the
'revisionist' interpretation of the 1930s in recent
years, are significant indicators of just how far the
Keynes/Beveridge axis has ceased to command a
consensus in contemporary Britain. Orwell's national
family, alongside that political switch of sympathy,
has also become a thing of the past.

The way in which these events have been
articulated in the national consciousness can be
demonstrated by two recent attempts to use them for
political purposes. During the Falklands War of 1982,
for example, the Sun newspaper published the news of
the sinking of HMS 'Coventry' and 'Atlantic Conveyor'
under the title 'Our Darkest Hour', a choice of
vocabulary meaningless to those not culturally
attuned to the belief that 1940 was a period in which
Britain was only saved from defeat by a supreme
effort of national will and unity, of which the
Churchill government was the central and organizing
element.(25) The Sun thus attempted to appropriate
for the Thatcher government the ethos of Churchillian
resistance to dictatorship, backed by a united
national will and spearheaded by the combined armed
forces, deftly combined in 'our', 'darkest hour'
being in directly linked contrast to the 'finest
hour' of Churchillian rhetoric. Conversely, during
the 1983 election campaign, the Labour Party issued a
handbill, a photograph of a dejected unemployed man
with his children in the 1930s, under the title 'The
Bad Days Are Back'. Below the photograph, a message
from Michael Foot read: 'This General Election is the
past versus the future. As Labour rebuilt Britain
after the last war, so we are now ready to rebuild
Britain after Tory destruction'. As the result of the
General Election clearly showed, this attempt to
appropriate the mythology of the Thirties signally

failed. Partly, perhaps, this was because the
Conservatives had cornered the market during the
Falklands War, centring attention on the Churchillian
nationalism of the 1940 myth. The fact was that the
view of the 1930s that Labour was attempting to
mobilize was fading fast as a dominant element in the
myth. Michael Foot, having co-operated in the writing
of Guilty men in 1940, the book which did so much to
establish the mythology in the first place, fell
victim to its re-working after the Falklands War.
Somewhere between 1940 and 1980 the myth of the
Thirties had become divorced from the myth of 1940.
Deep in that ideological shift lies the basis of
Britain's new crisis of hegemony.

NOTES

1.   C.L. Mowat, Britain between the wars,
1968, p.657.
2.   T. Harrisson, Living through the Blitz,
1976, p.15.
3.   COS 603, Memo by Committee of Imperial
Defence Sub-Committee, Estimated Scale of Attack on
Britain, June 1937, CAB 53/32 (Public Record
Office).
4.   F.A.L. to Prime Minister, 9 July 1940,
PREM 4/3/25 (Public Record Office); see M. Smith,
British air strategy between the wars, 1984.
5.   Home Intelligence, 1940. INF 1/292
(Public Record Office).
6.   Mass Observation, War begins at home,
1940.
7.   INF 1/292.
8.   War begins at home, pp. 413-25.
9.   INF 1/292.
10.   Ibid.
11.   Mass Observation, Britain 1939, 1940,
Introduction.
12.   Documentary News Letter, July 1940,
Editorial.
13.   G. Orwell, 'Poetry and the Microphone'.
CEJL, vol. 2, 1968, p.381
14.   J.B. Priestley, Postscripts, 1941, 23
June 1940, p. 18.
15.   Postscripts, 20 October 1940, p. 98.
16.   I. McLaine, Ministry of morale, 1979, Ch.
6.
17.   P. Addison, The road to 1945, 1975, Ch.
4.
18.   Daily Mail, 31 December 1940.

19.   London can take it, 1940, Ministry of Information Crown Film Unit (Imperial War Museum).
20.   T.S.Eliot, Four quartets, 1979, pp.43, 48.
21.   G. Orwell, 'The Lion and the Unicorn', CEJL, vol. 2, 1968, pp. 74-133.
22.   Love on the dole, dir. John Baxter, 1940 (BFI).
23.   Went the day well, dir. A. Cavalcanti, 1942 (British Film Institute).
24.   Miss Grant goes to the door, Ministry of Information, 1940; Mr Proudfoot shows a light, Ministry of Information, 1940; London can take it, GPO Film Unit for the Ministry of Information, 1940; Listen to Britain, dir. H. Jennings and S. McAllister, Crown Film Unit, Ministry of Information; Diary for Timothy, dir. H. Jennings, Crown Film Unit, Ministry of Information (all available from Imperial War Museum); see M. Smith, 'Narrative and Ideology in Listen to Britain', in J. Hawthorn (ed.), Narrative from Mallory to motion pictures, 1985.
25.   Sun, 27 May 1982.

CONCLUSION

To describe a country is to define its identity, but in that every description of something as complicated and as multi-faceted as an entire nation must also be partial and subjective, to describe a country is also to appropriate its identity. An 'achieved hegemony' relies on just such an appropriation of identity, the construction of uncontested signs of community, of 'sameness' as well as of uncontested signs of 'foreignness', of 'difference'. We have argued in these pages that the struggle for control of the definition of national identity, of 'us' as opposed to 'them' in the interwar period, went on at a number of different levels simultaneously, ranging from everyday political vocabulary to the aesthetic arguments of academic commentators. We have by no means exhausted a discussion of the phenomenon of hegemonic adaptation in the interwar years: we have merely erected a few mile-posts to demonstrate just how extensively the study of such a phenomenon must operate. Cinema and literature have provided our examples, but popular literature, radio, sport, holidays, schooling and so many other areas also need their analysts.

Ideology does not operate independently of the economic base in the construction of the social formation, though it does possess a 'relative autonomy' which allows it to become a site of struggle in its own right; indeed, the site of a struggle which becomes a precondition of any major change in the economic base. This struggle is fought out not only between classes but also within them. Thus the worries of F.R. Leavis or T.S. Eliot for the future of culture are as significant as attempts to form a discrete working-class literature, or attempts to combat the intrusion of Hollywood into British popular culture, in a struggle to achieve control of

252

the definition of national identity and to position
interest groups hierarchically in relation to that
identity. All this was played out against a
background of a developing process of attack and
counter-attack between and within social classes,
playing around cultural forms and their relevance to
the lived experience of those who made and used these
forms, as well as in relation to changing economic
circumstances. By the late nineteenth century in
Britain, an uneasy ideological truce had been
hammered out which produced a relatively stable and
viable class society. Yet the fears of Samuel Taylor
Coleridge or Matthew Arnold lived on in the truce,
worries about the possibilities of an unguided mass
culture of philistinism which would swamp high
culture. Their attack, however, was not simply or
even primarily against the working class but rather
against the hegemonic process for what it seemed
prepared to concede in the effort to attain and
maintain the cultural ascendancy of the middle class:
it was an attack against those members of their own
or similar social class (in economic terms) for
promoting, apparently consciously, the new mass
culture with its built-in hostilities to the higher
things in life. The relationship between the high
cultural elite and the middle class was by no means a
direct or uncomplicated one. On the contrary, as
heirs of the aristocratic tradition of anti-
materialism, the concerns of the elite were often at
variance with the world of industry, commerce and
imperialism. The homogenizing influence of the public
schools and of the Oxbridge system - in producing
both the new generation of cultural mandarins as well
as the captains of industry - should not be allowed
to disguise the differences in interest between the
two groups. Therein, however, lay an adaptive
strength as well as a potential lack of solidarity.
In railing against the materialism of the middle
class as progenitors of mass culture, yet at the same
time being unalterably tied to them at the economic
level (there was no question which side of the
barricades most of them would be on if it ever came
to that) they could act as a kind of high caste
within the middle class, a priesthood which would
contest the direction in which the control of culture
was moving without challenging the most basic
structures of the social formation. The relationship
between the elite and the middle class was like that
of an unhappy marriage, in which quarrels were
frequent but divorce was absolutely unthinkable
because of its effect on the children.

The other side of the coin was an equally divided working class bathing in the late nineteenth century in a 'culture of consolation', mapped out in cultural forms as diverse as music hall, professional sport or 'improving' recreations, delineated by a combination of the permeation of middle-class values and by resistance to such permeation. The combative edge of the working class may have been rubbed off but it still retained that consciousness which could easily re-emerge as confrontation if the hegemonic strategy failed to continue to adapt to the changing needs and directions of an ever-fluid social and economic situation. The Great War and the Great Depression threatened to bring those latent inter-class tensions into the forefront of life in interwar Britain. While the depression created renewed conditions for class confrontation, the Great War produced a revolt within the ranks of the elite which threatened to muddy a clear response on the part of dominant culture to this inter-class threat. In fact the working-class threat never materialized, at least not to the extent that it imposed an insufferable burden on dominant culture. This was partly the result of economic factors which made mass unemployment a divisive rather than a unifying influence on the working class, partly the result of piecemeal adaptation on an ad hoc basis at the political level, but also because of the legacy of the late Victorian and Edwardian 'culture of consolation' in preparing the working class for inexorable and inevitable bad times. The success of films like those of George Formby and Gracie Fields, shaped within the ideological parameters of what had become a traditional working-class culture, act as testimony to the continued non-combativeness of the working class as a whole, its self-defensive stance. Hollywood, moreover, offered a mythicized, classless world which legitimized American economic penetration as the harbinger of individual freedom, a brave new world of the near future. The marginalization of more radical cultural forms, the refusal of a clearly socialist working-class form of literature to emerge to challenge dominant culture, the continuing interest indeed in re-using traditionally canonical forms along the lines of the 'improving' tradition in working-class culture, all appear to demonstrate the signal failure of the working class to respond as the radicals hoped it would. This is not to suggest that the working class was duped or drugged en masse by mass culture, simply to suggest that the changing forms of mass culture continued to make sense of the world for a social grouping still prepared, for the time being at least, to make the most of a bad job. If the Depression had gone on longer, or if it had affected Britain in the same way it affected the United States or Germany, then no doubt the hegemonic process would have found it a great deal more difficult to cope. As it was, class friction was marginalized, localized and contained.

Yet we are not talking in this period about an 'achieved hegemony'; the unrest of the period had to be constantly worked upon, the idea of the national family to be constantly reiterated and redefined; the perceived threat of social breakdown ruled the minds of the dominant grouping. The revolt within the ranks of the elite may have been short-lived but the intrusion of the ultra-materialist American popular culture, signified in particular in cinema but equally clearly in popular music as in other cultural forms, threatened to take Britain's cultural future out of the hands of the elite. Eliot, Waugh and others responded with a brutally reactionary stance, Huxley and Greene ambivalently, but the Leavises responded with an aggressive assertion not just of the continuing vitality of the Great Tradition but of the need to hit back at the damaging effects, as they saw them, of mass culture by proselytizing. Their attitudes were to be communicated to a whole generation of teachers and lecturers and to be given institutional recognition in the post-Second World War developments in secondary and higher education. In this sense, the role of the Leavises was indeed hegemonic; coming from a conservative standpoint, they helped to ensure a continuing place for the values they held dear within a mass culture, and relating to that mass culture in terms of an arbitration of taste confined no longer simply to social caste but to training in sensibility. Though the Leavises would have despised the aims of the British Documentary Film Movement in using the techniques of the most dangerous of the mass media to reform it, their role too was to be equally hegemonic, transforming British cinema by targeting the working class as the natural heroes of traditional English values. Though their audiences remained small in the 1930s, their pervasive influence in subsequent decades in altering the direction of cinema, in establishing realism as a particularly British form of narrative on screens both large and small, was to make cinema and television the two showpieces of a rejuvenated British popular culture.

Conclusion

The survivors among the fellow-travellers, meanwhile, brought the social awareness they had learned in their radicalism back to traditional values, thus adapting those values to a new setting. George Orwell was to become the strident mouthpiece of the political centre, arguing for a specifically British revolution which would articulate traditional British values to a mass democratic society. By the late 1940s and into the 1950s and 1960s Leavisism, the documentary idea and Orwellism had become the referents of a new cultural order in Britain, providing cultural underpinning for the new order established in politics by John Maynard Keynes and William Beveridge. In a real sense, the Welfare State was twinned to Welfare Culture. There was no revolution because there was no need for one. That there was no need for one was a matter of perception. Perception lies in the realm of ideology, and it was in the realm of ideology that the interwar years produced something of a success story, however much the demands of post-1940 mythology demanded that the period should be pilloried and condemned.

BIBLIOGRAPHY

Addison, P., The road to 1945, Cape, 1975.
Aldcroft, D.H. & Richardson, H.W., The British
    economy, 1870 - 1939, Macmillan, 1969.
Aldgate. A., Cinema and history, Scolar press, 1979.
Aldgate, A. & Richards, J., Best of British,
    Blackwell, 1983.
Allott, K. & Farris, M. (eds), The art of Graham
    Greene, Hamish Hamilton, 1951.
Althusser, L., Lenin, philosophy and other essays,
    New Left Books, 1971.
Anderson, P., 'Components of the National Culture',
    in Cockburn, A. & Blackburn, R. (eds), Student
    power, Penguin, 1969.
Appleyard, J.A., Coleridge's philosophy of
    literature, Oxford UP, 1965.
Armes, R., British cinema – a critical history,
    Secker & Warburg, 1978.
Arnold, M., Culture and anarchy, 1869, repr. Penguin,
    1971.
Auden, W.H., Collected poems, 1927-1957, Faber, 1966.
Balcon, M., A lifetime of films, Hutchinson, 1969.
Baldwin, S., On England, Hodder & Stoughton, 1938.
Barr, C., Ealing studios, David & Charles, 1977.
Barthes, R., S-Z, Cape, 1975.
    – Image – music – text, Fontana, 1977.
Baxter, J., Science fiction in the cinema, Zwemmer,
    1970.
Bell, C., Civilisation, Chatto & Windus, 1928.
Belsey, C., Critical practice, Methuen, 1980.
Bennett, T. et al., Culture, ideology and social
    process, Batsford, 1981.
    – Popular television and film, BFI, 1981.
Berger, J., Ways of seeing, BBC, 1981.
Bergonzi, B., Reading the thirties, Macmillan, 1978.
Betts, E., The film business, Allen & Unwin, 1973.
Blatchford, R., My favourite books, Clarion Press,
    1900.
Boden, F.C., Pit-head poems, Dent, 1927.
    – Out of the coalfields, Dent, 1929.
    – Miner, Dent, 1932.
Bottomore, T.B., Elites and society, 1964, repr.
    Watts, 1967.
Boyle, A., The climate of treason, Hutchinson, 1979.
Brennan, G., The Spanish labyrinth, Cambridge UP,

1967.

Brittain, V., Testament of youth, Gollancz, 1933.

Briant, K., Oxford limited, Michael Joseph, 1937.

Brierley, W., Means test man, Methuen, 1935.

British Workman, The, 1913-14.

Britton, L., Hunger and love, Putnam, 1931.

Buell, F.W., W.H. Auden as social poet, Cornell UP, 1973.

Burgess, M. & Keen, T., Gracie Fields, W.H. Allen, 1980.

Calder, A., The people's war, Britain 1939 - 1945, Cape, 1969.

Carlyle, T., On heroes and hero-worship, James Fraser, 1841.

Carnegie Trust, Disinherited youth, Carnegie, 1943.

Carr, R., Spain, 1808 - 1939, Oxford UP, 1966.

Cato, Guilty men, Gollancz, 1940.

Caudwell, C., Studies and further studies in a dying culture, Monthly Review Press, 1971.
- Romance and realism, Harvard UP, 1970.

Caute, D., The fellow travellers, Weidenfeld & Nicholson, 1973.

Clark, J. et al. (eds), Culture and crisis in Britain in the 1930s, Lawrence & Wishart, 1979.

Clarke, I.F., Voices prophesying war, Oxford UP, 1966.

Coleridge, S.T., On the constitution of the church and state, 1830, repr. J. Barrell (ed.), Dent, 1972.

Colls, P. & Dodd, R., 'Representing the Nation; British Documentary Film, 1930 - 1945', Screen, 1985.

Commission on Educational and Cultural Films, The film in national life, Allen & Unwin, 1932.

Connolly, C., Enemies of promise, Routledge, 1938.
- The missing diplomats, Queen Anne Press, 1952.

Constantine, S., 'Love on the Dole and its Reception in the 1930s', Literature and History, 1982.
- Social conditions in Britain between the wars, Methuen, 1983.

Coombes, B., These poor hands, Gollancz, 1939.

Cox, C.B. & Hinchcliffe, A.P. (eds), T.S. Eliot: The waste land, Macmillan, 1968.

Crick, B., George Orwell: a life, 1980.

Cronin, A.J., The stars look down, Gollancz, 1935.

Crossick, G., The lower middle class in Britain, Croom Helm, 1977.

Cunningham, H., Leisure in the industrial revolution, Croom Helm, 1980.

Cunningham, V., Spanish Civil War verse, Penguin, 1980.

Curran, J., & Porter, V. (eds), British cinema history, Weidenfeld & Nicholson, 1983.
Curran, J., Gurevitch, M., & Woollacott, J. (eds), Mass communications and society, Penguin, 1979.
Curtis, T. (ed.), Wales, the imagined nation, Poetry Wales Press, 1986.
Davies, M. (ed.), Life as we have known it, L & V Woolf, 1931.
Davison, P., Meyersohn, R., Shils, E. (eds), Literary taste, culture and mass communication, 14 vols., Chadwyck Healey, 1975-80.
Davy, C.(ed.), Footnotes to the film, Lovat Dickson, 1938.
Dawson, C., Religion and the modern state, Eric Gill, 1935.
- Beyond politics, Sheed & Ward, 1939.
Durgnat, R., A mirror for England, Faber, 1970.
Dyer, R., Stars, BFI, 1982.
Eagleton, T., Literary theory, Blackwell, 1983.
Eliot, T.S., Selected essays, 1917-1932, Faber, 1932.
- After strange gods, Faber, 1934.
- The idea of a Christian society, Faber, 1939.
- The classics and the man of letters, Faber, 1942.
- Collected poems, Faber, 1974.
- Notes towards the definition of culture, Faber, 1948.
- Four quartets, 1944, rev. ed., Faber, 1979.
Ellis, J., Eye deep in hell, Croom Helm, 1977.
Field, A., Picture palace, Gentry Books, 1974.
Fledelius, K., et al (eds), History and the audio-visual media, University of Copenhagen, 1979.
Foakes, R.A. (ed.), Romantic criticism, 1800-1850, Ed. Arnold, 1968.
Ford, H.D., A poet's war, Oxord UP, 1965.
Forman, C., Industrial town, David & Charles, 1979.
Fowles, J., The Ebony tower, Cape, 1974.
Fox, R., The novel and the people, Lawrence & Wishart, 1937.
Francis, H., Miners against Fascism: Wales and the Spanish Civil War, Lawrence & Wishart, 1984.
Fry, R., Vision and design, Chatto & Windus, 1920.
Fussell, P., The Great War and modern memory, Oxford UP, 1975.
- Abroad, 1981.
Gathorne Hardy, J., The public school phenomenon, Cape, 1977.
Gibbon, L.G., A Scots quair, 1946, repr. Hutchinson, 1983.
Gibbs, P., England speaks, Heinemann, 1935.
Gilbert, B.B., British social policy, 1914 - 1939,

Batsford, 1973.
Gissing, G., The nether world, 1889, repr. Dent, 1974.
Gloversmith, F. (ed.), Class, culture and social change, Harvester, 1980.
Glynn, S. & Oxborrow, J., Interwar Britain: A social and economic history, Allen & Unwin, 1976.
Gramsci, A., Selections from the prison notebooks of Antonio Gramsci, Hoare, Q. & Nowell Smith, G. (eds), Lawrence & Wishart, 1971.
Graves, R. & Hodge, A., The long weekend, Faber, 1940.
Gray, R., 'Bourgeois Hegemony in Victorian Britain', in Bloomfield, J. (ed.), Class, hegemony, Lawrence & Wishart, 1977.
Green, M., A mirror for Anglo-Saxons, Longmans, 1961.
- Children of the sun, Constable, 1977.
Greene, G., It's a battlefield, Heinemann, 1934.
- England made me, Heinemann, 1935
- A gun for sale, Heinemann, 1938.
- Brighton rock, Heinemann, 1938.
- The pleasure dome, Taylor J.R. (ed.), Secker & Warburg, 1972.
- 'Subjects and Stories', in Davy, C. (ed.), Footnotes to the Film, Lovat Dickson, 1938.
Greenwood, W., Love on the dole, Cape, 1933.
- His Worship the Mayor, Cape, 1934.
- The cleft stick, Selwyn & Blunt, 1937.
- There was a time, Cape, 1967.
- How the other man lives, Labour Book Service, 1939.
Griffiths, R., Fellow travellers of the right, Constable, 1980.
Griffin, F., October day, Secker & Warburg, 1939.
Halsey, A.H., Trends in British society since 1900, Macmillan, 1972.
Hardy, F., John Grierson, Faber, 1979.
Hardy, F. (ed.), Grierson on documentary, 1946, rev. ed., Faber, 1966.
Harrisson, T., Living through the Blitz, Penguin, 1976.
Hawkes, T., Structuralism and semiotics, Methuen, 1977.
Hawthorn, J. (ed.), The British working class novel in the twentieth century, Edward Arnold, 1984.
Hayman, J., Leavis, Heinemann, 1976.
Hebdige, D., The meaning of style, Methuen, 1979.
Hoggart, R., The uses of literacy, Chatto & Windus, 1957.
Honey, J.R., Tom Brown's universe, David & Charles, 1977.

Hoskins, K.B., Today the struggle: literature and politics in England in the Spanish Civil War, University of Texas, 1969.
Howarth, T.E.B., Cambridge between two wars, Collins, 1978.
Huxley, A., On the margin, Chatto & Windus, 1923.
- Along the road, Chatto & Windus, 1925.
- Jesting Pilate, Chatto & Windus, 1926.
- Proper studies, Chatto & Windus, 1927.
- Do what you will, Chatto & Windus, 1929.
- Music at night, Chatto & Windus, 1931.
- Brave new world, 1932, repr. Chatto & Windus, 1955.
- The olive tree, Chatto & Windus, 1936.
- Brave new world revisited, Chatto & Windus, 1959.
- 'Where are the Movies Moving?', in Vanity Fair, July 1925.
- 'Our Debt to Hollywood', in Vanity Fair, August 1926.
Hynes, S., The Auden generation, Bodley Head, 1976.
Isherwood, C., Lions and shadows, 1938, repr. Signet, 1968.
- Christopher and his kind, Eyre Methuen, 1977.
Jackson, A., Semi-detached London, Allen & Unwin, 1973.
Jarvie, I.C., Towards a sociology of the cinema, Routledge, Kegan Paul, 1970.
Jennings, M-L., Humphrey Jennings, Riverside, 1982.
Johnson, R., 'The Proletarian Novel', Literature and History, 1975.
Johnstone, R., The will to believe: novelists of the nineteen-thirties, Oxford UP, 1982.
Jones, R., Cwmardy, Lawrence & Wishart, 1937.
- We live, Lawrence & Wishart, 1939.
Joll, J., Gramsci, Fontana, 1977.
Karpf, S.L., The gangster movie: emergence, variation and decline of a genre, 1930-1940, Ayer, 1970.
Keating, P., The working classes in Victorian fiction, Routledge, Kegan Paul, 1971.
Keegan, J., The face of battle, Penguin, 1978.
Klaus, H.G. (ed.), The socialist novel in Britain, Harvester, 1981.
Koestler, A., Arrival and departure, Cape, 1943.
Kojecky, R., T.S. Eliot's social criticism, Faber, 1971.
Korda, M., Charmed lives, Allen Lane, 1980.
Kracauer, S., From Caligari to Hitler, Dennis Dobson, 1947.
Lawrence, D.H., England, my England, 1924, repr. Penguin, 1979.

  - Lady Chatterley's lover, Penguin, 1960.
Leavis, F.R., New bearings in English poetry, Chatto
  & Windus, 1932.
  - Revaluations, Chatto & Windus, 1936.
  - Education and the university, 1943, rev. 1948,
  repr. Cambridge UP, 1979.
  - The great tradition, Chatto & Windus, 1948.
  - D.H. Lawrence, novelist, Chatto & Windus, 1955.
  - 'Scrutiny', a retrospect, Cambridge UP, 1963.
Leavis, F.R. & Q.D., Lectures in America, Chatto &
  Windus, 1969.
Leavis, Q.D., Fiction and the Reading Public, 1932,
  repr. Penguin, 1979.
Left Review, 1936-8.
Lehmann, J., The whispering gallery, Longmans, Green,
  1955.
Lehmann, J. (ed.), Ralph Fox: a writer in arms,
  Lawrence & Wishart, 1937.
Lewis, W., The art of being ruled, Chatto & Windus,
  1926.
Leyda, J., Films beget films, Allen & Unwin, 1964.
Llewellyn, R., How green was my valley, Michael
  Joseph, 1939.
London, J., The people of the abyss, 1903, repr.
  Nelson, 1919.
Low, R., History of the British film, 1918-29, Allen
  & Unwin, 1971.
  - Documentary and educational films of the 1930s,
  Allen & Unwin, 1979.
  - Films of comment and persuasion in the 1930s,
  Allen & Unwin, 1979.
Lucas, J. (ed.), The 1930s: a challenge to orthodoxy,
  Harvester, 1978.
MacCabe, C., 'Realism and the Cinema: Notes on Some
  Brechtian Theses', Screen, 1974.
  - 'Realism and Pleasure', Screen, 1976.
MacGill, P., The amateur army, Herbert Jenkins, 1915.
McGilligan, P., Cagney: the actor as auteur, Da Copo
  Press, 1980.
McLaine, I., Ministry of morale, Allen & Unwin, 1979
MacPherson, D. (ed.), Traditions of independence in
  the 1930s, BFI, 1980.
Madaraiga, S. de, Spain, Cape, 1961.
Maes-Jelinek, H., Criticism of society in the
  English novel between the wars, University of
  Liege, 1970.
Malcolmson, R., Popular recreations in English
  society, Cambridge UP, 1973.
Mangan, J.A., Athleticism in the Victorian and
  Edwardian public school, Cambridge UP, 1981.

Marquand, D., Ramsay MacDonald, Cape, 1977.
Marsh, D.C., The changing social structure of England and Wales, Routledge Kegan Paul, 1965.
Marx, K. & Engels F.W., Selected works, Lawrence & Wishart, 1968.
Mass Observation, Britain, 1939, Penguin, 1940.
  - War begins at home, Penguin, 1940.
  - Peace and the public, Pengun, 1947.
Mathias, P., The first industrial nation, Methuen, 1971.
Mayer, J.P., British cinemas and their audiences, 1948.
Middlemas, K. & Barnes, J., Baldwin: a biography, Weidenfeld & Nicholson, 1969.
Miles, P., 'Improving Culture: The Politics of Illustration in Evelyn Waugh's Love Among the Ruins', Trivium, 1983.
  - 'The Painter's Bible and the British Workman', in Hawthorn, J. (ed.), The British working class novel in the twentieth century, Edward Arnold, 1984.
Miles, P. & Smith, M., 'Hegemony and the Intellectuals in Interwar Britain', Trivium, 1985.
Mowat, C.L., Britain between the wars, Methuen, 1955.
Mulhern, F., The moment of Scrutiny, New Left Books, 1979.
Mulvey, L., 'Visual Pleasure and Narrative Cinema', Screen, 1974.
Murry, J.M., The price of leadership, SCM Press, 1939.
Muste, J.M., Say that we saw Spain die: literary reaction to the Spanish Civil War, University of Washington Press, 1966.
Naylor, J.F., Labour's international policy, Weidenfeld & Nicholson, 1969.
Neale, S., Genre, BFI, 1980.
Newsome, D., Godliness and good learning, Murray, 1961.
O'Brien, T.S., Civil defence, HMSO, 1950.
O'Connor, W.V. (ed.), Forms of modern fiction, Indiana UP, 1959.
Orwell, G., A clergyman's daughter, 1935, repr. Penguin, 1972.
  - Keep the aspidistra flying, 1936, repr. Penguin, 1973.
  - The road to Wigan pier, 1937, repr. Penguin, 1977.
  - Homage to Catalonia, 1938, repr. Penguin, 1980.
  - Coming up for air, 1939, repr. Penguin, 1971.
  - Animal farm, Secker & Warburg, 1945.
Orwell, S. & Angus, I. (eds), Collected essays,

journalism and letters of George Orwell, 4 vols., 1968, repr. Penguin, 1970.

Pawling, C., 'Orwell and Documentary', Literature and History, 1976.

Perry, G., The great British picture show, Hart-Davis, 1974.

Pilgrim Trust, Men without work, Cambridge UP, 1938.

Pimlott, B., Labour and the left in the thirties, Cambridge UP, 1977.

Powell, A., The music of time, Heinemann, 1951-75.

Preston, P., The coming of the Spanish Civil War, Methuen, 1983.

Priestley, J.B., English journey, Heinemann, 1934.
- Postscripts, Heinemann, 1940.

Pronay, N., 'British Newsreels in the Thirties', History, 1971 and 1972.

Pronay, N. & Spring, D.W. (eds), Propaganda, politics and film, Croom Helm, 1982.

Raymond, E., Tell England, Cassell, 1922.

Richards, I.A., Practical criticism, Kegan Paul, 1929.

Richards, J., Visions of yesterday, Routledge Kegan Paul, 1973.
- The age of the dream palace, Routledge Kegan Paul, 1984.
- 'The Lancashire Britannia', Focus on Film, December, 1979.
- 'The BBFC and Content Control in the 1930s', Historical Journal of Film, Radio and Television, 1981/82.

Roberts, R., The classic slum, 1971, Manchester UP.
- A ragged schooling, Manchester UP, 1976.

Robinson, R.A.H., The origins of Franco's Spain, David & Charles, 1970.

Rock, W., British appeasement in the thirties, Ed. Arnold, 1977.

Roddick, N., A new deal in entertainment: Warner Bros. in the 1930s, BFI, 1983.

Rotha, P., The film till now, 1930, repr. Cape, 1947.
- Documentary Diary, Secker & Warburg, 1973.

Rowntree, B.S., Poverty and progress, Longmans, 1941.

Rowson, S., 'A Statistical Survey of the Cinema Industry in Great Britain', Journal of the Royal Statistical Society, 1936.

Samuels, S., 'The Left Book Club', Journal of Contemporary History, 1966.

Sassoon, S., Memoirs of an infantry officer, Faber, 1930.

Sherriff, R.C., Journey's end, Gollancz, 1929.

Shelston, A. (ed.), Thomas Carlyle, selected writings, Penguin, 1971.

Bibliography

Shindler, C., <u>Hollywood</u> <u>goes</u> <u>to</u> <u>war</u>, Routledge Kegan Paul, 1979.

Short, K., <u>Feature</u> <u>films</u> <u>as</u> <u>history</u>, Croom Helm, 1983.

Sked, A. & Cook, C., <u>Crisis</u> <u>and</u> <u>controversy</u>, Macmillan, 1976.

Skelton, R. (ed.), <u>Poetry</u> <u>of</u> <u>the</u> <u>Thirties</u>, Penguin, 1964.

Skidelsky, R., <u>Politicians</u> <u>and</u> <u>the</u> <u>slump</u>, Macmillan, 1967.

Smith, D., <u>Socialist</u> <u>propaganda</u> <u>in</u> <u>the</u> <u>twentieth</u> <u>century</u> <u>novel</u>, Macmillan, 1978.

Smith, G. (ed.), <u>The</u> <u>letters</u> <u>of</u> <u>Aldous</u> <u>Huxley</u>, Chatto & Windus, 1969.

Smith, M., 'Orwell, War and Politics', <u>Literature</u> <u>and</u> <u>History</u>, 1980.
  - <u>British</u> <u>air</u> <u>strategy</u> <u>between</u> <u>the</u> <u>wars</u>, Oxford UP, 1984.
  - 'Narrative and Ideology in <u>Listen</u> <u>to</u> <u>Britain</u>, in Hawthorn, J. (ed.), <u>Narrative</u> <u>from</u> <u>Malory</u> <u>to</u> <u>motion</u> <u>pictures</u>, Ed. Arnold, 1985.

Smith, P. (ed.), <u>The</u> <u>Historian</u> <u>and</u> <u>film</u>, Cambridge UP, 1976.

Spender, S., <u>The</u> <u>new</u> <u>realism</u>, Hogarth, 1939.
  - <u>World</u> <u>within</u> <u>world</u>, Hamish Hamilton, 1953.
  - <u>The</u> <u>thirties</u> <u>and</u> <u>after</u>, Fontana, 1978.

Stansky, P. & Abrahams, W., <u>The</u> <u>unknown</u> <u>Orwell</u>, Constable, 1972.
  - <u>Orwell:</u> <u>the</u> <u>transformation</u>, Constable, 1979.

Stansky, P., <u>Journey</u> <u>to</u> <u>the</u> <u>frontier</u>: <u>Julian</u> <u>Bell</u> <u>and</u> <u>John</u> <u>Cornford</u>, Constable, 1966.

Stead, P., 'Hollywood's Message to the World ...', <u>Historical</u> <u>Journal</u> <u>of</u> <u>Film</u>, <u>Radio</u> <u>and</u> <u>Television</u>, 1982.

Stevenson, J., <u>Social</u> <u>conditions</u> <u>in</u> <u>Britain</u> <u>between</u> <u>the</u> <u>wars</u>, Penguin, 1977.

Stevenson, J. & Cook, C., <u>The</u> <u>slump</u>, Cape, 1977.

Sussex, E., <u>The</u> <u>rise</u> <u>and</u> <u>fall</u> <u>of</u> <u>British</u> <u>documentary</u>, University of California, 1975.

Symons, J., <u>The</u> <u>angry</u> <u>thirties</u>, Eyre Methuen, 1976.

Tawney, R.H., <u>Equality</u>, 1931, repr. Allen & Unwin, 1964.

Taylor, P.M., <u>The</u> <u>projection</u> <u>of</u> <u>Britain</u>, Cambridge UP, 1981.

Thomas, G., <u>All</u> <u>things</u> <u>betray</u> <u>thee</u>, 1949, repr. Lawrence & Wishart, 1986.
  - <u>Sorrow</u> <u>for</u> <u>thy</u> <u>Sons</u>, Lawrence & Wishart, 1986.

Thomas, H., <u>The</u> <u>Spanish</u> <u>Civil</u> <u>War</u>, 1961, repr. Penguin 1965.

Thompson, E.P., <u>The</u> <u>making</u> <u>of</u> <u>the</u> <u>English</u> <u>working</u> <u>class</u>, Gollancz, 1963.

- 'The Long Revolution', New Left Review, 1960.
Tolley, A.T., The poetry of the thirties, Gollancz, 1975.
Tomlin, E.W.F., Wyndham Lewis: an anthology, Methuen, 1969.
Tressell, R., The ragged trousered philanthropists, 1914, rev. 1955, repr. Granada, 1965.
Trevelyan, J., What the censor saw, Michael Joseph, 1973.
Waites, B. et al., Popular culture, past and present, Croom Helm, 1981.
Walker, A., Stardom, Penguin, 1974.
Watt, D. (ed.), Aldous Huxley: the critical heritage, Routledge Kegan Paul, 1975.
Waugh, Alec, A year to remember: a reminiscence of 1931, W.H. Allen, 1975.
Waugh, Arthur, Tradition and change, Chapman & Hall, 1919.
Waugh, E., Decline and fall, Chapman & Hall, 1928.
- Black mischief, Chapman & Hall, 1932.
- Put our more flags, 1942, repr. Penguin, 1943.
- Brideshead revisited, 1945, rev. ed. Penguin, 1960.
- The holy places, Queen Anne Press, 1952.
Wells, H.G., The shape of things to come, Hutchinson, 1935.
Weatherhead, A., Stephen Spender and the thirties, Associated Universities Press, 1975.
Wiener, M., English culture and the decline of the industrial spirit, Cambridge UP, 1981.
Williams, R., Culture and society, Chatto & Windus, 1958.
- The long revolution, Chatto & Windus, 1961.
- Orwell, Fontana, 1971.
- The country and the city, Chatto & Windus, 1973.
- Keywords, Croom Helm, 1976.
Wolmark, J., 'Problems of Tone in A Scots Quair', Red letters, 1981.
Woolf, L., Barbarians at the gates, Gollancz, 1939.
Woolf, V., To the lighthouse, 1928, repr. Penguin, 1964.
Wordsworth, W., 'Preface to the Lyrical Ballads', Longman Rees, 1800.
Working Man's Friend, The, Cassell, 1850-1.

INDEX

ABC Cinemas, 167.
Ackland, Valentine, 208.
Aero-engine, 185.
After strange gods, 98.
Althusser, Louis, 9.
Animal farm, 243.
Another country, 2.
Anstey, Edgar, 192, 193, 195.
Arnold, Matthew, 6, 72, 84, 85-6, 87, 253.
Asquith, Anthony, 74, 76, 218.
Attlee, Clement, 65.
Auden, W.H., 4, 59, 67-8, 73, 95, 119, 120, 191, 200, 207, 210, 213-14, 218.
Barbarians at the gate, 210-1.
Balcon, Michael, 30, 167, 168.
Baldwin, Stanley, 14, 20, 22-3, 53-4, 198, 219, 223, 25.
Barnett House, 35.
Bates, Ralph, 210.
Baxter, John, 244.
Beaverbrook, Lord, 233.
Betjeman, John, 47, 226.
Bell, Julian, 206.
Berkeley, Busby, 176.
Beveridge, William, 194, 248-9, 256.
Bevin, Ernest, 233.
Black mischief, 81.
Boden, F.W., 156-7.
Bombing, 222-7.
Bond, Ralph, 187.
Boulting brothers, 168.
Brave new world, 88, 102, 104, 106, 112, 113, 114, 115-21.
Brave new world revisited, 114.
Brideshead revisited, 2, 72.
Brierley, Walter, 154-6.
Brighton rock, 82.

British Film Censors, 169-71, 224.
British Broadcasting Corp., 11, 82, 229, 239-40.
British Council, 90.
British Workman, The, 128-9, 131.
Brittain, Vera, 57, 63-4.
Britten, Benjamin, 189, 191.
Britton, Lionel, 100, 136-41.
Brooke, Rupert, 42, 62, 64, 213.
Burgess, Guy, 70, 73.
Cagney, James, 172, 174-5, 176.
Campbell, Roy, 209.
Capra, Frank, 172-3.
Carlyle, Thomas, 41, 85.
Carnegie Trust, 35.
Caudwell, Christopher, 136, 206, 207.
Cavalcade, 195.
Cavalcanti, Alberto, 189, 191, 195, 245.
Chamberlain, Neville, 14, 221, 223, 225, 229, 235, 247.
Chaucer, Geoffrey, 41.
Chesterton, G.K., 220.
Churchill, Winston, 232, 235, 236, 240, 247, 249.
Cinematographic Films Act (1927), 166; (1936), 168-9.
Close harmony, 113.
Coalface, 189-91, 192.
Cobbett, William, 41.
Coleridge, Samuel, 6, 84, 85, 253.
Colman, Ronald, 176.
Comfort, Alex, 229.
Coming up for air, 47, 51, 82, 113, 227-8.
Conservative Party, 18, 20, 21, 65, 198, 219-20, 224-5, 234, 236, 245.

267